CONTENTS

THE NEW AGE MUSIC GUIDE

THE NEW AGE

Profiles and Recordings

MUSIC GUIDE

of 500 Top New Age Musicians

Patti Jean Birosik

COLLIER BOOKS   MACMILLAN PUBLISHING COMPANY   NEW YORK
COLLIER MACMILLAN PUBLISHERS   LONDON

To those who dream dreams,
and have the courage
to make them come true

Copyright © 1989 by P. J. Birosik

Collier Books
Macmillan Publishing Company
866 Third Avenue, New York, NY 10022
Collier Macmillan Canada, Inc.

Library of Congress Cataloging-in-Publication Data
The New Age music guide.
   1. New Age music—Discography. I. Birosik, Patti
Jean.
ML156.4.N48M48   1989   016.78164   89-9928
ISBN 0-02-041640-7

Macmillan books are available at special discounts for bulk purchases
for sales promotions, premiums, fund-raising, or educational use.
For details, contact:

   Special Sales Director
   Macmillan Publishing Company
   866 Third Avenue
   New York, NY 10022

10 9 8 7 6 5 4 3 2 1

Printed in the United States of America

PREFACE

New Age music is the strongest, and in my opinion healthiest, trend to emerge since the birth of rock 'n' roll in the fifties. As with early rock 'n' roll, there exists considerable confusion as to how to categorize the various musical strains that are being marketed. Currently no less than fourteen separate subgenres are being called New Age music. These include New Age East/West, Electronic/Computer, Environmental/Nature, Folk, Jazz/Fusion, Meditation, Native American/Indigenous, Pop, Progressive, Solo Instrumental, Sound Health, Space, Traditional, Vocal, and World Music.

To help ease this confusion I have asked some of the outstanding recording artists and journalists in the various subgenres to help me define their musical specialty, to explain how it relates to the concept of New Age music, and to list some of the notable recording artists creating this music. Of course, each time someone creates a definition, the musical form seems to mutate speedily into something new. This is the way vital, growing, powerful music must behave; after all, evolution ensures continuation of the species.

Artists listed in this book were selected based on specific criteria. Radio airplay on a New Age–formatted station—such as KTWV, WBMW, KGRX—or within a syndicated New Age radio program, major distribution into retail stores, and media coverage were all important parts of the selection process. Vocal music had to feature positive consciousness lyrics while instrumental selections needed to meet the outlines specified by Steven Halpern in the introduction to this book.

More than two hundred companies and six hundred fifty artists were sent query letters informing them of the ongoing compilation of this guide and requesting sample cassettes with biographical and marketing information. The final inclusions represent the best from a broad spectrum of New Age music subgenres as well as a few seminal artists who have directly influenced today's musicians through their bold and experimental approach to music for the new millennium.

Each artist profile includes a selection that I like to call discography highlights. While many profiles feature a complete listing of all recordings released by a certain artist, many others offer only those releases that can be deemed New Age music using the criteria described above. Some reasons for this are obvious: some artists record and release both New Age and non-New Age products; some record companies and/or artists did not have access to or submit complete discography information; some releases were out of print and not available to the public.

The records listed in each artist profile are listed alphabetically to aid in location and purchase by the consumer. Dates for records are not listed for several reasons: no copyright or date of release appeared on the product sent to the author, nor was this information included in biography or discography information made available during compilation; there was a large gap between date of creation by artist and date of release by record company; there were several conflicting dates of release for the product; the product had been re-released one or more times through a variety of record companies. Since this is a guide to facilitate the location and purchase of New Age music, and to that end dates are much less important than titles, dates for records were omitted. It is hoped that in the future, however, accurate dates will be an integral part of all New Age release packaging.

Of those releases selected for inclusion in the discography portion of the artist profiles, at least one record was selected for discussion in the profile itself. Selection was based on artistic innovation, creativity, and practicality. Space limitations for this book precluded the lengthy discussion that most releases merit; in virtually all profiles, however, the reader will learn valuable instrumentation, production, biographical, and stylist information that will aid in purchase selection. Much of this information was submitted to the author by the record company or artists themselves, so the author cannot be held liable for any errors or inaccuracies obtained from such information. Once again, the author hopes that complete information on instrumentation, production location, and specifics will be included in all New Age release packaging.

At the end of each entry is a category listing for each artist. While some artists do indeed produce only meditation music or New Age

Jazz, it is recognized by the author that some artists oftentimes cross subgenres between and within releases. With the help of the selected contributors, the author has endeavored to append proper appellations for each artist. When frequent style differentiations occurred within an artist profile, particularly with very progressive or experimental artists, it was decided to either append two separate category listings or to choose the most prominent style as a guide for the reader. These categories are to be used by the reader as a general guide rather than a concrete classification in order to aid in the location of suitably pleasing music. Scattered throughout the book, readers will find useful mini-guides to each subgenre and its artists. These boxes will enable fans of Kitaro, for example, to find other East/West artists who create compatible releases. It is hoped that these mini-guides will encourage consumers to take a chance on new artists as well as on musicians who were previously unknown to them. Some of the most enjoyable music heard during the compilation of this book was released by small record companies or the artists themselves; in other words, the artist does not have to be famous to be "good."

During the course of researching and compiling this guide, I had several conversations with New Age music "pioneers" who were upset that I was including vocal music (or electronic or environmental or something else) in the book. Like the early faction disputes in rock 'n' roll (remember the horrendous mod and rocker "wars" in England?), the arguments among various subgenre supporters have spread through the media like wildfire, causing irreparable damage to the reputation of a beneficial, nurturing, and, at worse, benign style of music. Such terms as "Yuppie muzak" or "wallpaper sound" have been bandied about by those usually ignorant of the vibrant, aural spectrum that New Age music has to offer. I hope that as you read this book, learning about the subgenres and getting acquainted with the artists and record companies, you will ignore the controversy and concentrate on what really matters: the music and how it makes you feel.

New Age music encourages personal empowerment, earth connectedness, space consciousness, and interpersonal awareness. These themes are repeated over and over; one look at some of the titles of New Age music releases will illustrate the point. Rock 'n' roll was based on an enjoyably disruptive set of chords as well as excessive volume. It didn't merely influence, it sledgehammered its message. New Age music is more subtle but no less effective; it is created by conscientious artists who are knowledgeable about the effects of sound on the mind of the listener. Instead of being taken as pure entertainment, New Age music can be "used" to induce a wide variety of mental and emotional responses. New Age music is the ultimate blend of art and science.

New Age music's consciousness-changing abilities can increase the mental and emotional health of those who listen to it. Whether used as ambient or foreground sound, the music can evoke feelings of peacefulness, joy, relaxation, gentle stimulation without distraction, intimacy, and sometimes even bliss. It possesses antinoise pollution qualities when used in homes, offices, and retail outlets. It aids mental concentration (or defocusing) for superior meditation, inner awareness or "out of body" traveling. New Age music's healing properties are well documented in many books, such as Steven Halpern's *Sound Health* (San Francisco: Harper & Row, 1985), and is used in hundreds of hospitals, clinics, mental institutions, and prisons the world over. Its capability for inducing physical relaxation has been discovered by massage therapists, doctors, and nurses as well. No other music has had this kind of wide-reaching effect on mental and physical health to date.

So how do you get the most benefit from New Age music? By creating an "artists' palette" of releases. Use the artist profile section to select appropriate music for a variety of moods and uses. If you cannot locate a particular record in your local retail outlets, use the record company section to write or call for mail order or further information.

A personal library of New Age music will enhance all your daily activities. You might select, for example, a Yanni or Vangelis tape to slip into your portable cassette player while jogging. This kind of majestic and fully orchestrated New Age music inspires confidence and a sense of capability and inner strength. If you feel slow or sluggish, you might want to try listening to upbeat selections from Oregon, Dallas Smith, or Susan Mazer. For improved concentration or study, try an ambient release, such as Brian Eno's *Music for Airports* or one of the nature sounds releases. If your home is located near busy intersections, a freeway, or ongoing construction, you might want to experiment with a variety of the environmental tapes that have been included in this book. Depending on your mood, you may choose to experience the natural sounds of waves gently breaking on the beach, a thunderstorm, or a night on Loon Lake. While these types of recordings do not always feature music, they are nonetheless effective in replacing noise with beneficial sounds.

The idea is to have fun with the music, to be creative, and to enjoy the results. Don't be afraid to experiment. If one type of New Age music doesn't please your ear, another surely will. Use this book to learn about your "sound options," then become your own "radio station" and "broadcast" an ever-changing pattern of sound. Try to create an atmosphere, change or heighten a mood. Plan an intimate evening, and program suitably romantic, supportive, and relaxing music. Or recline alone on a sofa or bed, slip on some headphones, and "journey" to the inner recesses of your own mind or the farthest reaches of the galaxy. Don't be afraid to let the music wash over you, to lift you up and carry you to a distant horizon. You may see colors, fantastic scenery, or animals, or you may not. Either way it's okay, as long as the music makes you feel good.

Feeling good is the key to New Age music. Whether it's instrumental or vocal, solo or ensemble, New Age music was created to be a positive force in your life. You have the power to choose music that will mentally stimulate or relax, emotionally uplift and ease the heart, cleanse the soul, inspire the mind, or move the body. With the wide variety of musical styles presented in this book, everybody will find something to enjoy.

Lastly, I'd like to stress that New Age music is still in its infancy and as such features musicians on both international record labels and independent labels operated by the artists themselves exclusively for the distribution of their own music. Because the industry is growing and changing so rapidly, it has been impossible to identify and categorize every artist working in the New Age genre. I apologize for the inevitable omissions and hope that emerging artists will feel free to contact me through the publisher of this book so that I can consider them for an updated volume.

Having spent most of my life working in the music business, I am encouraged by the resurgence of popular instrumental music, spiritual as opposed to "fundamentalist" music, and vocal music featuring positive lyrics. With the daily threats of urban violence, ecological rape, and nuclear holocaust, it's reassuring to see a large and growing grass-roots movement of positive thinkers, artists, and musicians dedicated to the preservation and improvement of life on this delicate Earth. As "New Age" ideals of hope and universal love take hold in the hearts of people around the world, we will, with time, be able to enjoy the fruits of a new era. New Age music can be a vital part of this developing consciousness worldwide, for music is truly the only universal language since it expresses the inexpressible. It is my fervent belief that New Age music is for the new millennium to come.

ACKNOWLEDGMENTS

In any large-scale endeavor there are many individuals whose contributions make the end product a success. I'd like to thank the following: for their unique insight into the various subgenres of New Age music—Steve Halpern, Paul Horn, Suzanne Doucet, Anna Turner, Jonathan Goldman, Bodhi Rains, Michael Stillwater, R. Carlos Nakai, Lee Abrams, Don Slepian, Apurvo, Dallas Smith, Rick Bleiweiss, Shel Kagan, and Lucky Clark; record company executives and publicists for their enthusiasm and recognition of the potential of this book as an educational tool for the public as well as the music industry itself; my agent, Madeleine Morel, for her enthusiasm, support, and willingness to pay for my Thai chicken pizza habit; my editor, Elisa Petrini, for believing that this book could be used to enlighten as well as entertain, and for her calm receipt of a million memos from yours truly; my friends who went above and beyond the call of duty during the months I had to stay glued to the computer screen; and finally, the creators of this wonderful new music—the musicians, composers, producers, and technological inventors who had the vision as well as the "ears" to usher in a "New Age" of music and planetary harmony. Without you, this book would not exist.

INTRODUCTION

Notes on New Age Music

by Steven Halpern

Halpern is an internationally acclaimed authority on the use of sound and music for health and well-being, as well as one of the first audio pioneers creating New Age music. He is the composer, producer, and principal recording artist of over forty-five recordings, including his world-famous Anti-Frantic Alternative *series for relaxation and pure listening pleasure. Halpern is founder and president of both Halpern Sounds and Sound Rx recording companies. A popular lecturer and seminar leader, he is the author of several books, including* Sound Health *and* Tuning the Human Instrument, *the music editor for* New Frontier *magazine, and contributor to numerous other magazines and journals. Halpern is a member of the National Academy of Recording Arts and Sciences and a charter member of the New Age Music Network. He has received both an M.A. and Ph.D. in the Psychology of Music.*

For thousands of years, people around the world have honored and acknowledged the healing, ceremonial, and uplifting role of music. From this perspective New Age music is really a return to roots, to a belief in the primordial power of sound. It is music that provides, as Lee Underwood has said, "emotional, psychological, and spiritual nourishment. It offers peace, joy, bliss, and the opportunity to discover within ourselves our own highest nature."

For many the New Age represents an explosion of human curiosity and creativity, of unlocking the undiscovered potential within each person. This spirit infuses New Age music as well. Those of us who were involved with the rock scene of the sixties may recall the insights of such premier music theorists as Robert Palmer, Michael Ventura, David Walley, Ben Fong-Torres, and Nik Cohn, who helped articulate the consciousness of the era. In jazz, too, we saw the high-energy explorations of such artists as John Coltrane and Pharaoh Sanders chronicled by such writers as Amiri Baraka, Charles Kiel, and Frank Kofsky. Here was community and dialogue, with music as a medium of cultural exchange.

In the same way New Age music was born of a shared consciousness. At such events as the San Francisco Festival in Honor of Comet Kohoutek in 1973, many composers/performers, meeting for the first time, discovered that they were all hearing "spacey" music. We had a sense of sharing in the birthing process of a new sound vision, of becoming the vehicles or instruments through which this new (hitherto unmanifested) form of music became audible. For such artists as Joel Andres, Iasos, and myself the process was the expression of our own meditative disciplines. Other explorers whose personal visions were formed by their meditative disciplines and who helped lay the groundwork for what we now term New Age music include Kitaro, Andreas Vollenweider, Vangelis, C. H. Deuter, Klaus Schulze, Paul Horn, Suzanne Doucet, Brian Eno, and Paul Winter. Although we received inspiration independently (since we all composed in isolation and all of our works were different), we found more in common with each other than with artists creating any other form of pop, rock, jazz, or classical music. And so a movement was born.

But what, exactly, *is* New Age music?

Traditionally musicologists define a form of music based on several stylistic criteria, typically involving harmony, melody, rhythm, timbre, and texture. Let's examine each of these.

Harmony.   Most true New Age music is based on harmony and consonance, rather than dissonance. Consonance doesn't mean just using syrupy major chords (as opposed to minor chords), but it does mean that many of the favorite voicings found in rock and jazz, such as a C7 #9 or a C7 b5, are conspicuously absent. Grating chords have more tension in them and thus tend to engender more stress in the listener. In fact, researchers have recently determined that mice exposed to discordant music developed difficulties in learning and memory, even incurring structural changes in their brain cells. They suffered disruptions in the levels of their messenger RNA and their neurons showed signs of wear and tear from stress. Dr. Gervasia Schrekenberg, a neurobiologist, and Dr. Harvey Bird, a physicist, suspect that disharmonious music might affect any mammalian brain, including the human brain. Further research awaits funding as of this writing, but clearly offers an extraordinary opportunity that begs to be explored. Hence, dissonant harmonies, which strain rather than uplift, are consciously avoided in New Age music.

Melody.   Most everyone who hears someone sing or play a scale—*do-re-mi-fa-so-la-ti . . .*—knows what's "supposed to" come next: the final *do,* the culmination of that pattern. And yet it's precisely this melodic inevitability that keeps us locked into predetermined states of awareness when listening to music. Indeed, we've all been culturally conditioned to respond to particular patterns in sound whether we are aware of it or not! Our cultural expectations are fulfilled by most music that has been heard on this planet—until New Age music, that is.

Listen to some of the classic New Age recordings, such as *Inside,* by Paul Horn, my own *Spectrum Suite,* or *Interdimensional Music* by Iasos. Even after repeated listenings, most people cannot remember the sequence of sounds in these works. Clearly they represent a totally different approach to composition. Their compositional style leaves them without the sound "hooks" that characterize virtually all popular music. When we eliminate the straitjacket of predetermined patterns, we open up new ways of organizing and experiencing sound for ourselves. Such music makes us feel good, for as Stephen Hill so eloquently states in the book *Music from the Hearts of Space,* it "creates a way to enter a space that is always there, as close as the heart, a slightly different frequency . . . a breath away. We enter the space by allowing it to enter us. . . . Such music takes us beyond ourselves and through ourselves." This is obviously not a description of standard format radio fare.

Rhythm.   Perhaps the most striking aspect of New Age music is its use of rhythm—or, more accurately, its lack of it. Since long before recorded history rhythm has been the backbone of music. From Cro-Magnon man pounding on skins and bones to rock drummers programming today's digital drum synthesizers, the mathematical subdivision of time into discreet building blocks or measures has been a key organizing principle of composition and performance. Most popular music listeners expect this timekeeping function to be handled by the percussive sounds of a bass (kick) drum, snare drum, tom-tom, or cymbals.

Classical music aficionados may rarely encounter a drum kit, but they still note the presence of a dominant pulse.

By radical contrast New Age music is *not* based on a pulse. Granted, one subgenre pioneered by Terry Riley, Steve Reich, and Klaus Schulze relies heavily on pulse to create very potent and powerfully hypnotic effects. But many other recording artists have opened up the space–time continuum in the rhythmic domain, in some cases actually doing away with the pulse entirely. This shift has created an extraordinary sense of timelessness for the listeners, who no longer have the same perceptual and contextual cues to help them to anticipate the next beat. No longer are music or musicians slaves of "the time machine."

New technology has made it possible to create sounds that can be sustained almost indefinitely. Consider the limitations of composing on a harpsichord. It's a wonderful instrument, but with its very crisp attack, short sustain, and rapid tone decay it can only produce music based on notes of brief duration, such as quarter notes, eighth notes, and sixteenth notes, rather than notes of longer duration, such as half notes—never mind whole notes tied together over several measures. The musical instrument itself is incapable of affording those compositional options. Similarly, a trumpet or woodwind player can sustain a tone only as long as breath allows.

Now consider the options a composer has today: unlimited sustain at the flick of a switch (of the electronic reverb and echo device), plus an ever-expanding palette of sounds generated by keyboard synthesizers. Technology has become an active partner in the creation of the new music.

Existing acoustic instruments have benefited from this technology as well. Even without electronic enhancement, through certain artists, the venerable grand piano has found a new voice because they learned to listen "with different ears" and to play with a different touch. They came to hear the symphony in the overtones, which could then be enhanced by certain pedal and microphone techniques. In these subtle dimensions of sound the spaces between the notes often speak as eloquently as the primary notes themselves. (This, by the way, is an important point. Some writers have tried to establish a false distinction between acoustic and electronic music. Certainly there are differences, but at the fundamental level of reality it is all one order of vibration. Thus, it's what and how you play, plus what comes through, that makes the music what it is, or isn't.)

From the time New Age was born, much of what set this new genre apart was its lack of traditional, riveting rhythmic core. The compositions were more spacious and open-ended. According to the musicians who invented the music, "If it features a big beat, yes, you can dance to it—but no, it isn't New Age music."

Timbre. The fourth component of our paradigm is timbre. Because harsh or shrill sounds tend to increase stress and tension, certain instruments and tones are specifically eschewed in New Age music. Not coincidentally these very sounds are some of the most popular features in Top 40 music and in some classical compositions as well. In the pioneering research of Dr. Hans Jenny, documented in his book *Cymatics,* we can actually see photographs of the effects of sound on solids, liquids, and gases. The harmonic attacks and overtones of violins, trumpets, heavy-metal electric guitars, and synthesized percussion are clearly disruptive—and so not suitable for the New Age music genre. By contrast, electric piano, harp, flute, bells, and "eq'd" string ensembles are soothing—indeed, for millennia instruments have been revered for their healing potential.

Texture. "Space" is a vital dimension of New Age music; so much so that one of the early appellations for the genre was simply "space music," referring both to its texture and to the state that it tended to evoke in the listener. By "space" we mean the electro-acoustic enhancement of instrumental tones, through reverb and echo; in New Age music such enhancement is not simply a "special effect," but rather an integral part of the music itself.

It is this aspect that directly links New Age music to the most traditional uses of sound. In the caves where the same Cro-Magnon hunters painted exquisite figures of animals on the walls there is a huge room, deeper within the cave, that archaeologists have identified as a music room. Ancient shamans, priests, and yogis at every age since, well aware of the awe-inspiring capacities of certain natural sound chambers, have used them to amplify the ceremonial and consciousness-raising aspects of music. Special acoustic properties were incorporated into the ziggurats of Mesopotamia as well as into Christian cathedrals. The phenomenon of echo, whether organically or digitally derived, gives us a glimpse of the world beyond our senses. Echo and reverberation thus carry strong religious or otherworldly symbolism. This awareness of the primacy of psychoacoustic space is one of the characteristics that distinguishes New Age music. When you listen to a recording made this way, you feel as if you are listening inside one of the magnificent structures such as the Taj Mahal, the Great Pyramid, or a Gothic cathedral.

Beyond these conventional criteria there are other distinguishing features of authentic New Age music, the first being the psychic state of the composer. Research conducted by Psychotronic Research Group, John Diamond, M.D., and Patrick Flanagan, among others, has shown that the "vibrational" (emotional or physical) state of the artist when composing or recording can affect our response to the music. We react differently to music an artist plays from a state of balance and love than to sound arising from a wish to glorify the ego, or, worse, from anxiety. I noted earlier that a high percentage of New Age musicians are into various forms of meditation/holistic health/cosmic awareness, which offer a special kind of collective unconscious. A composer who has "composed" him/herself through meditation, yoga, communing with nature, et cetera, has raised his/her own vibrational rate. And it is to this state, as well as the notes of the music itself, that the listener resonates.

The second distinguishing feature is New Age music's effect on the listener. Simply ask yourself how the music makes you feel. If you feel speeded up, hyper, aggressive, saddened, depressed—or if you experience no change at all—you're probably listening to music that is actually pop, rock, fusion, jazz, or Muzak, rather than New Age music. True New Age music will take you out of yourself, evoking a different spectrum of responses than other music. You won't necessarily see colors more vividly or hear more acutely (although some listeners have experienced this), but your body may feel lighter and your general mood will be uplifted and refreshed.

These effects come from actual, measurable physiological changes that New Age music produces. True New Age music can deepen and regularize the breath, improve digestion, lower blood pressure, and balance the two hemispheres of the brain. It also can enhance learning and induce deep relaxation. Brain-wave measurements through electroencephalography (EEG) and biofeedback equipment have shown that true New Age music can induce an effortless alpha state (8 to 12 cycles per second) with potential for deeper relaxation, going into the theta state (4 to 7 cycles per second). Electrical conductivity (GSR) tests on the surface of the skin show similar effects, consistent with the specific physiological coordinates of relaxation. It is this healing power that has brought New Age music into common use in both hospitals and executive boardrooms—representing a long-overdue reversal of the trend that limited the role of music to "entertainment" or as backdrop for dancing or as a soundtrack for movies or ads.

As a listener try to approach New Age music on its own terms. Don't try to force traditional left-brain constructs and modes of analysis on this right-brain phenomenon. Some New Age pieces are equally adaptable as background or foreground music. Some music is intended exclusively as ambient sound—the kind some derisively (and unfairly) term "aural wallpaper." (Speaking as a composer I can attest that it is actually quite tricky to create music interesting enough to withstand attentive listening yet not conflict with or distract from the primary activity.) But other recordings are are so powerfully engaging that the listener has no real choice but to surrender to the music. I would include in this category several of the selections on Iasos's *Interdimensional Music,* Constance Demby's *Novus Magnificat,* and Michael Stearns's *Chronos.* Indeed, to attempt to read a book, write in a journal, or carry on a casual conversation while listening to this type of music is futile. Such music grabs hold of the nervous system as surely as the "heartbeat" rhythm of rock, but it takes you to a different place.

Try listening with your eyes closed. With a good set of headphones listening to this music becomes a meditation in itself. Try lying down with your feet pointed toward the speakers. Our entire body responds to sound, and this technique opens up a whole new dimension. When listening with a close friend or lover, position yourselves back to back. Our bodies act as amplifiers and speakers for the music. Don't be surprised if the music sounds and feels different, depending on who you are with. Use the music to enhance any life activity: dining, studying, meditating, driving, brainstorming, working, walking, and lovemaking.

More than artists in any other genre New Age musicians are consciously aware of the concept of "the music of the spheres." They see themselves as working with the concordance of harmonies that underlie the orderly processes of the universe. This belief is grounded in physical rather than metaphysical law. In fact, our bodies do function as human instruments, producing an electromagnetic field that resonates with the electromagnetic field of the Earth itself. Science confirms the fact that the dominant resonant frequency of our planet—approximately 7.83 to 8 hertz (cycles per second)—is also the natural resonating frequency of a human body at rest or in a "balanced" state. Few means for achieving "balance" are as easy or enjoyable as listening to beautiful, uplifting sound. That is the most important function of New Age music—to keep our human instruments in tune, so they can play more harmoniously in the symphony of life.

Stay tuned!

THE NEW AGE MUSIC GUIDE

A

Philip Aaberg

High Plains Windham Hill
Philip Aaberg
  Windham Hill
Piano Sampler
  Windham Hill
Sampler '86 Windham Hill
The Shape of the Land
  (w/Ackerman and
  Hedges) Windham Hill
A Winter's Solstice
  Windham Hill

For keyboardist Aaberg, variety has been a welcome fact of life. He's been equally at home in orchestras and rock bands, performing with artists as diverse as Peter Gabriel and Rudolph Serkin. *High Plains*, released in 1985, is a lovely, moving collection of original pieces for solo piano. He says, "I am now experimenting with the digital sampling of different piano sounds. The piano is such a personal instrument that you can really find your own voice in it." New Age Solo

William Ackerman

Childhood and Memory Windham
  Hill
*Conferring with the
  Moon* Windham Hill
*In Search of the Turtle's
  Navel* Windham Hill
It Takes a Year Windham Hill
Passage Windham Hill
Past Light Windham Hill
Sampler '82 Windham Hill
Sampler '84 Windham Hill
Search for the Turtles Windham
  Hill
The Shape of the Land (w/Aaberg
  and Hedges) Windham Hill
Winter Solstice Windham Hill

A hyraulic engineer-turned-guitar player, Ackerman began Windham Hill records by distributing three hundred of his own cassettes to neighbors in Palo Alto, California. He is now CEO of Windham Hill Productions, which includes Magenta Records, Lost Lake Arts Records, Open Air Records and, of course, Windham Hill, the best known New Age record label. His music cuts across folk, jazz, and European classicism, and he is widely considered a pioneer of New Age music in the United States. His captivating steel-string picking is original and uplifting. Ackerman himself describes his sixth album, *Conferring with the Moon,* as a synthesis of everything he can remember. *Passage* emphasizes stirring chords and rich and mellow steel-string guitar work through peaceful and melodic instrumentals. Adding accents to Ackerman's performance are violins, cello, piano, and English horn. **New Age Folk**

John Adams

Light over Water
  New Albion
Shaker Loops New Albion

Recently dubbed "the most promising American composer" by *High Fidelity* magazine, John Adams creates highly polished music for string septet. His warm, resonant sound is best displayed in pieces "Shaker Loops" and "Phrygian Gates" on the *Shakes Loops* album. But his return to electronic music with *Light over Water* best embodies his bold personal vision. At times rather dark, this dramatic album travels deep into space exploring black holes as well as blinding novas. Consisting of three extended instrumentals, *Light over Water* is a symphony for brass instruments ensemble and Adam's synthesizers. **New Age Electronic**

Obo Addy

African American Flying Heart

Addy is a master drummer in the Ghanian tradition, the son of a *wonche,* or master drummer. Since moving to America, Addy has added domestic influences such as electric guitar to his music, creating a happy fusion of percolating percussion and lyrical melody that inspires dancing. *African American* is a cheerful celebration of life perfectly suited to movement or casual listening. **New Age World**

Aeoliah

Angel Love Sona Gaia
Crystal Illumination
  Antiquity
Inner Sanctum
  Sona Gaia
Light of Tao Sona Gaia
Majesty Sona Gaia

Keyboardist Aeoliah is also a visionary artist who creates the cover art for his releases. His concerts incorporate sound, light, and color in a production called "Universal Light." On *Angel Love* delicate yet majestic layers of piano and synthesizers combine to create a beautiful atmospheric sound for meditation or relaxation. New Age pioneer Paul Horn describes Aeoliah's music as "an integral part of the expanding global fabric of higher consciousness." Aeoliah's recordings have also been used in therapy by Dr. Elisabeth Kubler-Ross. **New Age Meditation**

Aeolus (Robert Aeolus Myers)

Aeolian Melodies Global Pacific
Rays Global Pacific

Multi-instrumentalist Aeolus creates vivid sound paintings. *Rays,* dedicated to the transformation of man, offers a wide range of emotions, colors, and states of consciousness through the use of synthesizers, recorder, double ocarina, kalimba, and subtle vocalizations. "Aeolian Melodies" is a tapestry of soothing harmonies and resonant overtones featuring a similar range of instruments—flutes, recorders, clarinet, bells, kalimba, and synthesizers—all performed by Aeolus himself. The exploratory spirit of the album is evoked by his original poem on the insert card entitled "On Angels Becoming Human":

You are alone.	You reach out . . .	You turn it.
	you wait	
No light.	A door . . .	You remember.
	the knob.	
No sound.	You hold it.	
No memory.	You wonder.	You open the door.

New Age Traditional

Laura Allan

Reflections (w/Horn) Unity

On this debut album New Age vocalist Allan joins with renowned flutist Paul Horn to create a light, ethereal sound that is pure enchantment. Accompanying herself on zither, she creates a relaxing, softly enveloping mood that is gentle on the ears and on the mind. As always, Horn weaves a musical masterpiece with each solo he takes, his flute the perfect complement to Allan's lyrical and pure voice. *Reflections* is filled with sweet and lovely melodies to soothe the heart and raise the spirit. New Age Vocal

Marcus Allen

Breathe (w/Canyon) Rising Sun
Petals (w/Canyon, Bell, Smith) Rising Sun
Quiet Moments Rising Sun
Rising Sun Collection Rising Sun
Solo Flight Rising Sun
Summer Suite (w/Bell, Canyon, Smith) Rising Sun

Solo Flight showcases the soaring, melodic piano artistry of Allen. *Quiet Moments* features solo piano works for a relaxing musical journey, while the more meditative *Breathe* features Sky Canyon (Jon Bernoff) accompanying Allen on vibes. Allen and Canyon are joined by Dallas Smith and Teja Bell on *Petals,* a beautiful blend of acoustic and electronic instruments that offers lush, orchestrated music well suited to both active and passive listening. New Age Meditation, New Age Solo

Justo Almario

Forever Friends Meadowlark
Plumbline Meadowlark

Flute and tenor sax player Almario has dozens of soul and jazz albums to his credit, collaborating with such groups as the Commodores, Freddie Hubbard, and Mongo Santa Maria. But *Forever Friends* is different; as the

NEW AGE EAST/WEST MUSIC

by Bodhi Raines*

Percussionist Raines, a former English professor, is the editor of New Music News *(a trade publication for New Age/Global music), as well as a recording and performing artist.*

Typically, Western (European, North American) composers exult in layers of harmonies and complex notation for many instruments, while Eastern (Indian, Asian) composers delight in exploring the subtleties and depths of melody and rhythm, working with microtones and rhythmical divisions. Out of the interaction between East and West—through the meetings of musicians sharing ideas and art forms—comes New Age East/West music. American jazz fused with traditional Japanese music, rock music featuring sitar, and now New Age music influenced by Eastern philosophies as well as instrumentation continue a musical trend of world integration. Some East/West selections feature vocals or vocal effects while others make use of the wealth of exotic instruments found around the world, such as tabla (drums), gourds, and shakuhachi (bamboo flute).

AMAKUDARI   AZUMA

AMBHOJ AND DEVAKANT   TIMOTHY BISHOP-PRASANNA

APURVO   KRISHNA CHAKRAVARTY

*Artist listing compiled by Patti Jean Biroski.

artist himself explains, "It gave me the opportunity to explore the more melodic and mellow." Utilizing Lyricon and vocals as well as sax and flute, Almario creates a sensual rhythm that is delicately moving rather than scintillating. New Age Jazz

Carlos Alomar

Dream Generator Private Music

Ever since he began performing, multi-instrumentalist Alomar has had a vision of making music far beyond the usual confines of his rock/r&b roots. For over a decade he has served as David Bowie's musical director, but as he says, "In doing this [solo] album, I wanted to take my audience to a different world." Through the aid of a Photon Guitar synthesizer, Macintosh Plus computer system, and an assortment of more than thirty synthesizers, drum

CHAITANYA HARI DEUTER

AKI DOMO

RICHARD GARNEAU

SRILA GURUDEVA

PETER MICHAEL HAMEL

LOU HARRISON

HIROSHIMA

LUCIA HWONG

DAVID HYKES

INVINCIBLE RECORDS

ALEX JONES

BIBI BHANI KAUR

SAT KARTAR KAUR

SINGH KAUR

AL GROMER KHAN

OSAMU KITAJIMA

KITARO

MASAYUKI KOGA

RILEY LEE

CECIL LYTLE

MILA

JOHN KAIZAN NEPTUNE

PUSHKAR

DON REEVE

KIM ROBERTSON

RAHUL SARIPUTRA

SOMEI SATOH

RAVI SHANKAR

ELAN SICROFF

GURUMANDER SINGH

LIV SINGH

VIKRAM SINGH

SANGIT SIRUS

TOMOKO SUNAZAKI

WILL TUTTLE

YAS-KAZ

MASAKAZU YOSHIZAWA

machines, and effects generators, Alomar was able to create an orchestrally rich set of elaborate yet subtle compositions. Why an instrumental record? "I have the opportunity to make the right statement without sacrificing what I want. The advantage to doing an instrumental recording is just that—there are no words. No matter what your native language, you can listen to my album and enjoy it as is." **New Age Electronic, New Age Pop**

Amakudari
Amakudari Attic

The group Amakudari creates lushly textured yet elegantly delicate music that is cinematic in scope and eloquent with emotion. Guitar, bass, cello, sitar, keyboards, and lots of percussion create an East Meets West fusion that is very melodic and spacious, exploring the full colors of the New Age music spectrum. **New Age East/West**

Ambhoj and Devakant

Jewel in the Lotus
Synchronicity/Chidvilas

This duo has created soft, flowing music featuring a beautiful yet haunting flute, silky violin caresses, acoustic guitar, and warm, rich viola. Simple and sweet melodies invite the listener to gently melt inside them, to curl up contentedly within these mesmerizing auditory vignettes. Perfect music for a rainy or any other day. New Age East/West

American Gramaphone Records

Sampler American Gramaphone

Mannheim Steamroller, Checkfield, Ric Swanson and Urban Surrender, Ron Cooley and John Rutter are featured on this eclectic (in mood and tone) but highly satisfying introduction to the world of American Gramaphone. Perennial New Age favorite Mannheim Steamroller takes up the bulk of the record, with six selections chosen from a wide variety of the group's state-of-the-art albums, including the Fresh Aire series. American Gramaphone has long been at the apex of modern technology, and this sampler demonstrates that they are also at the apex of good sound. New Age Progressive

(Michael) Amerlan

Ascendances Caeleste Arc

Synthesist Amerlan has created an emotion-filled, lyrical tone poem on

Ascendances. Soothing washes of sound relax the body and quiet the mind. At times subtly cosmic, other times as delicate as a newly opened flower, Amerlan's music is a good example of pretty, electronic New Age music. New Age Electronic

Ananda

Amazonia Sonic Atmospheres

In Sanskrit the word *ananda* describes the highest plane of spiritual existence. This quintet performs world music that melds elements of classical, jazz, and international folk music, creating a sound that blends the unusual textures of oboe, flute, and twelve-string guitar with pulsating Latin rhythms and the harmonies of contemporary jazz. Relying principally on oboe and flute leads, Ananda does indeed ease the listener onto another plane of existence. New Age World

Ancient Future

Asian Journal Music of the World
Natural Rhythms Philo
Quiet Fire Narada Lotus
Visions of a Peaceful
　Planet Beauty

Ancient Future has sought to create a new music that synthesizes a wide array of diverse Western and Eastern forms. Jazz, classical, Northern Indian, and Balinese have been the predominant influences, with hints of African and South American accents. Exotic instruments such as the esraj, gamelan, and charango are used as well as the scalloped fretboard guitar, violin, flute, and cello. From these the group weaves a mesmerizing, intricately rhythmic ensemble sound that is both nuanced and direct. *Quiet Fire* is an exhilarating and beautiful example of the best that New Age World Fusion music can be. Embracing both the physical and metaphysical aspects of music, Ancient Future explores the positive power of sound on the psyche and the soul. **New Age World**

Ruth Anderson

New Music for Electronic and Recorded Media 1750 Arch

New Music offers Anderson's electronic compositions from the early seventies, but the selection "Points" is especially noteworthy. Anderson spent considerable time studying the direct relationship between music and meditation when New Age music was being pioneered, and "Points" is comprised of aurally rendered sine waves. Limited by its mathematical origins, Anderson's "music" is not melodic, but the resonant tones do have a relaxing effect on the mind, possibly enhancing meditation. **New Age Electronic**

Joel Andrews

An Angel Sings/Ambience JA/VF
Kuthumi JA/VF
Meditations #2 Golden Harp
The Violet Flame JA/VF

Powerful, metaphysically inspired harp music from Andrews can be enjoyed on *The Violet Flame,* which traditionally is a flame of purification. Masterfully channeling energy from another dimension, Andrews easily raises the listener's consciousness level to the point of potent spiritual awakening. Solo harp meditations encourage the listener to relax and to let go of daily stress and care, to vibrate in tune with the music. *Meditation #2* captures the clarity of Andrew's harp instrumentals as he uses inspired music to open the chakras. The result is an audio cleansing. **New Age Meditation**

Darol Anger and Barbara Higbie (w/Mike Marshall)

The Duo Rounder
Live at Montreux
  Windham Hill
Tideline Windham Hill

Anger, Higbie, Marshall, and compatriots in the group Montreux perform New Age acoustic music that is energizing, lyrical, uplifting, and influenced by Third World rhythms. Higbie performs on keyboards, Anger plays violin, cello, and mandolin, while Marshall adds guitar and mandolin on this trio of albums. The compositions mix jazz, New Age, classical, and ethnic influences into an eclectic but thoroughly enjoyable form of loosely structured instrumental music. The mood ranges from relaxed to kinetic on each release. **New Age Jazz**

Anudeva
(See Tsumi)

Anugama

Classic Fantasy Nightengale
Morning Breeze Nightengale
Open Sky Nightengale

Anugama creates a warm cascade of musical harmony that flows through soft synthesizer compositions. The fluid music carries a healing ability and inspires feelings of harmony and liveliness. The seven compositions on *Morning Breeze* feature light, transparent melodies, like a delicate caress of wind at the birth of a new day. **New Age Sound Health**

Apurvo

Flow of Love (w/Sun) Soundless
   Sound
*Inside the Cathedral of
   Life* Soundless Sound
Journey Home Soundless Sound
*Love Live from the
   Heart* Soundless Sound
*Prince James/Dolphin
   Lullaby* Soundless Sound
Soundless Sound I Soundless
   Sound

Keyboardist Apurvo says it best: "People tell me they have reached a quieter space inside themselves, through listening to Soundless Sound, than they had ever before achieved. This, I know, is not unique to my music but is endemic to the style that we are creating, a new way of channeling information onto the planet in such a way that it quiets, calms, and relieves while bringing people out of their worries and into their natural harmony." On *Inside the Cathedral of Life,* Apurvo brings us

the joys of simplicity as well as the grandeur of an orchestra. Her solo piano music, such as *Soundless Sound I,* can be enjoyed for relaxation, meditation, and recreation. Her 1987 release, *The Adventuresome Angels,* is perfect for children of all ages, blending synthesizer suites with uplifting words. **New Age East/West**

Dan Ar Bras

Acoustic Green Linnet
Douar Nevez WEA
The Earth's Lament WEA
*Music for the Silences to
   Come* Shanachie

Ancient rhythms, meditative melodies, cutting-edge technology—these are the tools of guitarist Ar Bras, a master musician who draws equally from Celtic traditions and from contemporary textures. On *Music for the Silences to Come,* keyboards, bass, sax, and Linn drums meld beautifully with his acoustic and electric guitars. The effect is a combination of mesmerizing drones and synthesized orchestral tapestries—energizing music that is both passionate and soothing as well as a particularly effective spiritual balm. **New Age World**

David Arkenstone

Valley in the Clouds Narada
   Mystique

"If I could sum up the feeling I'm trying to create in the listener with one word, it would be adventure," says Arkenstone. *Valley in the Clouds* carries a sense of high adventure with

10

its sweeping motifs, rich percussion, and crystalline melodies. Piano, guitar, flute, bass, and a variety of synthesizers are his instruments, and he plays them all himself. The album represents a meeting place, a harmony among Arkenstone's many directions: acoustic and electronic, classical and rock. **New Age Electronic**

Christofer Ashby

Light Impressions New World
New Age of Christmas New World
Renaissance New World
Time Present, Time Past New World

Beginning his musical career at age seven, Ashby has toured extensively over thirteen countries as a solo guitarist. He is a Fulbright scholar and, in 1986, was the first American guitarist to tour China. *Renaissance* is a unique collection of beautiful compositions for classical guitar and flute that are peaceful and flowing, serene and meditative. His New Age renditions of works by classical composers are quite outstanding. Superbly performed by this virtuoso, the music has a warm, expressive quality of lasting appeal. **New Age Solo**

Ash Ra Tempel
(See Manuel Gottsching)

Atmosphere Collection

A Day on Cape Cod Rykodisc
Island Jungle Rykodisc
Midnight Rainshower Rykodisc
Tropical Surf Rykodisc
Waterfall Rykodisc
A Week in Hawaii Rykodisc

The Atmosphere Collection is a series of compact disc releases that feature the ever-needed, ever-welcome sound of peace on Earth. *A Week in Hawaii* is a series of four ambient environmental recordings capturing the essence of that island haven as digitally recorded by Dr. Toby Mountain, re-creating paradise right in your own living room. From the rhythmic crash of *Tropical Surf* to the soothing patter of a *Midnight Rainshower*, the refreshing sounds of Mother Nature, sans music, will soothe and invigorate. **New Age Environmental**

Audion Records

Best of Both Worlds Audion
First Editions Sampler Audion

Best of Both Worlds showcases many new faces destined to become important figures on the increasingly popular electronic music scene: Daniel Grey, Russell Brower, and So'Ho to name just a few. The other artists have already made international names for themselves: Emerald Web, Jim Bartz, Wendy Carlos, Garry Hughes, Laraaji, Wavestar, Kevin Braheny, Don Slepian, Barry Cleveland, and Synergy. Their styles are varied, but all share an understanding and feeling for the new musical tools that technology has given us today. Many of the featured artists have made significant contributions to that technology themselves. All have retained a sense of warmth and humanity, making these electronic compositions accessible, visual, and passionate. **New Age Electronic**

William Aura

Aurasound Higher Octave
Aurasound II Higher Octave
Dreamer Higher Octave
Fantasy Higher Octave
Half Moon Bay Higher Octave
Lovely Day Higher Octave
Paradise Higher Octave
Timeless Higher Octave

Half Moon Bay is one of a series of smooth, meditative releases by Aura, and it could very well be his best to date. Working with traditional New Age instruments—synthesizer, guitar, flute, and piano—Aura creates earthy and personable music. The song "Mirada" is a classic, charged with ethereal passion. The album was created with the use of "holophonic" sound, a revolutionary sonic technique that imparts a strong, three-dimensional quality to the music. **New Age Traditional**

Azimuth

Azimuth ECM
Azimuth 85 ECM
Depart ECM
The Touchstone ECM

Crossing the border between jazz and New Age Jazz Fusion, Azimuth creates exquisitely lovely music with unusual instrumentation: piano, organ, voice, trumpet, flügelhorn, and synthesizers. *The Touchstone* is a nonfrenetic release that will please fans with its understated elegance. Azimuth avoids overly intellectual arrangements in favor of easily accessible, gently rhythmic performances. The group makes music that is interesting yet easy on the ears. **New Age Jazz**

Azuma

Asian Wind
Azuma Private Music
Far from Asia Nippon Columbia
Moonlight of Asia Nippon
　　Columbia

In his native Japan, Azuma has long been considered a distinguished and visionary composer. Now American audiences can enjoy the warm, organic sounds of shakuhachi (Japanese flute) and stringed koto, as performed on *Azuma*. Crystalline timbres catch the ear. Breathy sounds and shimmering synth lines swell to orchestral proportions, then fall back to a hush underscored by a Zen sense of silence. At times soft and spacious, at times dense and driven by sequencer pulses and insistent backbeats, *Azuma* blends the digitally crisp sounds of the future with subtleties of ancient Japanese music. As he explains, "By drawing on my heritage I hope to provide a basis for the future energy of my audience in their daily lives." **New Age East/West**

Azymuth

Cascades Milestone
Crazy Rhythm Milestone
Flame Milestone
Light as a Feather Milestone

Outubro Milestone
Rapid Transit Milestone
Spectrum Milestone
Telecommunication Milestone
Tightrope Walker Milestone

On *Crazy Rhythm,* Azymuth's ninth album in as many years, the Brazilian instrumental trio continues to refine and expand the boundaries of its unique blend of samba, jazz, and funk. As group member/producer Jose Bertrami explains, "We were trying to develop our own sound within samba and jazz while trying to escape the patterns and limitations of both." This is not dance music, although its infectious cheerfulness does make you want to move; it is world music, music from the heart to uplift, inspire, and energize. **New Age World**

B

Thor Baldursson

(See Les Hurdle)

Patrick Ball

Celtic Harp Fortuna
Celtic Harp Vol. 2 Fortuna
Celtic Harp Vol. 3 Fortuna

Ball's wire-strung Celtic folk harp music is pure magic. He plays his unusual instrument as the ancient masters intended, with his fingernails rather than fingertips, a technique lost for nearly two hundred years. George Winston describes Ball's debut album, *Celtic Harp,* as "one of the most beautiful . . . I've ever heard, from start to finish." It features compositions by the seventeenth-century harpist Turlough O'Carolan which were unique in its own day, influenced by both the Irish folk traditions and the influx of Italian baroque compositions of the time. Weaving intricate textures, Ball renders the centuries-old material compelling from the first note. It's pure astral travel music: clear, resonant, and achingly beautiful. **New Age World**

Baffo Banfi

Hearth Innovative Communications
Ma, Dolce Vita Innovative Communications

Banfi creates rather chirpy, flowing synthesizer melodies that touch your heart with an invitation to a dance. *Hearth* is full of lovely electronic tunes that convey happiness and beauty through selectively created and arranged tonal patterns. Banfi plays like a modern-day Vivaldi, cheerfully enjoining you to merge into the music, to let the stress and tension of modern life slowly slip from your shoulders, and to emerge refreshed and energetic once again. **New Age Electronic**

Tom Barabas

Magic in December Soundings of the Planet

Piano Impressions Soundings of
  the Planet
Soaring (w/Dean Evenson)
  Soundings of the Planet
You're the End of the Rainbow
  Soundings of the Planet

Truly a global musician, solo pianist Barabas began his musical career at the Liszt Conservatory in Budapest, Hungary, then emigrated with his family to Venezuela. Developing a taste for jazz and rock music there, he soon evolved his own compositional style using grand piano and multiple synthesizers. Barabas's keyboard work on *Piano Impressions* conveys a message of universal love in line with his declared goal of "raising planetary consciousness." **New Age Traditional**

Richard Barbieri
(See Janson Barbieri)

Pete Bardens

Seen One Earth Cinema/Capitol

Former founder of the seminal progressive rock band Camel as well as guest performer with Van Morrison on his *Wavelength* album, keyboardist Bardens creates New Age Space music with a sense of adventure. His latest flight of musical fancy is *Seen One Earth,* a dazzling, densely textured electronic album that evokes a full spectrum of moods. Bardens is one of the best explorers to be found voyaging through the new frontiers of electronic/space music today. **New Age Progressive**

Russ Barenberg

Behind the Melodies
  Rounder

Barenberg is an extremely versatile and talented guitarist who combines folk, traditional, and jazz influences. *Behind the Melodies* is an upbeat release that will have you moving your feet as his fingers fly over the strings and the talented backup band swings along. Enhanced by South American flutes, the opening track is especially plaintive, giving a preview of other, slower selections to come. This multitempo mix will be appreciated by those who value tasty guitar licks in addition to a well-integrated ensemble sound. **New Age Folk**

Jim Bartz

*Pictures of Earth and
  Space* Audion

Bartz began exploring the boundaries of progressive rock influenced by the Moody Blues, Genesis, and Patrick Moraz. Within a short time the young composer developed increasingly unpredictable, exotic original pieces utilizing his unique guitar technique, which combines technical expertise with a deep love of strange new sounds. *Pictures of Earth and Space* is an aurally enchanting journey through worlds both far and near, very shamanic in quality as well as texture. This is progressive space music for the mental pioneer. **New Age Progressive**

Robbie Basho

Best of. Vol. 1 Windham Hill
Sampler '81 Windham Hill
Twilight Peaks Vital Body

Twilight Peaks is part of the Art of Relaxation series. Mesmerizing, melodic guitars sing through a series of intricate harmonic phrases, the repetition of tone slowly easing the listener into a mentally and emotionally receptive state. It's easy to get caught up in the rise and play of the strings as they move; stress seems to just slip away. This is New Age Solo acoustic guitar instrumental music nonpareil. **New Age Solo**

Peter Baumann (see also Tangerine Dream)

Repeat Repeat Portrait
Romance '76 Virgin
Strangers in the Night Portrait
Transharmonic Nights Virgin

Private Music Records founder and multi-instrumentalist Peter Baumann has a musical vision that is international in scope yet individual in focus. In 1971, he joined Tangerine Dream, the group that would soon establish itself as a groundbreaker of electronic pop music. Then Baumann expanded his horizons by releasing solo records and producing other artists. With *Repeat Repeat* and *Strangers in the Night,* he began to integrate computer-controlled synthesizers with traditional acoustic instruments such as guitar, bass, and drums, yielding music that is progressive yet accessible. **New Age Progressive**

Jeff Beal

Liberation Antilles/New Directions

Trumpeter/composer Beal's compositions are inspired by the study of Bartok, bebop, and big-band jazz. His first big-band chart, written at age thirteen, was performed at a Stan Kenton clinic. He has since won numerous awards including an unprecedented eleven "db" awards from *Downbeat* magazine. His instrumental style draws from those of Miles Davis, Freddie Hubbard, and Wynton Marsalis, but he creates an unusual setting for jazz-oriented trumpet by juxtaposing a rich symphonic palette using electronic and natural instruments with the rhythms of jazz. Beal is one of the newest shining stars in the New Age Jazz firmament. **New Age Jazz**

Robert Bearns and Ron Dexter (The Golden Voyage Series)

Golden Voyage Vol. 1 Awakening
Golden Voyage Vol. 2 Awakening
Golden Voyage Vol. 3 Awakening
Golden Voyage Vol. 4 Awakening
Golden Voyage Vol. 5 Awakening

Bearns and Dexter's releases are gentle, neoclassical blends of music and environmental sounds. Accessible melodic themes are delicately woven by classical guitars, flutes, piano, horns, strings, synthesizers, and the vibraphone. The Golden Voyage experience is a galactic exploration through celestial harmonics, great for reducing tension or improving meditation. In fact, each

NEW AGE ELECTRONIC/COMPUTER MUSIC

by Don Slepian*

Described by Rolling Stone *magazine as "one of the genre's major talents," Slepian is an internationally known electronic musician, computer instrument designer, recording artist, and concert performer as well as a consultant in computer music.*

The emerging electronic music technology places within most artists' means the resources of a small orchestra. This new generation of intelligent musical instruments wields tremendous power, allowing for the creation of never-before-heard sounds impossible to achieve with traditional acoustic instruments. "Synthesizer" is one term that describes this large, growing class of dissimilar instruments that often combine tape recordings, computers, and samplers. "Samplers" allow a musician to combine little pieces of recorded acoustic sound such as a violin strain or a bird song with electronic tones, creating music that is alternately warm, spacey, delicate, profound, lively, or serene. Electronic composers can also devise personal, customized sounds. Many of the artists listed below work solely with electronic instruments, but others create electro-acoustic music by combining traditional instruments with state-of-the-art technology.

JOHN ADAMS	DOUG AND MATT BRODY
CARLOS ALOMAR	MICHAEL BROOKS
MICHAEL AMERLAN	PETER BUFFET
RUTH ANDERSON	RICHARD BURMER
DAVID ARKENSTONE	RAY BUTTIGIEG
AUDION RECORDS	WENDY CARLOS
BAFFO BANFI	STEPHEN CAUDEL
DAVID BEHRMAN	GEOFFREY CHANDLER
SERGE BLENNER	SUZANNE CIANI
KEVIN BRAHNEY	ALEX CIMA
THOM BRENNAN	BARRY CLEVELAND

*Artist listing compiled by Patti Jean Birosik.

CLUSTER

PETER DE HAVILLAND

DOUBLE FANTASY

EMERALD WEB

BRIAN ENO

LARRY FAST

G.E.N.E.

GHOSTWRITERS

JAN HAMMER

DON HARRISS

MICHAEL HOENIG

GARRY HUGHES

IASOS

INNOVATIVE
   COMMUNICATIONS RECORDS

JANSEN/BARBIERI

JEAN-MICHEL JARRE

EDDIE JOBSON

JEAN-PIERRE LABRECHE

LIFESTYLE RECORDS

MALAYSIAN PALE

ROBERT MARGOULEFF

MEGABYTE

PETER MERGENER AND
   MICHAEL WEISSER

MIND OVER MATTER

BRUCE MITCHELL

MOSAIC

NARADA RECORDS

MAGGI PAYNE

PEAK

ELAINE RADIGUE

GILES REAVES

KURT RIEMANN

STEVE ROACH

HANS-JOACHIM ROEDELIUS

SOMEI SATOH

JOHANNES SCHMOELLING

KLAUS SCHONNING

ROBERT SCHROEDER

KLAUS SCHULZE

KRISTIAN SCHULTZE

PETER SEILER

JOHN SERRIE

MICHAEL SHRIEVE

DON SLEPIAN

RICHARD SOUTHER

MICHAEL STEARNS

SYNCHESTRA

ISAO TOMITA

UPPER ASTRAL

VALLEY OF THE SUN RECORDS

VANGELIS

RICHARD VIMAL

RICHARD WAHNFRIED

WAVESTAR

YANNI

Golden Voyage volume has been used by hypnotists to relax their clients and by hospitals to promote patients' inner well-being. **New Age Traditional**

Beaver and Krause

Gandharva Warner Bros.

New Age Jazz is calmer, more spacious, and less frenetic than traditional jazz. On *Gandharva,* Paul Beaver and Bernard Krause create an especially innovative fusion of classical, jazz, and space music combining Moog synthesizer with cathedral organ, saxophone, and harp. This is jazz made for the heart rather than the mind; easily accessible and highly enjoyable. **New Age Jazz**

Bruce BecVar

Take It to Heart Shining Star/Backroads

A musician and guitar maker from Northern California, BecVar creates music that is a minimalist yet eloquent blend of melodic guitar and synthesizer instrumentals. Graceful and heartfelt music, it has a lyric patience that beguiles rather than demands. His instruments, like his original compositions, combine traditional tone formation with high-tech electronics. One of his guitars is on display at New York's Metropolitan Museum of Art. **New Age Pop**

David Behrman

Circling Six Lovely Music
Leapday Night Lovely Music

On the Other Ocean Lovely Music

Behrman's New Age Electronic compositions are gentle and accessible and far removed from sci-fi sound effects or cold, hard technological tones. *On the Other Ocean* in particular evokes a pastoral, quietly exploratory mood using computers and synthesizers. Guest contributors Maggi Payne and Arthur Stidfole add tasteful flute and bassoon parts to the soothing, meditative instrumentals. Cosmic in scope but intimate in tone, Behrman's music is warm, evocative, and lovely to listen to. **New Age Electronic**

Teja Bell

Dolphin Smiles (w/Kindler) Global Pacific
New Spirit of Christmas Music West
Petals (w/Allen, Canyon, Smith) Rising Sun
Snow Leopard Dancing World Arts/Global Pacific
Stellar Voyage (w/Dallas Smith) Rising Sun
Summer Suite (w/Allen, Canyon, Smith) Rising Sun

Bell creates a wonderfully uplifting message of joy and giving on *New Spirit of Christmas,* a modern classic crafted from an electronic orchestra, tubular bells, acoustic and electric guitars, along with violin. The influences he cites are equally eclectic: J. S. Bach, Jimi Hendrix, and Andrés Segovia. In talking about his music, Bell mentions *korkoro,* a Japanese word meaning "spirit of the heart." He lets *korkoro* make the music, "expanding the envelope of expression and the possibilities that lie within." A disciple of the martial arts (with black belts in both aikido and tai kwon do karate), Bell is currently working on an album of music inspired by the art of aikido. "Aikido is basically meditation in motion and lends itself to musical interpretation," explains Bell. His first album, *Petals,* demonstrates his talents on guitars, bass, and synthesizer in a classical-meets-jazz-fusion format. **New Age Jazz**

Pierre Bensusan

Bensusan 2 Rounder
Compilations Chant du Monde
Early Bensusan Lost Lake Arts
Musiques Lost Lake Arts
Pres du Paris Rounder
Solilai Rounder

He's been called a musician's musician, an orchestra of one, a poet of the guitar, a natural. His influences range from classical to modern jazz to the traditional music of Africa, Brazil, India, and beyond. Bensusan melds acoustic with electric sounds, redefining the possibilities of acoustic guitar. As George Winston puts it, "He plays the guitar as if it were the very soul of himself." His voice is an equally fluid instrument, and his songs on the album *Solilai* convey the softness of a flower, the passion of love, a soul on fire. **New Age Jazz**

William Bent

Sirius Lullabye Bentsounds

Solo composer Bent uses a complex array of synthesizers and various electronics to create the lovely, cosmically ethereal space music on *Sirius Lullabye.* Concentrating on the "human" qualities of electronic music, he promotes the accessible, warm, and inspired, encouraging inward voyaging through the use of drone, sustain, and repetition. This album is a gentle trip for New Age galactic voyagers. **New Age Space**

Jim Berenholtz

Turquoise Waters Earthsong

According to Berenholtz, the music on *Turquoise Waters* was received in a trance state and is intentionally aligned with shamanic traditions. The album features pervasive percussion mixed with vocal chants influenced by Native North American, Mesoamerican, and medieval Western traditions. Berenholtz, one half of the duo Xochimoki, is pioneering a new level of New Age Vocal music on this solo recording, a level of spiritual awakening that is inspired by the ancient mystics yet sounds relevant and meaningful today. (See also Xochimoki.) **New Age Vocal**

Erik Berglund

Beauty Sona Gaia

Berglund became fascinated with the harp after hearing the music of Joel Andrews. World-renowned harpist Mildred Dilling developed the design of the instrument he plays on *Beauty,* which is a modified single-action Celtic harp patterned after the Egan harp displayed in the Metropolitan Museum of Art. It is decorated with symbols based on those found in the *Book of Kells.* Produced by fellow artist Aeoliah, Berglund's *Beauty* yields a special feeling of warm elation through his sensitive interpretation of traditional works as well as his gentle, touching original compositions. Lovely, moving, stirring, the album lives up to its title. **New Age Traditional**

John Bernoff

(See Sky Canyon)

Beyond Records

The Voyage Beyond Sampler Beyond

The Voyage Beyond is a musical journey to the center of the listener's inner universe as conceived by label founder Suzanne Doucet. Artists featured include Doucet, Greg Stewart, Christian Buehner, Christaal, Al Gromer Khan, Pyramid, Karl Schaffner, Michael Shapiro, Lothar Grimm, and Helge Schroeder. Their individual electronic and acoustic sounds make the trip exciting, a thoroughly enjoyable overview of Beyond Record's eclectic style. **New Age Electronic, New Age Traditional**

Amin Bhatia

Interstellar Suite Cinema/Capitol

Synthesist Bhatia's *Interstellar Suite* is a masterwork debut. With an un-

wavering commitment to technical and "visual" excellence, Bhatia creates electronic music that thrills the listener with its symphonic sweeps of sound. Straddling the line between space and progressive music, Bhatia incorporates elements of both: long-sustained tones veer into unusually bright and resonant accents. This is pure dynamic power for New Age Space music fans. **New Age Progressive, New Age Space**

Timothy Bishop-Prasanna

Etheric Journeys 1 Chidvilas

Etheric Journeys 1 uses a heartbeat, synthesized water sounds, wind, harps, and "humming angels and dancing fairies" to quiet the mind and emotions. The music sounds tranquil and gentle, with delicate arrangements perfectly suited for headphones. This album is an effective antidote to civilization. **New Age East/West**

Serge Blenner

La Dimension Prochaine Life Style
Life Style Sampler 1 Life Style

A specialist in computer music, Blenner proves through his unique combination of acoustic and electronic sounds that it is possible to create "computer" music of great warmth and soul. Most important to him are "fantasy, and the use of the computer as an instrument of human creativity—a new electronic esthetic." *La Dimension Prochaine* is modern instrumental music—imaginative, melodious, and sensitive—that leads the listener into an aural adventure of a different kind. **New Age Electronic**

Steve Boone

Prelude to Lazaris Concept Synergy

Prelude to Lazaris is the instrumental theme music played prior to an appearance by the disincarnate entity Lazaris as channeled through Jach Purcel. Its swirling, colorful washes of synthesized sound and sparkling highs have made it a very popular album with both workshop participants and the public. Gently relaxing, the music seems to help "open the way" for altered states of consciousness. **New Age Meditation**

Ferne Bork
(See James Durst)

Christopher Boscole

Shimmer Nebula

Boscole's main love is solo piano pieces, and with the release of *Shimmer* he has evolved his own original acoustic music into a variety of New Age Jazz. His music is a strong, vigorous mix of high-caliber jazz, pop, and classical influences that generates good vibes. **New Age Jazz**

Philip and Pam Boulding
(See Magical Strings)

Kevin Braheny

Galaxies Hearts of Space
Lullaby for the Hearts of Space Hearts of Space
Starflight One Compilation Hearts of Space
The Way Home (aka *Perelandra*) Hearts of Space
Western Spaces (w/Roach and Burmer) Innovative Communications

Electronic composer Braheny is one of the foremost contemporary space music artists. His recordings are technically and musically sophisticated, spacious, serene, and very beautiful. As he says, "I modified or built my own equipment to ensure maximum sonic control and expressiveness. I try to get inside sounds and work from the inside out. My compositions flow from a sensual experience of sound, but they're designed by my knowledge of form and by my love, passion actually, for beauty." *Perelandra* is a New Age classic of refined and expressive synthesizer music that takes its name from C. S. Lewis's famous science-fiction novel. The three-part composition for synthesizer and choral voices is a lush and verdant evocation of Lewis's celestial paradise. On *Galaxies*, Braheny uses shimmering, floating electronics to explore the realm of celestial sound. *Galaxies* is a masterpiece, a crown jewel in the firmament of New Age Space music. *Lullaby for the Hearts of Space* was originally created live on the Hill/Turner syndicated radio show, "Music from the Hearts of Space," and blends synthesizer with exquisite saxophone meanderings for a space music classic. **New Age Electronic, New Age Space**

Thom Brennan

Mountains TMB Music

Inspired by artists as diverse as Terry Riley, Morton Subotnick, Tangerine Dream, and Brian Eno, Brennan has been creating musical improvisations since 1980. Combining an appreciation for sound textures and atmospheres, his music is mesmerizing, introspective, and hypnotic. *Mountains,* produced by Steve Roach, was recorded live in the studio to two-track, then digitally mastered, yielding clean, crisp notes and warm, resonant tones. The project was inspired by Brennan's remembrance of the lush valleys, mountains, sacred temples, and quiet shores of an island in the East China Sea. Brennan also co-composed "In the Heat of Venus," a twenty-minute epic tone poem with Steve Roach that can be heard on Roach's album, *Western Spaces.* Brennan states, "My music is not meant to be an exercise in melody or rhythm as much as an environment to sit in, just as you would go to the mountains, the desert, or the sea. Unlike most popular New Age music, mine does not rely solely on consonance or harmony. Discord is as important as consonance to create a range of moods and colors." **New Age Electronic, New Age Space**

Spencer Brewer

Emerald (w/Rumbel and
    Tingstad) Narada Lotus

Portraits Narada Lotus
Shadow Dancer Sona Gaia
Where Angels Dance Sona Gaia

Brewer's recordings have an impressionistic sensibility based on his amazing range, using scales and styles of music as diverse as Balinese, Gregorian, Gypsy, and jazz. *Portraits,* especially, demonstrates this eclectic quality, combining Brewer's keyboard work with a wide array of acoustic instruments. Its reflective compositions are sometimes quietly moody, other times brightly animated. **New Age World**

Doug and Matt Brody

Form and Illusion New World

The Brody brothers create modern, high-tech electronic music that pumps and vibrates, soars and glides on wings of shimmering synthesizers, enhanced by guitar, bass, keyboards, saxophones, and "many little boxes." In the spirit of Tangerine Dream and Jean-Michel Jarre, some selections have a pronounced European influence while others are classic space music. *Form and Illusion* will stimulate your intellect and energize your soul. (See also Mosaic.) **New Age Electronic**

Michael Brook

Hybrid (w/Eno) Editions EG

Brook brings a wealth of diverse influences and experiences into each of his original compositions. Born in Canada to English parents, he moved to New York to study Indian classical music with avant-garde composer La Monte Young. After a stint with the pop band Martha and the Muffins, Brook toured and recorded with Jon Hassell and Brian Eno. Brook has refined his haunting instrumental style into a technique he calls "infinite guitar" employing sustained tones. Brian Eno describes *Hybrid* as ranging from "dark, dense forests of sound to extremely sparse and open landscapes—views from several windows. . . . Structurally amorphous, like recordings of strange and unidentified gatherings." It combines state-of-the-art electronics with a variety of acoustic "world" instruments such as mbira, vibes, and conga drums for an unusual but delightful feel. **New Age Progressive**

Michael Brooks

Fragile Shoreline New World

Fragile Shoreline paints the serenity and vigor of nature through Brooks's melodic synthesizer works. With spacious, uncluttered electronic arrangements, *Fragile Shoreline* reminds the listener of the power of beauty, instilling a love of life. **New Age Electronic, New Age Space**

Joanna Brouk

Music by Joanna Brouk Hummingbird

A restrained yet stately piece for gongs, Brouk's release is enhanced by the mesmerizing and heart-stopping sound of the conch shell. When blown through a hole at one end, the conch shell emits a primal, almost unearthly, deep tone. Combined with gong percussion and reverberation, this unusual combination, rare on record, is well suited to inducing mystical, spiritual, or metaphysical states of consciousness. **New Age Meditation**

Gavin Bryars

Hommages Crepuscule
The Sinking of the Titanic Obscure

The Sinking of the Titanic is an experimental outing produced by the one and only Brian Eno. On it, Bryars combines organ, vibes, horns, harp, strings, and a host of other instruments with a repetitive tape loop of several lines sung from a hymn. Hypnotic and very moving, the music slowly builds until it is more than the sum of its parts; the music is a monument to both Bryars's and Eno's creative genius for arrangement and improvisation. **New Age Progressive**

Christian Buehner

Mirror Beyond
Nightflight Beyond
Sounds of the New Age Sampler Isis Music
Transformation Beyond
Transmission Beyond
Visions from Atlantis Beyond
Voyage Beyond Sampler Beyond

Synthesist Buehner is a composer, producer, and sound engineer who owns a cutting-edge recording facility in Munich, Germany. He does film scores and has created many guided meditation tapes in Europe. Buehner's music is very rich in texture and instrumentation with strong, pervading melodies. *Transmission,* especially, created with Suzanne Doucet, is a remarkable work that blends synthesizers, guitar, drums, pan flutes, bells, and chimes. It carries the listener on long lines of sound, a wave of warm light. **New Age Meditation**

Peter Buffet

The Waiting Narada Mystique

Buffet creates distinctive and epic musical visions with the help of several state-of-the-art synthesizers that "achieve the dynamics and feel that usually only come when you have people playing together." The music itself on *The Waiting* is cinematic in scope, drawing on many musical idioms and ethnic textures while featuring instruments as diverse as cellos, finger cymbals, gamelan bells, and Andean flutes. "Most people who hear it think it's very cinematic and visual. I've pushed to have a lot of acoustic sounds in the music, not to have it sound too electronic," Buffet adds. An extended, rich, original musical statement, *The Waiting* resounds with boldness and drama. **New Age Electronic**

Richard Burmer

Bhakti Point Fortuna
Mosaic Fortuna
Western Spaces (w/Roach and Braheny) Innovative Communications

The Indian word *bhakti* means an act of pure love and devotion. For Burmer, *Bhakti Point* is "an imaginary, wonderful place where the value of life is not simply a matter for intellectual discussion but a powerful feeling." The artist reflects this vision with his lush sonic tapestries drawing from his expertise with sitar, piano, and electronic music. *Mosaic* is a good relaxation aid but also somewhat playful, with short, bright electronic melodies mixing with subtly synthesized rhythmic flows. Each cut complements the next, yielding a fresh, pleasing totality. **New Age Electronic**

Richard Bush
(See Rocco Notte)

Ray Buttigieg

Compucircuit Cykxincorp
Etere Cykxincorp
Music for Movies Cykxincorp
Quantum Mechanics Cykxincorp

Similar in style to Klaus Schulze's solo works, Tangerine Dream, and a bit of Brian Eno's repertoire, Buttigieg creates New Age Electronic and Space music in a variety of moods and forms. *Music for Movies* is a collection of short soundtracks for the movies in your mind, while *Compucircuit* is orchestral, with separate movements that vacillate between the ethereal and the cosmic. **New Age Electronic, New Age Space**

C

Jeff Cain

(See Ghostwriters)

Don Campbell

Cosmic Classics Spirit Music
Crystal Meditations Spirit Music
Crystal Rainbows Spirit Music
Runes Spirit Music

Crystal Meditations is designed to bring the listener to a deep state of attunement and resonance with crystal energies; the music is particularly effective if used in conjunction with crystals for meditation and healing. The penetrating quality of the extremely slow, peaceful synthesizer and electric piano melts away tension with its sustained notes. The sounds are very simple and relaxing, with clear, bell-like notes creating pure, shimmering, soothing waves. Teachers of stress reduction at Harvard Business School found *Crystal Meditations* to be the most effective tape they utilized in their work. **New Age Sound Health**

Tony Campise

Bass Flute Loquat

Campise uses his bass and alto flutes to create a meditative environment on *Bass Flute*. His minimal notes spread slowly through the air, rising and falling like waves, to create a repeating, fading echo of each musical phrase. The selections are flowing and full of nurturing calm, enhancing relaxation. **New Age Meditation**

Sky Canyon (John Bernoff)

Breathe (w/Allen) Rising Sun
Petals (w/Allen, Bell, Smith) Rising Sun
Rising Sun Collection Rising Sun
Summer Suite (w/Allen, Bell, Smith) Rising Sun

Canyon says that he is "committed, through [my] musical expression, to the creation of a domain shift on the Earth." On *Summer Suite* he performs bright, jazzy melodies on vibraphone, synthesizers, and percussion, and is joined by Teja Bell, Marcus Allen, Dallas Smith, and Robert Powell. One extended suite on each side ensures sustained pleasure as the listener is invited to peregrinate through the various delights of this most pleasant of seasons. Natural sounds such as birdcalls are heard as the tape ends, a gentle reminder to awaken from reverie. **New Age Meditation, New Age Sound Health**

Wendy (aka Walter) Carlos

Beauty in the Beast Audion
By Request CBS
A Clockwork Orange CBS
Digital Moonscapes Columbia
Sonic Seasonings Columbia
The Shining Warner Bros.
Switched on Bach Columbia
Switched on
   Brandenburgs Columbia
The Well Tempered
   Synthesizer Columbia
Tron CBS

Predating New Age music's fascination with synthesizer textures by two decades, Carlos's work has changed the way we make and hear electronic music. Her revolutionary album, *Switched on Bach,* a mid-sixties collaboration with Bob Moog, was a breakthrough for the genre, proving to the world that synthesizers could indeed create music rather than sound effects or interesting noise. Since then Carlos has helped develop more than a dozen electronic instruments and processes that she uses extensively on her recordings. She has also thrown off the tuning and timbre

restraints that date back more than two hundred years and has created hybrid synthesized voices such as metal marimba, woodwind glockenspiel, and bowed timpani. Divided into four seasons, *Sonic Seasonings* blends computer music with live nature sounds into a soothing, ambient mix perfect for relaxation, meditation, and massage. With its haunting wolf cries and icy, crystalline desolation, the selection "Winter" is especially moving. The more recent *Beauty in the Beast* is an aural journey inspired by the exotic sounds of Bali, Africa, India, and the Middle East. Carlos's sometimes eerie, often lovely, lyrical instrumental stylings also have been featured on film soundtracks, notably for Stanley Kubrick's films *A Clockwork Orange* and *The Shining.* While her style expands and mutates with each new record, Carlos seems to enjoy incorporating classical themes and warm, organic world music instrumentation into her electronic repertoire. Her search for "new" sounds is exhaustive but yields a perfect blend of art and science. **New Age Electronic**

Danny Carnahan and Robin Petrie

Continental Drift Flying Fish
Two for the Road Flying Fish

Petrie's forte is hammered dulcimer, an ancient instrument enjoying a new popularity in this technological age. His work with Carnahan, who performs on mandolin, violin, and guitar, stands above most of the currently available neo-Celtic of-

NEW AGE ENVIRONMENTAL/NATURE SOUNDS

by P. J. Birosik

Historically, wildlife soundtracks—recordings of birds, animals, rain, the ocean—were used for documentary purposes only. Today, modern technology enables producers to arrange natural sounds into predetermined patterns. New Age musicians have utilized this breakthrough by blending their original compositions with a variety of natural sounds to create desired responses in the minds of their listeners. Natural soundtracks (without music) are used to deepen meditation, enhance studies, or combat noise pollution; for example, the sound of waves produces calming effects on patients, as has been documented in medical studies. Nature sounds mixed with music induces reverie and stimulates the imagination. When choosing an environmental recording, read the information carefully to determine whether it contains music plus natural sounds or just the sounds of nature.

ATMOSPHERE COLLECTION	ARIEL KALMA AND RICHARD
CHAZZ	TINTL
ALVIN CURRAN	NATURE RECORDINGS
MYCHAEL DANNA AND TIM	SCHAWKIE ROTH
CLEMENT	SOLITUDES
AKI DOMO	SYNCHESTRA
ENVIRONMENTS	TONY WELLS
JERRY FLORENCE AND	ANDREW WHITE
RANDALL LEONARD	HIROSHI YOSHIMURA
LOU JUDSON	

ferings. Joyful and complex, these compositions draw freely from the emotional reservoirs of European and American traditional music, jazz, classical music, and beyond. These pleasing, anti-frantic alternative tunes lay lightly on the ears and lend themselves to either ambient or dominant listening. **New Age Folk**

David Casper

Crystal Waves Hummingbird

Casper creates soothing, healing music—in his words, "psychophysiologically active sound." Using tuned crystal glasses, synthesizer, bells, gongs, horns, flute, cello, and other instruments, he creates music that floats gently; the title piece on his album *Crystal Waves* is a cascading, pure, shimmering sound. Each song on this release soothes the nerves, quiets the mind, or lifts the heart. An excellent release for either quiet contemplation or massage. **New Age Sound Health**

Oscar Castro-Neves

Oscar! Living Music

An honorary "life member" of the Paul Winter Consort, Castro-Neves is a virtuoso guitarist. His debut release, *Oscar!,* is filled with a percussive, joyful spirit that especially shines on such Brazilian-flavored tunes as "Bahia Calling" and "Street Corner Samba." On *Oscar!* he contributes piano, percussion, and vocal effects as well as Brazilian guitar, while Consort members add flute, piano, bass, and saxophone. The ensemble sound never overshadows Castro-Neves's tasty guitar licks and rhythmic phrasing on these jazzy selections. **New Age World**

Stephen Caudel

Wine Dark Sea Landscape

Caudel's solo album, *Wine Dark Sea,* utilizes synthesizers and guitars to create an atmospheric, moody, and emotional sound. The music ranges from majestic to delicate, en-ergetic to relaxed, inspired to inspiring. Rock, pop, and progressive influences underpin the selections, yet this is definitely New Age Electronic music in spirit and execution. **New Age Electronic**

Malcolm Cecil
(See Robert Margouleff)

Celestial Harmonies Records

Keys of Life (compilation) Celestial Harmonies

Keys of Life could very well be the ultimate New Age piano recording because it demonstrates the diverse but equally compelling talents of some of the most exciting modern composers: Florian Fricke, Hans Otte, Peter Michael Hamel, Herbert Henck, Cecil Lytle, and Terry Riley. Each piece is a mini-masterpiece, evoking a profusion of colorful mind-pictures. For those who love piano—really love piano—this release is a must. **New Age Solo**

Celestial Odysseys

Galactic Odyssey Valley of the Sun

Galactic Odyssey features exciting futuristic-style electronic music, expanding potentials of sound with contemporary synthesizer technology. The music creates a textured otherworldly environment, evoking the mystery and adventure of an intergalactic musical journey, pulsing with joyful energy and modern rhythms. New Age Space

Louis Cennamo
(See Stairway)

Krishna Chakravarty

Ananda Fortuna

On *Ananda*, Chakravarty, one of India's few female sitar masters, plays the ancient raga "Raga Pancham-Malkauns" with dedication and fire, accompanied by tabla and tamboura. This is an evening raga— very spiritual in nature, it is used to calm the soul prior to nightfall and rest. Although perhaps technically not New age music, the beautiful traditional Indian classics, with their stirring rhythms and subtle phrasings, are prized by East/West and world music fans. New Age East/West

Geoffrey Chandler

Starscapes Unity

Starscapes features New Age Electronic music with spacey overtones. Chandler's music embraces the celestial through a variety of innovative and powerful synthesized sounds, some of which are surprisingly warm and acoustic, while other tones spark and shimmer like novas. New Age Electronic

Chandresh

Inner Landscapes Nightengale

Enter the fairy-tale world of *Inner Landscapes* on the sweet yet lofty notes of Chandresh's grand piano. Gentle solo piano improvisations transport you into the land of make-believe, a state of deep detachment and gentle contemplation. New Age Solo

Jim Chappell

Dusk Music West
Tender Ritual Music West

Personal emotional moments return to us through Chappell's piano music. *Tender Ritual* is playful and pensive, refreshing music that stimulates the imagination while it combines classic and modern influences into a melodic, rhythmic tapestry of sound. *Dusk* is more romantic, ageless music, a soundtrack to the sunset. This music nourishes the heart and arouses the senses. New Age Solo

Chazz

A Time to Dream Mystic

Chazz uses acoustic, electronic, and natural sounds to create for the listener *A Time to Dream.* These spaciously arranged compositions evoke a gentle, quiet atmosphere, through groupings of bird song, bells, shakuhachi flutes, running water, guitar, piano, synthesizer, and an ethereal male choir. While the music itself ranges from hauntingly beautiful to lush and sensual, sometimes the instruments drop out to leave only the extended resonance of the environmental sounds for a totally relaxing effect. New Age Environmental, New Age Meditation

Checkfield

Distant Thunder American
  Gramaphone
Spirit Pausa
Wing, Water, and
  Stone American Gramaphone

Checkfield's music is like a fresh, clean breeze. The group predominantly features acoustic guitars and synthesizers, and the music is rooted in American folk tradition. On *Wind, Water, and Stone* additional instruments (violin and flute) add warmth and texture, and the melodies range from uplifting and cheerful to tranquil. On *Distant Thunder* the selections have a common theme: the majestic beauty of nature and the seasons. The title cut offers an impressionist view of an impending summer storm created with synthesizer, strings, and winds. New Age Folk, New Age Pop

Ray Cheser

Soft Motion New World

Cheser's synthesizer sounds reveal the versatility of technology when challenged by imagination. He says, "I strive for a sound that you can appreciate with your mind but truly hear with your heart." The album *Soft Motion* laces gentle melodies with undulating rhythms in a landscape of energizing harmonies. Playful undercurrents and reflective passages combine to create the sensation

of subtle movement through the stillness of tranquility. New Age Pop

Sri Chinmoy

Existence-Consciousness-Bliss Aum
Flute Music for Meditation Sri
  Chinmoy Center

Recorded during Chinmoy's 1984 Peace Concert tour, the peaceful flute improvisations on *Existence-Consciousness-Bliss* are inspired and spiritual in nature, lending themselves easily to meditation, contemplation, or quiet activities. In addition to the flute, Chinmoy plays the exotic esraj and sings and chants in traditional Hindu form. *Flute Music for Meditation* uses deep tone and resonance to provide a relaxing environment for inner focusing and meditation as well as precise movement meditational exercises like tai chi and yoga. New Age Meditation

Christaal

Mystic Traveler Beyond
The Voyage Beyond
  Sampler Beyond

As Christaal started exploring psycho-spiritual states of consciousness through meditation, he found that what he was experiencing internally could not be translated into songs with lyrics, so he began composing instrumental New Age music. Christaal says that *Mystic Traveler* was created to describe musically "the state which an individual finds himself in when he makes the decision to step on that very difficult path toward self-awareness." The record weaves flute, violin, and synthesizer into evocative guitar themes, creating hauntingly beautiful, highly melodic compositions. **New Age Traditional**

Suzanne Ciani

Neverland Private Music
Seven Waves Finnadar
The Velocity of Love Skylark/RCA

Ciani began her career as a performance artist in the early seventies, designing sounds around the buchla, one of the more sophisticated custom electronic instruments available at that time. Where synthesizers had previously been used for special effects and shock value, Ciani took the technology and imbued it with sensuality. Relying on theme, interesting arrangements, and plaintive melodies, she has developed lush electronics that communicate sheer emotion. "My music is very personal," Ciani states. "It really springs up from this deep reservoir of Jungian dreamlike emotions. It represents an original venture into what I consider a new classical tradition." *The Velocity of Love* features beautiful, slowly moving crystal fantasies. It soars, it lifts, it's music for the spirit as well as the ears. It is also one of the most requested records on New Age radio today—a new classic. **New Age Electronic, New Age Traditional**

Alex Cima

Cosmic Connection Polydor
Machines Wavefront

Music from the 21st Century GNP-Crescendo
Solid State GNP-Crescendo

Southern California-based engineer-synthesist Cima has traveled light-years into the galaxies of electronic and computer music, both as a solo artist and with his groups, Lem and On-line. Space music of the first degree, his soundscapes create images ranging from lonely lunar craters to breathtaking supernovas exploding into life. On the compilation *Music from the 21st Century*, Cima's selections take you on a sonic tour that is the aural equivalent of a ride in the space shuttle. You can actually feel the booster rockets churning. **New Age Electronic**

Clannad

Clannad Shanachie
Clannad 2 Shanachie
Clannad in Concert Shanachie

Clannad is at the forefront of the modern Irish music movement, combining traditional vocal pieces with beautiful instrumentals. The group has swiftly gained acceptance within the New Age community because of its intricate and delicate nonvocal pieces featuring harp, flute, and other traditional instruments. Its exquisite, lilting lead vocals and uplifting harmonies are soul stirring. If you've shied away from New Age World music or Irish-influenced music, try Clannad; there is simply no group better at mixing ancient and contemporary. **New Age Vocal, New Age World**

Tim Clement
(See Mychael Danna)

Barry Cleveland

Mythos Audion
Stones of Precious Water Chacra
Alternative

Cleveland plays electronic guitar using such processing devices as clocked multiple digital delays and tape loop systems as well as unorthodox playing techniques employing violin bows, Thumbo, the Masley Bowhammer, and E-Bow. This combination produces unique sounds that the average listener may not have heard before, some of which are strange but many of which are beautiful. On *Mythos* he is joined by members of Emerald Web on flutes, recorders, light percussion, and synthesizers. The resulting sound is progressive, vibrant, and highly individualistic—an exciting and rich three-dimensional landscape for mental pioneers. Great for headphones. **New Age Electronic, New Age Progressive**

Cluster

After the Heat Sky
Cluster Brain
Cluster II Brain
Cluster and Eno Sky
Curiosum Sky
Sowiesoso Sky

Cluster is one of the most successful groups to pioneer electronic music without succumbing to progressive rock arrangements. Particularly prolific, the duo is comprised of Hans-Joachim Roedelius and Dieter Moebius performing on a wide variety of keyboards, synthesizers, and electronic instruments. Influenced by avant-garde and minimalist sounds, their music often features repetition of sonic phrasing, cyclical motifs, and unexpected—yet not irritating—experimental aural departures. Teamed with Brian Eno on *Cluster and Eno,* they sculpt weird yet beautiful existential music with broad sweeps of sound and exotic images. This is music to feed the brain rather than nourish the heart; however, New Age Electronic music aficionados will relish its interesting textures and innovative arrangements. **New Age Electronic**

Jon Coe
(See Mirage)

Charles Cohen
(See Ghostwriters)

David Collett

Balance Spirit Music

Reviewer Ron Kendricks might have said it best: "Collett's music sounds like how the harmony between stars might sound." The music on *Balance* was composed to be used for relaxation, meditation, and self-healing. Acoustic guitars, gentle arrangements, and rich choral effects create music that encourages you to become less stressful, more tranquil, at peace with yourself and the world. **New Age Sound Health**

Ron Cooley

The Ancient and the Infant American Gramaphone
Daydreams American Gramaphone
Rainbows American Gramaphone

The Ancient and the Infant is a wonderfully balanced set of tunes combining jazz, rock, New Age, and classical elements into a cohesive whole. Cooley blends his acoustic guitar beautifully with oboe, strings, and other instruments. As he says, "I think the theme of [this album] is the realization that there's a lot to be learned from the old, from the past." **New Age Jazz, New Age Pop**

Jessie Allen Cooper

Heaven Sent Cooper Sound Waves
Soft Wave Sona Gaia

Cooper presents a personal blend of New Age and jazz that is notable for its earthy yet soothing quality. *Heaven Sent* features nature sounds recorded "on top" of the music, reflecting Cooper's concern for the environment. His second album, *Soft Wave,* is more rhythmically structured and makes use of synthesizers as well as acoustic instruments to create a pleasing, broad spectrum of sounds, tied together by the ongoing sounds of surf. *Soft Wave* will encourage you to drift into reverie. **New Age Jazz**

Steven Cooper

Crystal Garden Valley of the Sun

Key West Afternoon Valley of the Sun
Transcendence Valley of the Sun

Close your eyes and imagine yourself in a beautiful flower garden on a spring morning; growing among the flowers are quartz crystals that amplify your pleasurable experience. Cooper's *Crystal Garden* successfully captures this idyllic daydream using glistening harps, ethereal choral voices, and shimmering arrangements. This stream-of-consciousness album is fantastic for meditation. **New Age Meditation**

Scott Cossu

Islands Windham Hill
Sampler '82 Windham Hill
Sampler '84 Windham Hill
She Describes Infinity Windham Hill
Still Music FSM
Wild Dance Windham Hill

Cossu creates lighthearted, piano-based New Age Jazz. *She Describes Infinity* adds strings, guitar, and tasteful percussion to the keyboard melodies, creating an emotional range from gentle and calming to lively and uplifting. Cossu's music glides rather than percolates for an easygoing flow. **New Age Jazz**

Stephen Coughlin

Archways Fortuna
East Window East Window Productions
The Song of the Reed Fortuna

NEW AGE FOLK MUSIC

by P. J. Birosik

New Age Folk music is typically acoustic, deriving its influences from traditional folk and ethnic sources such as Celtic or bluegrass. But unlike most historical or contemporary folk music, it is instrumental music (without lyrics). New Age Folk usually has an uplifting sound, created with such instruments as six- and twelve-string guitars, Celtic harp, flute, and dulcimer. Some New Age Folk artists combine original compositions with classical folk music on their releases.

WILLIAM ACKERMAN	BENNETT HAMMOND
RUSS BARENBERG	TOM MCFARLAND
DANNY CARNAHAN AND	MEADOWLARK RECORDS
ROBIN PETRIE	BILLY MILLER
CHECKFIELD	NO STRINGS ATTACHED
GEORGE CROMARTY	MARK O'CONNOR
PEPPINO D'AGOSTINO	JUDITH PINTAR
MALCOLM DALGLISH AND	CHRIS PROCTOR
GREY LARSEN	ANDY STATMAN
WILLIAM ELLWOOD	ALLAN STIVELL
GARTH	WINDHAM HILL RECORDS

Coughlin has enriched the stream of New Age music in the West by drawing on the haunting and mystical melodic traditions of India, North Africa, and the Near East. His fluid flutes and reeds yield subtle, highly melodic music, as best displayed on *The Song of the Reed*. The soothing, healing sounds on this record enhance almost any quiet activity from meditation and relaxation to reading and daydreaming. On *Archways,* Coughlin collaborates with Moulabakhsh Funk, blending the sounds of jazz, classical, and East/West into one gentle stream that is sensual and rich in its ebbs and flows. A student of G. S. Sachdev, Coughlin's sound is based on a cross-cultural storehouse of world music influences. **New Age World**

George Criner

Behind the Sun
  Novus/RCA
New England Vanguard

Pianist Criner fuses a strong personal vision with elements of rock, jazz, and classical music, citing influences as diverse as Led Zepplin, Ravel, and Ahmad Jamal. He is especially inventive in the way he builds a musical theme, gradually expanding it to include exciting eclectic overtones and intricate harmonies. *Behind the Sun* is for the discriminating, adventurous sonic wanderer. **New Age Pop**

George Cromarty

Grassroots Guitar Thistle
Here They Are—the Gold Coast Singers World
The Only One Thistle
Wind in the Heather
  Dancing Cat

Cromarty is a guitarist, songwriter, and poet who has collected folk songs from all over the world and sings in more than twenty languages. *Grassroots Guitar* is a solo guitar album showing influences from various folk, ethnic, and classical styles in both theme and technique. The arrangement in general is spare with emphasis on motion. *Wind in the Heather* was produced by George Winston and is a more sophisticated yet very heartfelt effort. The guitar notes seem to float effortlessly, hanging on a breeze. **New Age Folk, New Age Solo**

Robin Crow

Creator Fortress/Global Pacific

Guitarist Crow has a delicate touch that wrings maximum emotion from each note he plays. On *Creator,* he adds keyboards, woodwinds, bass, and percussion to create moving, slightly moody selections showing contemporary and jazz fusion influences. Not suitable for meditative purposes, *Creator* is nonetheless an enchanting record that hypnotizes with its dazzling textures. **New Age Jazz**

Crystal

Rainbow Voyagers Crystal

This self-released cassette features smooth, flowing synthesizer washes with additional electronic punctuation. The selections are subtly crafted and tastefully accented throughout, although somewhat monotonic. **New Age Space**

Shawna Culotta and Edith Leicester

Foxglove Turquoise

Traditional ethnic tunes (Israeli, English, and Irish) mixed with original compositions performed on harp, flute, and synthesizer make *Foxglove* a warm and beautiful acoustic instrumental debut for this duo. Culotta's masterful harp sounds blend perfectly with Leicester's eloquent and lyrical flute playing; they are backed up by Randy Marchany and Wes

Chappell (of No Strings Attached) on dulcimer, bouzouki, and synthesizer, as well as Rick Ruskin on guitar, and Dave Miles on percussion. **New Age World**

Alvin Curran

For Cornelius New Albion
Maritime Rights New Albion

Curran is a composer and performer of instrumental electronic and environmental music. A primary concern in his work is to extract and refine the harmony, melody, and rhythms found in all natural sounds and render them as music. *Maritime Rights* is part of a series of environmental works that take place on, over, or near bodies of water and are inspired by such sounds as those of rowboats, ships' horns, foghorns, and entire seaports. Bells, gongs, whistles, and other instruments merge in an ever-thickening texture creating an imaginary panoramic soundscape. **New Age Environmental**

Cusco

Apurimac
Higher Octave

The German progressive ensemble Cusco creates a dynamic blend of contemporary electronic music with traditional Peruvian rhythms. *Apurimac* was inspired by a journey to the Apurimac River in the Peruvian Andes, which is considered to be the sacred source of the Amazon. Led by Michael Holm and Kristian Schultze, Cusco utilizes everyday instruments—bass, drums, guitars, keyboards—for a uniquely visionary, gentle, and majestic sound. You feel almost teleported to the Andean countryside. This album is an amazing American debut from a group that has achieved well-deserved superstar status in Japan. **New Age World**

D

Peppino D'Agostino

Acoustic Spirit Shanachie

Guitarist D'Agostino truly does have an "acoustic spirit" as well as an obvious ability to create extremely expressive, emotional songs. Many of the selections are up-tempo and blissful, perfect for traveling down two-lane blacktop under a hot afternoon sun. Joining D'Agostino for the ride are Windham Hill artists Darol Anger, Mike Marshall, and Michael Manring, who add bass, mandolin, and violin on a couple of tracks. One song on *Acoustic Spirit* is dedicated to the memory of guitarist extraordinaire Robbie Basho, an influencing spirit indeed on this folk- and jazz-inspired acoustic guitar album. **New Age Folk**

Malcolm Dalglish and Grey Larsen

Banish Misfortune June Appal/Lifedance
The First of Autumn June Appal
Jogging the Memory Windham Hill
Thunderhead Flying Fish
Winter Solstice Windham Hill

This duo's *Banish Misfortune* is a strictly Irish album, while *The First of Autumn* is split between Irish and traditional American music. *Thunderhead* finally surpasses those influences to become universal music; it's an exceptional collection of intricate yet smoothly flowing melodies. Its arrangements have a vibrancy and depth that are often lacking in traditional acoustic instrumental releases. Combining dulcimer, flutes, fiddles, guitar, and other instruments, Dalglish and Larsen span the range from instrumental folk ballads to haunting airs. **New Age Folk**

Mychael Danna and Tim Clement

Another Sun Chacra Alternative
The Electronic Orchestra (Danna solo) Harris

Elements (Danna solo) Harris
A Gradual Awakening Fortuna
Summerland Fortuna

Summerland is a musical landscape evoking languid summer days and blending graceful electronic impressions with the sounds of nature such as whirring cicadas and liquid bird song. Moving into New Age Environmental music, *A Gradual Awakening* has the duo blending rich electronic textures, tone colors in deep green and silver-gray, and streaming water sounds with the poignancy of a flute, the clarity of a guitar, and the haunting cries of native Canadian animals and birds. As Danna says, "The deepest reason for music is not an intellectual adventure but a chance to transcend the mundane and touch the spirit for a moment." **New Age Environmental**

David Darling

Amber (w/Alex Jones) Narada
  Lotus
Cycles ECM
Journal October ECM
Woodlands (w/Tingstad and
  Rumbel) Narada Lotus

Cellist Darling and pianist Alex Jones have achieved a true collaboration on *Amber,* a gracefully fluent musical conversation. Their sounds are subtle and delicate, their themes spiritual, and their kaleidoscopic playing styles combine to create sheer magic. At one moment the cello will provide a sonorous wash of tone to underpin the venturesome piano. Then roles reverse and it is the piano that provides the rhythmic foundation for the cello's flights of melodic improvisation. As featured cellist in the Paul Winter Consort, Darling has played on five albums with that group as well as appearing on over thirty albums with artists as varied as Tom Rush and Spyro Gyra. (See also Radiance.) **New Age Pop**

Gino D'Auri

Passion Play Sonic Atmospheres

D'Auri creates spatially enhanced flamenco guitar channeled via electrocrystals through deep digital reverb into the spaciousness of a thousand and one reflections. *Passion Play* is sensuous, romantic, almost unbearably intimate; you don't want the music to end. D'Auri doesn't just "play" the guitar; he caresses, embraces, and subtly teases it, wringing out heartrending melodies. This is music for lovers. **New Age Solo**

Larry David

Lunar Sky Eastern Gate
Peace Offering (w/Alex
  Jones) Eastern Gate

Pianist David's *Lunar Sky* features a subtle interplay of classical and contemporary styles on original compositions of varied tempos and emotional shadings. On *Peace Offering* David plays his own arrangements and structurings of six original songs by Alex Jones. The result is subtle, evocative, and richly rewarding. **New Age Pop**

Bill Davila

Spirit Windows Davila

Spirit Windows is a far-out blend of classical and ethnic music, drawing additional inspiration from jazz and world folk music. Davila plays guitar, synthesizer, ocarina flute, tamboura, percussion, and tabla on this wonderful, multitextural soup of a record, creating pleasantly exotic yet accessible sounds. Davila also hosts and produces "Journey Through the Realms of Music" on KPFK-FM and created the soundtrack for PBS's "The West of the Imagination" television series. **New Age World**

Peter Davison

Forest Avocado
Glide Avocado
Mountain Avocado
Music on the Way Avocado
Stargazer Avocado
Traces Avocado
Winds of Space
  Higher Octave

Winds of Space features pleasantly relaxing, emotionally uplifting tunes influenced by jazz, classical, rock, and blues. The piece "Soft Light" is particularly joyful. Davison composed and produced the album as well as played all the instruments—synthesizers, saxophone, and flutes. This is textural space music that lends itself well to focused, quiet activity. Davison derives his inspiration from nature and states that his music is his commitment to our planet. **New Age Jazz, New Age Space**

Alex de Grassi

Antiplano Novus
Clockwork Windham Hill
Sampler '82 Windham Hill
Sampler '84 Windham Hill
Slow Circle
  Windham Hill
Southern Exposure
  Windham Hill
Turning, Turning Back
  Windham Hill

Turning, Turning Back is a series of lighthearted tone poems performed by a modern master of the guitar. De Grassi's technique is impeccable: fine finger picking, open-chord structures (with the occasional closed chord), and gentle, lyrical rhythms. Colorful, lovely melodies are his specialty, and all of his albums repay the listener's effort. **New Age Solo**

Peter de Havilland

Bois de Boulogne
  Venture/Virgin

De Havilland is a musician who has ably embraced the latest in electronic technology yet not sacrificed the goal of creating strong evocative music. The title of his debut release is taken from the lovely wooded park in Paris that has a reputation as a rather risqué, almost dangerous place. De Havilland translates these mixed messages into warm, joyful songs that are also delicate, hypnotic, and sometimes edgy, shaped by his early training in classical piano. **New Age Electronic**

Jordan de la Sierra

Gymnosphere Unity
Song of the Rose Antiquity/Music Design
Valentine Eleven Music Design

De la Sierra says, "I am a possiblist. My life and work is dedicated to serving humanity's aesthetic evolution. Music, art, and poetry are my three children. With them I am laboring to build a bridge that will stretch from the shores of my life and time into a domain of gracious possibilities." His album *Valentine Eleven* features joyous, electro-symphonic pop songs with a big-world beat. De la Sierra likens it to "a psycho-acoustic journey into a new frontier." The music is sensually rich, the notes hanging like heavy, ripe fruit waiting to be plucked in some hedonist's version of heaven. This is music to dance to, skate through, actively listen to. *Song of the Rose* offers unedited piano improvisations that are spacious, intimate, and contemplative. The liner notes, written by Stephen Hill (of the radio show "Music from the Hearts of Space"), detail the extraordinary experiences that brought this release to the light of day. **New Age Pop, New Age World**

Richard del Maestro

Language of the Heart Expansion
Relax Expansion

Language of the Heart is filled with lush melodic synthesized sounds. The compositions combine surreal imagery with a delicate series of electronic passages to yield a refreshingly balanced, emotionally varied listening experience. Del Maestro tempers his New Age Pop music with jazz and classical influences, making *Language of the Heart,* in particular, very accessible to those just discovering New Age and contemporary instrumental music. **New Age Pop**

Constance Demby

Light of This World (Best Of) Sound Currents
Live at Alaron Sound Currents
Novus Magnificat Hearts of Space
Sacred Space Vol. 1 Sound Currents
Skies Above Skies Sound Currents
Sunborne Sound Currents

This visual/musical artist began formal meditation practice in the seventies and used the experience to develop spacious new forms of contemporary classical music. After experimenting with many ethnic acoustic instruments, Demby designed and constructed two large-scale sonic steel instruments: the Space Bass and the Whale Sail. The deep, otherworldly sounds that resonated from these instruments gave her the foundation on which to pioneer a whole new plane of sacred and meditative music. In 1982 she combined dulcimer, piano, and synthesizer to create the brilliant, inspirational original compositions of one of the first New Age classic recordings, *Sacred Space Vol. 1.* It encouraged listeners to go inside themselves, to explore their own budding spirituality. "Going inside means looking at your inner self," comments Demby. "You have to temporarily give up ego control and allow the music to take you into perhaps new and unexplored territories." In 1986 came *Novus Magnificat,* another New Age classic recording that is still topping radio play lists everywhere. This tour de force is a favorite among space music fans, too, as it features a host of synthesizers, percussion, organ, strings, and a chorus of voices created by Demby, plus some electronic effects by Michael Stearns. The record is a New Age symphony, articulating humanity's highest spiritual potentials. Stories abound of the positive effects *Novus Magnificat* has had on its listeners, and there have even been testimonials from doctors and nurses about its beneficial effects in hospitals. As Demby proclaims, "Music is the highest of the arts," it helps "make a connection of spirit through sound, transporting ourselves to our higher reaches, ascending through the music to the great overview." **New Age Traditional**

Bill Denny, Jr.

Intertribal Peyote Chants Vol. 1
  Canyon
Intertribal Peyote Chants Vol. 2
  Canyon
Intertribal Peyote Chants Vol. 3
  Canyon

Denny's three albums feature the sacred rites of the Native American Church of North America. During these rites, singers chant in orderly succession and partake of their sacramental water and peyote in a traditionally prescribed format. The chants themselves are hypnotically rhythmic and accompanied by repetitious pulsating drumming, along with other percussion effects. Some of these chants were experienced by participants in the various Harmonic Convergence gatherings that took place in August 1987 and celebrated the beginning of a new time cycle of purification. Now others with New Age and Native American interests can share the uplifting experience of these moving and compelling tapes. **New Age Native American**

(Georg) Chaitanya Hari Deuter

Aum Kuckuck
Basho's Pond Chidvilas
Buddham Sharnam Gachchami Chidvilas
Call of the Unknown (compilation) Kuckuck
Celebration Kuckuck
Cicada Kuckuck
D Kuckuck
Ecstasy Kuckuck
Flowers of Silence Chidvilas
Haleakala Kuckuck
Land of Enchantment Kuckuck/Celestial Harmonies
Nirvana Road Kuckuck
Sambodhi Music Chidvilas
San Chidvilas
Silence Is the Answer Kuckuck
Tea from an Empty Cup Chidvilas

Deuter was one of the first artists of his generation to effectively merge the West and the East both musically and philosophically. He was also one of the first to integrate the sounds of nature into his music, not as decorative effects but as vitalizing elements. Through travel as well as through his study with Gurdjieff and the Sufis, Deuter found pan-cultural inspiration early in his recording career. Lilting Indonesian, Indian, and Japanese harmonies waft through the soft melodies found on *Basho's Pond,* an early New Age classic recording. A mosaic of flute, harp, guitar, cello, tamboura, tabla, mandolin, and other instruments makes this release a sheer joy to listen to. Deuter weaves a magic carpet of melodies, transporting the listener above the clouds, lifting spirits with sparkling sound. The doors to a Zen monastery open up in *Tea from an Empty Cup;* bells, gongs, zither, and chimes ring out with grace and delicacy while the plaintive sound of a shakuhachi flute gently fills the room. Sit silently and allow the flute melodies to flow through on this one. *San* is another masterpiece of delicacy and grace, with guests Renu on harp and Rupesh on congas tying together the lyrical melodies and uplifting harmonies. Deuter's current Rajneesh-inspired music is beautiful, meditative, and arranged for quiet listening, especially on *Land of Enchantment.* As Deuter explains, "The message in the music is Light . . . derived from an understanding that life is a gift, and from an acceptance of the miracle that it is that everything exists." **New Age East/West, New Age Traditional**

Ron Dexter

(See Robert Bearns)

Do'a

Ancient Beauty Philo
Companions of the Crimson Colored Ark Philo
Light upon Light Philo
Ornament of Hope Philo

Do'a's self-composed music—the name comes from a Persian word signifying the call to prayer and meditation—fuses classical, jazz, folk, and ethnic elements into truly New Age world music. Mixing modern, traditional, and in some cases even archaic instruments, *Ornament of Hope* begins with a haunting, ethereal solo flute line that is soon punctuated with percussive guitar lines and then joined by a multiplicity of polyrhythmic melody lines. The mix may sound complicated, but it works. This is powerful and optimistic music. **New Age World**

John Doan

Departures Narada Lotus
Guitar Sampler Windham Hill

A versatile performer, composer, and storyteller, Doan has appeared frequently on radio and television in the United States and Europe, a testimony to his prowess on the harp guitar. This unusual instrument, popular on vaudeville stages a century ago but rarely seen today, features unfretted bass and treble strings on either side of an ordinary six-string guitar neck. Through it Doan has gained more power, resonance, texture, and expressiveness than previously possible with a standard guitar or harp. George Winston has said,

"John has restored my faith . . . there is still new and exciting music for the guitar." Doan's selections on *Guitar Sampler* reveal folk, Latin, classical, and pop influences, while *Departures* evokes an earlier era when life was innocent and simple. **New Age Solo**

Terence Dolph

Gongs for Meditation Pythagoras
Gongstream I Pythagoras
Gongstream II Pythagoras

The dramatic crashes of gongs in symphonic compositions were just a starting point for violinist Dolph's exploration of these ancient percussion instruments. The delicate, soft, and subtle effects possible with gongs inspired him to create a harmonic language based entirely on these instruments. On *Gongstream I* and *Gongstream II*, the blending and interplay of rhythms and timbres form the raw material, which the symphonically trained Dolph then leavens with violin and ocean stones (containing resonating chambers made by a boring clam). The simply arranged selections feature the gong's rich, lush tones while the stones give out syncopated pops, aqueous whispers, and strange but pleasant gulping sounds. These pieces are specifically created to enhance meditation, relaxation, body work, and holistic health applications. **New Age Meditation, New Age Sound Health**

Aki Domo

Sunrise Walk Along a Tahitian Seashore Invincible

Twilight Walk Along a Creek Invincible
Vista (w/V. Heldenleben) Invincible

Journey the energy fields just beneath the surface of Mother Earth and discover a new world. Japanese synthesist Domo has created a novel, panoramic *Vista* that is powerful, hypnotic, and truly visionary electronic music. On *Twilight Walk Along a Creek* and *Sunrise Walk Along a Tahitian Seashore,* Domo sculpts true three-dimensional sound images through a new process developed by Mirror Image Labs and Invincible. You'll experience all the sounds of nature with a fullness you've never heard before. Add to this Domo's sensitive, gentle, and surprisingly organic electronic inventions, and you've got a listening experience not to be missed. **New Age East/West, New Age Environmental**

Double Fantasy

Universal Ave. Innovative Communications

This group's secret is its free and easy sound, which melts New Age with "groove" music, electronics with jazz, served up in a laid-back style—a musical summer breeze, if you will. Electronic repetitions mix tastefully with guitar and other electro-acoustic instruments to create a soundtrack that is at times slow and moody, at other times rhythmic and pulsating with life. *Universal Ave.* will please both New Age Space music fans as well as aficionados of electronic music. **New Age Electronic, New Age Space**

NEW AGE JAZZ/FUSION

by Dallas Smith*

Smith is a writer, teacher, and pioneer of the electric wind synthesizer in addition to being a nonstop touring performer with numerous albums to his credit. He performs with electroacoustic harpist Susan Mazer.

New Age Jazz fusion represents a gentle rebellion against overly spacey New Age music and overly frenetic jazz. The music also avoids abstract dissonance—more associated with avant-garde jazz or classical compositions—in favor of mood, texture, and flowing movement. Through a blend of composition and improvisation, jazz crosses into New Age territory when it avoids standard "swing" rhythms, when its instrumentation is enhanced by synthesizers and the use of digital reverb, and when it is not repetitious or inaccessibly intellectual. New Age Jazz fusion is distinguished from other New Age subgenres, especially space music, by its rhythm and identifiable melodies. Its typical instrumentation includes: woodwinds, horns, percussion, keyboards, and string instruments.

JUSTO ALMARIO	RON COOLEY
DAROL ANGER AND BARBARA HIGBIE	JESSE ALLEN COOPER
	SCOTT COSSU
AZIMUTH	ROBIN CROW
JEFF BEAL	PETER DAVISON
BEAVER AND KRAUSE	STEVE DOUGLAS
TEJA BELL	D'RACHAEL
PIERRE BENSUSAN	FRIEDEMANN
CHRISTOPHER BOSCOLE	DAVID FRIESEN

*Artist listing compiled by Patti Jean Birosik.

JERRY GOODMAN	ANTONIO FORCIONE
TOM GRANT	NIGHT ARK
DAVID HAYES	OREGON
HIROSHIMA	JEAN-LUC PONTY
INVINCIBLE RECORDS	JOHN RENBOURN
NANCEE KAHLER	THE TONY RICE UNIT
PETER KATER	RISING SUN RECORDS
BEN TAVERA KING	LEE RITENOUR
STEVE KUJALA	TERRY RYPDAL
YUSEF LATEEF	VLADISLAV SENDECKI
LATITUDE	JOHN SERRIE
JOAQUIN LIEVANO	SHADOWFAX
LIFE STYLE RECORDS	RICHARD SHULMAN
LYLE MAYS	BEN SIDRAN
SUSAN MAZER	SIRI NAM SINGH
MEADOWLARK RECORDS	MARK SLONIKER
PAT METHENY	DALLAS SMITH
MOSAIC	JORGE STRUNZ AND
ALPHONSE MOUZON	ANDESHIR FARAH
MUSIC WEST RECORDS	RIC SWANSON
NARADA RECORDS	JOHN THEMIS
KENNETH NASH	FRED WACKENHUT
JOHN KAIZAN NEPTUNE	TIM WEISBERG
JAMES NEWTON	WINDHAM HILL RECORDS
EDUARDO NIEBLA AND	

Double Image

In Lands I Never Saw Celestial
Harmonies

Double Image is comprised of
composer/performers David Fried-
man and David Samuels who use vibraphone, marimbaphone, and percussion to create ethereal music that
sings and rings as clear as a thousand
crystals. The instrument combination
is rather unusual in New Age music,
but it works extremely well. *In Lands
I Never Saw* lifts the spirit while
soothing the mind and relaxing the
body. **New Age Meditation**

Suzanne Doucet

Brilliance (w/William
 Wickman) Isis
Reflecting Light II Isis
*Sounds of the New Age
 Sampler* Isis
Transformation
 (w/Buehner) Beyond
Transmission (w/Buehner) Beyond
*The Voyage Beyond
 Sampler* Beyond

Doucet is the owner of the Only
New Age Music record store, a
founder of the New Age Music Network, as well as president of both Isis
and Beyond record labels. A singer/
songwriter since 1963, with more
than fifteen pop albums released in
Europe, Doucet became involved
with the New Age movement in
1970 after taking a year-long vision
quest journey and studying meta-
physics, music therapy, and psychology. *Brillance,* co-composed with
William Wickman, features Doucet

on synthesizer creating cosmic
drones, sparkling arpeggios, and vibrant, uplifting melodies aimed directly at the emotions. The music
soars, swoops, and heads out into
space with crystalline precision on
warm jet streams of sound. On *Reflecting Light Vol. II,* Doucet explores
two complementary mind-states inspired, she says, "by reincarnation
experiences and the desire to describe musically the states over
there." Both releases are New Age
Traditional. **New Age Traditional**

Steve Douglas

The Music of Cheops Cheops

Similar in concept to Paul Horn's
Inside the Great Pyramid album,
Douglas's *Music of Cheops* features his
solo saxophone improvisations recorded inside the king's chamber of
the great pyramid in Egypt. The
music is New Age Jazz, with more
emphasis on the jazz than on the
meditative, less frenetic New Age
stylings. However, there is plenty of
emotional fuel on these selections,
which sound modern and ancient at
the same time. **New Age Jazz**

D'Rachael

Gong with the Wind (w/Dean
 Evenson and Kramer) Soundings
 of the Planet
Joy to the World (w/Dean
 Evenson) Soundings of the Planet
Lifestreams (w/Dean
 Evenson) Soundings of the Planet
Peaceful Pond (w/Dean
 Evenson) Soundings of the Planet

Tropic of Paradise (w/Dean Evenson) Soundings of the Planet
Whistling Wood Hearts (w/Dean Evenson and Kramer) Soundings of the Planet

D'Rachael plays piano, vibes, guitar, and flute, but it is with the stringed harp that she creates magic. Her collaborations with flutist Dean Evenson are fresh, spontaneous compositions that emanate a gentle yet vibrant mood. On *Peaceful Pond* she teams with Dean and Dudley Evenson to create rich, serene music through the harmonious interplay of flute, harp, cello, keyboards, and handharp. *Tropic of Paradise* is a symphony of natural sounds created with flute, harp, sitar, guitar, autoharp, violin, and bells, evoking waterfalls flowing into crystal-clear lagoons as exotic birds share their song of tropical paradise. **New Age Jazz, New Age Traditional**

Paul Dresher

Nightsongs New Albion
This Same Temple Lovely Music

The arresting album cover art on *Nightsongs* does not give away all the surprises tucked inside the jacket. Dresher performs mental music with the New Performance Group of the Cornish Institute. On one track, a single note hangs suspended, then doubles, triples, becoming a multilayered melody with thick textures oozing out of the vinyl until it coalesces into a slow, satisfying movement. Perhaps not suitable for New Age Traditional music fans, this album is a must for those looking for the more progressive side of the genre. **New Age Progressive**

James Durst and Ferne Bork

Alive in Concert Songs for a Small Planet
How Can I Keep from Singing (Bork solo) FootBridge
Light Up the Sky WorldWind/Songs for a Small Planet
Planetary Citizen (Durst solo) PhoeniXongs/Songs for a Small Planet

Singer/songwriters Durst and Bork are in the vanguard of New Age Vocal musicians. Their instrumentation on *Light Up the Sky* ranges from sparse (classical guitar and English horn on "Let the Joy Do Its Part") to full (synthesizer, bass, drums, cello, oboe, and electric guitar on the title track). Combining original compositions with New Age and folk favorites by songwriters Tom Paxton, Amanda McBroom, and Bob Gibson, the duo performs material that expresses social concerns, the desire for change through personal growth, and the empowerment of individuals in societies throughout the world. **New Age Vocal**

Durutti Column

The Guitar and Other Machines Venture/Virgin

The Durutti Column is the brainchild of Vini Reilly, composer, guitarist, and sole member of the group to date. This is modern music on the cutting edge, blending both classical and pop influences for an atmospheric, uplifting, mysterious sound. "Music can be an emotional safety valve . . . a lament against the present absence of future," he says. Starting out gently, *The Guitar and Other Machines* builds to a bright, melodic, and memorable musical force that envelops the listener. This is progressive music for a new age. **New Age Pop**

John Dyson
(See Wavestar)

E

Brook Medicine Eagle

For My People Earthsong
Singing Joy to the Earth Earthsong

Eagle is a healer, teacher, and singer from the Crow reservation in Montana. Her path is that of "bringing spirit, aliveness, joy, harmony, abundance, and oneness to all our relations." *For My People* features vocal harmonies, drums, rattles, and other instruments along with the traditional Crow chants. It is Eagle's intent that this music be used to "align the consciousness of people around the world." Although enjoyable, *Singing Joy to the Earth* is not designed for casual listening but for education. **New Age Native American, New Age Vocal**

Paul Edwards

All Through the Night Revere
Silent Night Revere

All Through the Night features luxurious, lush, and gentle treatments of traditional lullabies. Electronic composer Edwards's peaceful, relaxing, and sleep-inducing sound mixes flute, guitar, choir, chimes, and crickets, integrating each seamlessly into fluid, simple melody lines and textured harmonies. **New Age Pop**

Elevation Express

Going Up Invincible
Homecoming Invincible

Stimulate new levels of awareness in your meditations with the beautiful electronic orchestral music of Elevation Express. On *Going Up* electronic lines weave deftly with a lively tempo to create great music for relaxation or recreation. Subtle Latin undercurrents warm up the compositions and add texture to the music. *Homecoming* features a sixty-beat-per-minute heartbeat background tempo and vibrating electronic effects to help the listener achieve a deeply relaxed state of mind. **New Age Meditation, New Age Sound Health**

William Ellwood

Openings Narada Lotus
Renaissance Narada Lotus

A self-taught guitarist, Ellwood started with folk and rock "while searching for more subtle instrumental forms," as he puts it, such as baroque, renaissance, and classical. Ellwood conceives his creativity as a kind of alchemy "transforming the evolving face of reality into a melodic setting" and has called the process of his art "the Tao of picking." On *Renaissance,* keyboards, percussion, flute, and bassoon join his steel-string and classical guitars to expand the sumptuous compositions with color and warmth. **New Age Folk**

Emerald Web (Bob Stohl and Kat Epple)

Aqua Regia Stargate
Catspaw Audion
Dragon Wings and Wizard Tales Stargate
Light of the Ivory Plains Fortuna
Love Unfolding Stargate
Nocturne Fortuna
Sound Trek Stargate
Valley of the Birds Stargate
Whispered Visions Stargate

This electronic instrumental duo creates ethereal, progressive New Age music using a wide variety of instruments including synthesizers, flutes, Lyricon, shakuhachi flute, and sampling equipment. *Photonos,* Emerald Web's videocassette release, is a feast of pulsating multicolored mandalas and swirling lasers, digitally orchestrated with impressionistic melodies that reflect many cultures and times. *Light of the Ivory Plains* ranges from etheric and richly romantic selections to heavily rhythmic, energetic electronics. *Nocturne* features more reflective, twilight themes as well as the Celtic harp of Patrick Ball. Yet, through all these moods, Emerald Web's music is always like an intimate conversation. **New Age Electronic**

Daniel Emmanuel

Rain Forest Music North Star
Wizards North Star

Combining synthesizer with acoustic instrumentation, Emmanuel creates nurturing, healing, visionary New Age music. *Rain Forest Music* is particularly successful, inspiring aural images of verdant lushness, an overhead canopy filled with brightly colored birds, chattering wildlife, and sweet aural fragrances. **New Age Sound Health**

Brian Eno

Another Green World Obscure
Apollo, Atmospheres, and Soundtracks Editions EG
Before and After Science Editions EG
The Catherine Wheel (w/David Byrne) Warner Bros.
Day of Radiance Editions EG
Discreet Music Editions EG
Dune Polygram
Evening Star (w/Robert Fripp) Antilles
Fourth World Vol. 1 (w/Hassell) Editions EG

Here Come the Warm
Jets Editions EG
Moebius, Roedelius, Eno Best
More Blank than Frank Editions
EG
Music for Airports Editions EG
Music for Films Editions EG
My Life in the Bush of Ghosts
(w/David Byrne) Warner Bros.
No Pussyfooting (w/Robert
Fripp) Antilles
On Land Editions EG
The Pearl (w/Harold
Budd) Editions EG
Plateaux of Mirror (w/Harold
Budd) Editions EG
Possible Musics
(w/Hassell) Editions EG
*Taking Tiger Mountain by
Strategy* Editions EG
Thursday Afternoon Editions EG
*Working Backwards
1983–1973* Editions EG

Musician, producer, and philosopher Eno is a primal force in contemporary music. Assailing previously established musical boundaries through his involvement with Roxy Music, David Bowie, Talking Heads, and U2, Eno also created prototype New Age albums with his Ambient Music Series, synthesizing elements of rock, minimalism, and electronics. *Here Come the Warm Jets* and *Taking Tiger Mountain by Strategy* in 1973 featured Eno's progressive compositions as well as a stellar cast of guest musicians, including Phil Manzanera, Robert Fripp, Andy MacKay, John Wetton, and Phil Collins. But it was 1975's *Another Green World* that found him concentrating his studio talents on the subtle colorations of the synthesizer rather than vocally oriented electro-pop tunes. The music was subtle, lush, nonintrusive, a forerunner to today's New Age Space music. *Discreet Music* continued this trend. "I was trying to make a piece that could be listened to and yet ignored . . . in the image of Satie who wanted to make music that could 'mingle with the sound of knives and forks at dinner.' " The album's soothing quality arises from two simple melodic lines, digitally processed to create waves of uplifting and inspiring sounds. Of the popular *Music for Airports,* another ambient release that gives a sense of place rather than story line in terms of composition, Eno says, "One of the things music can do is change your sense of time so you don't really mind if things slip away or alter in some way. It's about getting rid of people's nervousness." His collaboration with Harold Budd and Laraaji on the rest of the Ambient Music Series *(On Land, Day of Radiance,* and *Plateaux of Mirror)* has yielded some of the most achingly beautiful and haunting ethereal audio images put to tape. New Age Electronic, New Age Progressive, New Age Space

Roger Eno

*Apollo, Atmospheres, and
Soundtracks* (w/B. Eno) Editions
EG
Dune (w/B. Eno) Polygram
Music for Films Vol. II (w/B.
Eno) Editions EG
*New Voice on the Wild
Frontier* Editions EG

During his brother Brian's tenure with the glitter-rock band Roxy

Music, Roger Eno pursued a more classically oriented path, becoming an accomplished pianist and supporting himself by working as a music therapist at a hospital for the handicapped. He brings a sensitive, emotive approach to the keyboards, evoking sensual, colorful, and vibrant passages on *New Voice on the Wild Frontier* as well as powerful majesty on the soundtrack to the film *Dune*. **New Age Sound Health**

Environments

Be-In/Dusk ATC
Bells/Breeze ATC
Blizzard/Thunderstorm ATC
Dawn/Dusk ATC
Heartbeat/Wind in Trees ATC
Intonation/Summer ATC
*Meadow/Night in the
    Country* ATC
*Pacific Ocean/Carribean
    Lagoon* ATC
Sailboat/Stream ATC
Seashore/Aviary ATC
Thunderstorm/Gentle Rain ATC

Environments is an excellent series of pure, innocent, lovely, ambient nature sounds. No need for additional music here; each audio environment, recorded with state-of-the-art technology, is complete unto itself. Whether you choose to enjoy the intensity of a blizzard or the calm peacefulness of a night in the country, these releases can transport you to another place and time. **New Age Environmental**

Kat Epple
(See Emerald Web)

Rick Erlien

Ascending Colors Kicking Mule

Mixing classical and jazz influences, solo pianist Erlien creates luminous mellow sounds on *Ascending Colors*. This is music to stimulate the imagination, in a gentle way, to indulge in some breathless imaginings. The record is consistently lyrical and pleasant, suitable for concentrated listening rather than for background. **New Age Solo**

Eternal Wind

Eternal Wind Flying Fish
Terra Incognita Flying Fish

Eternal Wind—both the group and the eponymous album—invokes the music of many cultures. Interweaving wood blocks, saxophone, trumpet, guitar, tablas, flute, and other instruments, Eternal Wind creates a swirling vortex of evolving musical repetitions that uplift the listener into a transcendental state. **New Age World**

Dean and Dudley Evenson

Desert Dawn Song Soundings of
    the Planet
Evensong Soundings of the Planet
Gong with the Wind
    (w/D'Rachael and
    Kramer) Soundings of the Planet
Joy to the World (w/D'Rachael)
    Soundings of the Planet
Lifestreams (w/D'Rachael)
    Soundings of the Planet
Peaceful Pond (w/D'Rachael)
    Soundings of the Planet

54

Sampler (compilation) Soundings
of the Planet
Soaring (w/Barabas) Soundings of
the Planet
Tree O2 (w/Kramer and
Verdeaux) Soundings of the
Planet
Tropic of Paradise (w/D'Rachael)
Soundings of the Planet
Whistling Wood Hearts
(w/D'Rachael and Kramer)
Soundings of the Planet

Flutist Dean merges pop, rock, and classical influences while Dudley plays open-tuned autoharp and uses her voice as a complementary instrument on many of their "peace through music" themed releases, such as *Peaceful Pond* and *Tree O2*. A good introduction to the Soundings of the Planet players can be found on the *Sampler* cassette. Selections feature gentle instrumentation such as flute, harp, and cello in symphony with such natural forest sounds as birdcalls and the flow of mountain streams. The Evensons are cofounders of Soundings of the Planet studio, record company, and musical group; with Jonathan Kramer they have completed a Citizen's Diplomacy concert tour of the Soviet Union. **New Age Traditional, New Age World**

Exchange (Gerald O'Brien and Steve Sexton)

Into the Night Audion

As a member of the seventies group Klaatu, keyboardist O'Brien was a progressive music explorer even before his songwriting involvement with such contemporary pop groups as Loverboy and Glass Tiger. Sexton was a member of pop band Red Rider as well as top session keyboardist for many multiplatinum recording artists. Their collaboration, *Into the Night,* merges their individual commercial and experimental influences into a seamless tapestry of sound. Although no instrumentation is listed on the liner notes, the listener can enjoy synthesized accents of South American flute and percussion layered between swirling electronic lines. **New Age Progressive**

F

Franco Falsini

Cold Nose Polydor

This electronic space music album is the soundtrack for the Italian film *Naso Freddo* (cold nose). Known primarily for his more progressive works, Falsini here uses synthesizer and guitar to create a darkly melodic, mesmerizing mood. At times spacious, atmospheric, and ambient in tone, *Cold Nose* is, at other times, a lushly rich tone poem that resonates and thrills. **New Age Space**

Ardeshir Farah

(See Jorge Strunz)

Larry Fast (Synergy)

Audion Passport
Computer Experiments Vol. 1 Audion
Cords Passport
Electronic Realizations for Rock Orchestra Passport
Games Passport
Metropolitan Suite Audion
Semi Conductor Passport
Sequencer Passport

Under his own name as well as the "group" name Synergy, Fast has released a series of stunning albums demonstrating his singular talent for incorporating harmony and traditional structure into the characteristically minimalist electronic composition. *Metropolitan Suite* was inspired by the changing face of New York City from 1900 to 1930. Its tracks fairly hum with rhythmic throbbing as the lush, cyclical soundscape encompasses all sorts of high-tech vibrancy. Like his associates Wendy Carlos and Robert Moog, Fast designs and customizes electronic equipment in order to realize his personal aural imagery on tape. Much of Fast's work is sophisticated electronic avant-garde music, and devotees of experimental or modern classical music will find it intelligent and rewarding. However, *Computer Experiments Vol. 1* is rather dissonant and falls outside the realm of New Age. **New Age Electronic**

Morton Feldman

The Early Years Odyssey
Morton Feldman Odyssey
Music of Our Time Odyssey

Keyboardist Feldman is an avant-garde composer whose work embraces both spaciousness and meditative qualities. On *Music of Our Time* the delicate tinkling of chimes mixes with high, airy, yet powerful choral voices to create an intense aural experience perfect for focused voyaging or mystical meditations. **New Age Space**

Deborah Fier

Firelight Ladyslipper
In Your Hands Freedom Music

"Music is a feeling, a device," says Fier. "It draws out an emotional response. It lets you relax." Fier is a singer, songwriter, and keyboardist who creates well-crafted personal and political songs with jazz/blues/folk roots. *In Your Hands* features both heartfelt instrumentals and intellectually stimulating lyrics. There's strength and spiritualism running through each track, as well as spontaneity and humor. Fier also conducts sound health workshops, for as she says, "The tones of music can open one up and can dispel anger and pain." **New Age Vocal**

Stephen Longfellow Fiske

I Believe in You Songs for a Small
    Planet
Seeds of Peace Songs for a Small
    Planet

Touch New World
*Transformation: The 100th
    Monkey* Songs for a Small
    Planet

Since the early seventies, singer-songwriter Fiske has been an activist in the New Age movement. His decision to become a conscientious objector during the Vietnam War forced him to closely examine his spiritual beliefs and led him to explore yoga, meditation, and other spiritual disciplines. Fiske gained national fame by composing new lyrics to the American national anthem, which he titled "The Peacemakers Planetary Anthem." His records include both instrumental and folk-inspired word-and-music selections, delivered with either playful or political attitudes. Of the songs on *Touch*, Fiske says, "I feel a New Age song could be any style. . . . [There's] a quality of connectedness with an underlying universal and unifying truth or wisdom. [It] need not preach, proselytize, or hit you over the head with a message . . . but somewhere the listener has the opportunity to come away with a sense of connectedness to a higher wisdom or deeper source within. There is a quality of upliftment about it." **New Age Vocal**

Jerry Florence and Randall Leonard

Music from the Heart Vol. I Hay
    House

For New Age music listeners yearning for peace and deep relaxation, *Music from the Heart* could be a ticket to the bliss zone. Mixing warm heart music with ocean and other natural sounds, Florence and Leonard avoid many of the clichés of previously released environmental/ music records while delivering a soundtrack perfect for deep meditation, guided reverie, or yoga. The repetitive and sustained synthesizer tones move slowly, creating a sense of serenity, while the other instruments are carefully arranged to softly soothe your psyche and calm your nerves. **New Age Environmental, New Age Meditation**

Antonio Forcione
(See Eduardo Niebla)

Francisco

Cosmic Beam Experience CBE

Francisco has created an instrument he terms the "beam" using a steel girder and some customized electronic gear. With it he sculpts sound not just within human hearing range but above and below it as well. In the seventies, during a live performance, the awesome power of the instrument was revealed when it cracked the concrete floor it was resting on! The sounds created are eerie yet primitive, mystifying and transcendent, alternately reminiscent of a synthesizer and some alien creature's harp. This is great voyaging music. **New Age Progressive, New Age Space**

Friedemann

Indian Summer Narada Equinox

Indian Summer is energetic, boldly stated New Age Jazz. Freidemann plays both acoustic and electronic guitar, accompanied by synthesizers, brass instruments, and a Chinese hammered dulcimer played by keyboardist Johannes Wohlleben. Each selection is light, lyrical, and engaging. Friedemann says, "Although the record does not have any singing on it, it at last gives voice to my own musical language." **New Age Jazz**

David Friedman
(See Double Image)

David Friesen

Amber Skies Palo Alto
Heart to Heart (w/Horn) Golden Flute
In Concert (w/Horn) Golden Flute
Inner Voices Global Pacific
Live from Russia (w/Horn) Golden Flute
Shared Visions (w/Halpern) Halpern Sounds

Bassist Friesen explores jazz, New Age, and world music both as a solo artist and as a performer with Chick Corea, Paul Horn, Ralph Towner (from the group Oregon), and others. *Inner Voices* has a spiritual, reverent feel due in part to his reworking of three traditional hymns, "Amazing Grace," "O Come Emmanuel," and "What Child Is This?" ("Greensleeves"). The rest of the album is original material with the track "Peace Be Still" beginning and ending with a Chinese gong that sets the mood for meditation—a palpable quietness. As Friesen says, "All the

59

NEW AGE MEDITATION MUSIC

by Apurvo*

Apurvo is a recording artist who performs solo and with modern dance companies and theater groups. She also edits The World of Harmony, *a magazine dedicated to music and meditation.*

New Age Meditation music is intentionally created to expand awareness into deeper and higher levels of consciousness. Some releases are instrumental; others feature chanting or singing styles that induce meditation. Such music removes negativity in the listener through careful arrangement of each note and tone pattern. As Osho Rajneesh said, "Meditation is the art of hearing the soundless sound, the music of silence." However, not all meditation music is serene and gentle in nature. Dynamic meditation music often combines drumming and pulsing music to stimulate an active response within the listener, such as dancing or graceful movement.

AEOLIAH	JOANNA BROUK
MARCUS ALLEN	CHRISTIAN BUEHNER
JOEL ANDREWS	TONY CAMPISE
APURVO	SKY CANYON
STEVE BOONE	CHAZZ

*Artist listing compiled by Patti Jean Birosik.

music that I write is spiritual to me. It's written to show forth the glory of the kingdom of God, his love toward mankind." Having played bass on dozens of albums for other artists, Friesen brings a special perspective to the instrument for his own solo work, "keeping it interesting [by] bowing notes and stacking chords with the help of a digital delay so that it can sound like a string choir of several basses." **New Age Jazz**

Eugene Friesen

Callings (w/P. Winter Consort) Living Music
Canyon (w/P. Winter Consort) Living Music
Concert for the Earth (w/P. Winter Consort) Living Music
Missa Gaia (w/P. Winter Consort) Living Music
New Friend (w/Halley) Living Music

SRI CHINMOY

STEVEN COOPER

CHAITANYA HARI DEUTER

TERENCE DOLPH

DOUBLE IMAGE

PAUL EDWARDS

ELEVATION EXPRESS

JERRY FLORENCE AND
  RANDALL LEONARD

SYLVAN GREY

GYUME TIBETAN MONKS

THE HABIBIYYA

STEVEN HALPERN

AKIRA ITOH

KANO

KARMA

LIV SINGH KHALSA AND SAT
  WANT KAUR KHALSA

VAN KRUEGER

LARAAJI

JONATHAN LEE

FRANK LENTZ

ALVIN LUCIER

INGRAM MARSHALL

KIM MENZER

KARMA MOFFETT

NIGHTENGALE RECORDS

OM

SWAMI KRIYA RAMANANDA

KIM ROBERTSON

TONY SCOTT

AVTAR SINGH AND KULWANT
  SINGH

LIV SINGH

DAVID SUN

JOHANNES WALTER

RICHARD WILKINS

STEPHEN WINFIELD

HENRY WOLFF AND NANCY
  HENNINGS

Cellist Friesen has taken his instrument far beyond its traditional chamber ensemble and orchestral roles to a position as "lead instrument" through both solo performances and his work with the Paul Winter Consort. *New Friend* features Friesen with fellow Consort member Paul Halley in a collection of instrumental compositions for cello and keyboard that sound fresh, bright, and invigorating. Arrangements feature jazz improvisations influenced by melodic pop—a touchingly warm blend of sounds that grows richer with repeated listenings. **New Age Traditional**

Edgar Froese

Ages Virgin
Aqua Virgin
Epsilon in Malaysian Pale Virgin
Macula Transfer Brain

Froese creates synthesized, etheric space music that is both tranquil and tropical in flavor. On *Epsilon in Malaysian Pale,* he combines environmental sounds with flute and electronic instruments to create music that is alternately intoxicating and delicate, shimmering and subtle. Froese's multitextured pieces are a virtual sound garden. **New Age Space**

G

Mazatl Galindo
(See Xochimoki)

Kay Gardner

Emerging Ladyslipper
Moods and Rituals Ladyslipper
Moon Circles Ladyslipper

Gardner composes lyrical, improvisational, and experimental music designed for meditation, relaxation, and healing. One-time student of Jean-Pierre Rampal, she is a superb flutist sings, and plays the guitar, piano, tin whistle among other instruments. Her theories on the healing properties of music have been expressed in dozens of workshops and lectures, and she is a pioneer in the current movement to revive the ancient art of healing through music, color, sound, and light. *Emerging*'s all-instrumental tunes are extremely relaxing since they are "based on E," says Gardener. "And [the musical note] E is related to the solar plexus, or the center of the body. It was also writ-ten in a minor mode, which tends to settle things." Gardner's refreshing, invigorating music is the perfect antidote to modern life. **New Age Sound Health, New Age Traditional**

Richard Garneau

*The Fruits of Our
   Labors* (compilation) Global
   Pacific
Sunwheel Global Pacific

Garneau is an internationally acclaimed sitarist who trained with the foremost masters in his field, including Ravi Shankar and Nikhil Banerjee. Mixing this heritage with jazz, blues, and New Age Fusion, Garneau matches Eastern virtuosity with Western compositional style on *Sunwheel*. Featuring sitar, guitar, cellos, flute, tabla, strings, and percussion, *Sunwheel* blends tropical notes with melodic tones to create a warm, fragrant breeze of an album that inspires mental "mini-vacations." **New Age East/West**

63

Garth

Spirit Voyage Sun Energy

Per the liner notes, *Spirit Voyage* is an audio exploration based on the artist's belief that "we are born into mystery." Featuring electric and acoustic guitar, flute, piano, synthesizer, and violin, Garth's music is influenced more by folk traditions than space or electronic noodlings. The journey is peaceful, calming, and cleansing by turns as the selections move from playful to thoughtful, celestial to earthy. **New Age Folk**

Dr. Robert Gass (See On Wings of Song)

Alleluia Spring Hill
Hara Hara Spring Hill
Humanity Spring Hill
Many Blessings Spring Hill
Om Namaha Shivaya Spring Hill
On Wings of Song Spring Hill
Trust in Love Spring Hill

Teacher, lecturer, and musician Gass holds a doctorate in clinical psychology from Harvard; his music reflects his rich background in humanistic psychology, spiritual studies, and politics. Over the last fifteen years he has conducted seminars that have attracted more than one hundred thousand people. During eight of those years he directed the dynamic thirty-person On Wings of Song choral group, producing eight albums geared to applying the principles of individual transformation to social change. *Om Namaha Shivaya* features ninety minutes of this gentle Sanskrit chant and is ideal for meditation, relaxation, or easy listening. *Humanity* is more upbeat, energetic, and danceable with full orchestration. *Many Blessings* combines spiritual folk songs and chants from a myriad of the world's cultures. These albums are among the finest examples of New Age Vocal music released to date. As Gass says, "We can all know the ultimate Truth if we just open our hearts and find our answers inside." **New Age Vocal**

Adam Geiger

Impressions Lura Media

Subtitled "A New Day," *Impressions* evokes the transcendent quality of the dawn. Using synthesizer and piano, keyboardist Geiger conjures up a wide variety of colors and moods, from peace and calm to majesty and splendor. The feeling is warm rather than spacey, intimate and romantic. **New Age Pop**

Geist

4 Hands and 2 Hearts Dancing in a Universe of Strings Pathways

The harp (a very ancient instrument) and the Chapman Stick (a very modern instrument) make an unusual pairing, but the results here are definitely worth it. Expressing a *geist* (spirit) not heard anywhere else, harpist Diana Stork and stick player Teed Rockwell create moving music that subtly pulses with joy and vibrancy. The duo's music aims to aid personal inner transformation and growth. **New Age Progressive**

G.E.N.E. (Grooving Electronic Natural Environments)

Fluting Paradise Chacra Alternative
Life Is a Melody Chacra Alternative

Crystal Binelly and Cleo de Mallio are the nerve center and heart of the G.E.N.E. project, a duo dedicated to harmonizing with "the subtle rhythms of nature. This then stimulates a corresponding musical response in [us] which can then be expressed through [our] synthesizers in limitless ways." According to G.E.N.E., what is most important for them is to succeed in channeling and sharing nature's loving message with all those who seek to listen. **New Age Electronic**

Michel Genest

Ascension Sona Gaia
Crystal Fantasy Sona Gaia

Crystal Fantasy is visionary synthesizer music, as the song titles on it—"Mystic Wanderer," "Sacred Temple Dance," and "Radiant Rainbow Prism"—suggest. Although it is Genest's first album in the world of electronic music, *Crystal Fantasy* is perfect for meditation, stress reduction, relaxation, or massage. A former rock guitarist, Genest utilizes keyboards and synthesizers "instead of paint and canvas . . . substituting sounds on tape [to] create a music sound painting." Synthesizing the sounds of nature such as birds, wind, and water, Genest creates pure, perfect, crystalline imagery, evocative of moonlight glistening on a stream. *Ascension,* inspired by the view of California's majestic Mount Shasta, uplifts with its melodic, lovely, quiet beauty. **New Age Space**

Edward Gerhard

Guitar Sampler 1988 Windham Hill
Night Birds Reckless (CD version, Xenophone)

Night Birds, Gerhard's debut release, features solo acoustic guitar gems—real instrumental "songs" that begin intriguingly, soar to memorable heights, then have a refreshing denouement. Gerhard's playing is clean, precise, fluid, and colorful. His musical palette is diverse, using complex tunings to achieve a broad range of textures and moods. The result is a lyrical melding of folk and classical influences sure to delight any New Age Solo Instrumental fan as well as novice listeners. This music doesn't need words to sing. **New Age Solo**

Ghostwriters

Objects in Mirrors Red
Remote Dreaming Mu-Psych Music

Jeff Cain and Charles Cohen are the two veteran composer/performers who comprise Ghostwriters. As long ago as 1971, these local "godfathers" of electronic music in Philadelphia envisioned a broader application for their exotic music than science-fiction films, so they began to collaborate with choreographers, visual artists, and theater companies. *Remote Dreaming,* rich in filmic atmosphere and emotion, displays their special style of electronic music. Structured improvisations and seminarrative sound images weave a tapestry of exquisite textures, evocative melody lines, and effervescent environments. The release is excellent for both casual listening and as an aid for relaxation, meditation, and inward journeying. **New Age Electronic**

Dan Gibson
(See Solitudes)

Mila Gilbert
(See Mila)

Eliza Gilkyson

Pilgrims. Gold Castle

Pilgrims is an impassioned statement from New Age vocalist Gilkyson. Her beautiful, clear, resonant voice shimmers over compositions performed with understated elegance on primarily acoustic instruments. This is an intensely personal work, delivered in a melodically rich and lyrically perceptive style. Gilkyson dedicates the album to all "pilgrims on the road to self-understanding" and explains that the "songs [address] personal, political, and spiritual issues. It is a concept record based on Jungian male/female archetypes that show how inner balancing can lead to greater self-understanding and ultimately affect the state of the world." **New Age Vocal**

Chris Glassfield

Island New World

Island is a collection of carefree and flowing melodies reminiscent of sun-warmed evenings. Glassfield has created a series of romantic guitar compositions that open the senses to an "island of relaxation." **New Age Solo**

Patrick Gleeson

Rainbow Delta PVC/Jem

Synthesist Gleeson straddles the progressive and space music subgenres with *Rainbow Delta.* He sculpts a three-dimensional soundscape that is easy to get lost in; alternately inspiring and transcendent, then exploratory and mysterious. **New Age Progressive, New Age Space**

Global Pacific Records

The Fruits of Our Labors
(compilation) Global Pacific

Some of the best New Age and world music to be released in recent years is now available on this sampler album from Global Pacific Records. It features sixteen instrumental selections from Steve Kindler, Bob Kindler, Paul Greaver, Aeolus, Penny Little, and Ben Hurley, Ben Tavera King, Richard Garneau, and Sulubika. With such diverse artists, the release encompasses a wide variety of sounds, instruments, and styles, while serving up a thoroughly satisfying eclectic mix. **New Age Traditional, New Age World**

Golden Voyage Series

(See Robert Bearns and Ron Dexter)

Jonathan Goldman

(See Lyghte)

Jerry Goodman

Ariel Private Music
Electric Guitarist (w/John McLaughlin) Columbia
It's Alive Private Music
Like Children (w/Hammer) Nemporer
My Goal's Beyond (w/John McLaughlin) Elektra
On the Future of Aviation Private Music
World of Private Music Sampler Private Music

Hinted at within tracks of the all-acoustic *My Goal's Beyond* (1971, with John McLaughlin and Billy Cobham), Goodman's prodigious talent blossomed during his tenure with the Mahavishnu Orchestra. Now, on *Ariel*, violinist Goodman has created a positive, exciting, New Age Jazz album with real melodic and lyrical strength. Goodman's fusion roots give his instrumentals compelling intensity and passion, meshing rock textures with classical dynamics in tightly arranged compositions. His violin style employs the phrasing and sonorities of an electric guitar but with the bends and slurs you can get only on a bowed instrument. *It's Alive* captures live on the concert stage the spontaneity and exuberance that has been a hallmark of Goodman's music throughout his career. This is energizing, chakra stimulating, foreground music. **New Age Jazz**

Edward Larry Gordon

(See Laraaji)

Steve and David Gordon

Astral Journey Sequoia
At the River's Edge Sequoia
Celestial Suite Sequoia
Garden of Serenity Sequoia
Images Sequoia
Lightspring Sequoia
Misty Forest Morning Sequoia
Oneness Sequoia
Peaceful Evening Sequoia
Radiant Sea Sequoia
Still Waters, Clear Sky Sequoia

David and Steve Gordon's aim is to "create a light-filled abundant reality of happiness for ourselves and our planet." To help make this happen, they have produced more than two hundred fifty self-help and spiritual potential tapes as well as the eleven New Age music tapes listed above. The music ranges from acoustic piano and guitar punctuated with sounds of nature to electronic, meditative space music. *Images* is a compilation of the most-requested music from their earlier releases. The Gordons' latest series of tapes, called the "Inner Music Series," includes three releases of longer, more meditative pieces. "Each tape is different but will create a specific experience of an overall meditative feeling you can use as a tool for meditation or just music," says Steve. The instrumentation is varied: *Lightspring* features island and conga drums and creates a feeling of energy and balance with very energetic, bubbly melodic patterns; *Oneness* emphasizes Tibetan temple bells and Chinese wind chimes to express in music the sounds you might hear if you transformed the meditation experience into sound; *Garden of Serenity* is dominated by Japanese shakuhachi flute, as well as the feeling of peace that permeates a small quiet garden secluded behind stone walls. What's next for these New Age pioneers? Steve answers, "I think that we're going to see a return to a re-enchantment of the world where each day the things you do in your life take on a mythical, magical quality, [and] each act becomes sacred." **New Age Traditional**

Manuel Gottsching

Ash Ra Tempel VI Cosmic
   Couriers
Blackouts Virgin
Correlations Virgin
New Age of Earth Isadora

Ash Ra Tempel VI features New Age Space music inventions for electric guitar that range from lengthy space journey pieces to sweet lullabies. Creating a galaxy of innovative sounds, this album demonstrates how to make a guitar sound like an interstellar orchestra. Although more poplike in tone and composition, *New Age of Earth* is still an excellent electronic voyage album. Harold Grosskopf and Lutz Ulbrich join Gottsching to form the German cosmic rock band, Ashra, on *Correla-*

tions. If you like Pink Floyd, Van Der Graaf Generator, or Go, you'll like Ashra's *Blackouts* as well. **New Age Space**

Tom Grant

Heart of the City Pausa
Just the Right Moment Pausa
Mystified Timeless
Night Charade Gaia
Take Me to Your Dreams Pausa
Tom Grant Pausa
You Hardly Know Me WMOT

Grant mixes appealing instrumentals with smooth, romance-infused vocals on his New Age Jazz fusion release *Night Charade*. The music is built around the sound of acoustic piano with influences drawing more from John Coltrane, Miles Davis, and Herbie Hancock than from fifties and sixties pop. Grant's years of touring experience have honed his delivery to a razor-sharp edge; the music is sensuous, evocative, and stimulating, more foreground than ambient soundtrack. **New Age Jazz**

Paul Greaver

Joy Global Pacific
*The Fruits of Our
   Labors* (compilation)
   Global Pacific
Returning Global Pacific

Greaver, an accomplished acoustic guitarist, is known for his exquisitely melodic compositions that have been influenced by his extensive travels throughout the world, daily meditation, and his spiritual beliefs. As he says, "I write and perform music not merely to impress and entertain the intellect but to go deeper and touch the heart. I offer music that I feel is nourishing, relaxing, and revitalizing." On *Joy*, the selections range from optimistic, exuberant cuts to delicate, shimmering pieces that move rather than astonish. Mixing folk and pop influences with classical training, Greaver manages to come up with a "guitar record" that emotes, inspires, and thoroughly satisfies. **New Age Pop, New Age Solo**

Green Linnet Records

*Flight of the Green
  Linnet* Rykodisc
*Traditional Music and
  Beyond* Green Linnet

Traditional Music and Beyond is the first Green Linnet sampler and features carefully selected Irish/Celtic songs from artists such as Kevin Burke, Robbie O'Connell, Touchstone, Phil Cunningham, Triona Ni Dhomhnaill, and The Irish Tradition. This upbeat and emotional collection is a great introduction to the world of Green Linnet music. The CD-only release *Flight of the Green Linnet* features Relativity, Silly Wizard, Patrick Street, Mick Moloney, Matt Molloy, the Tannahill Weavers, and others. **New Age World**

(New Age) Gregorian Chants

New Age Gregorian Chants Valley of the Sun

It has long been known that the spiritual voice has the therapeutic effect of generating serenity and personal power. This amazing tape synthesizes the melodies of famous Gregorian chants to capture the essence of the songs without the oftentimes distracting words. The result is New Age Gregorian chants that flow like music and are ideal for meditation, self-hypnosis, deepening concentration, and quiet self-empowerment. The beautifully modulated vibrations are haunting, inspiring, and uplifting. **New Age Vocal**

Sylvan Grey

Ice Flowers Melting Fortuna

This is meditative music for the Finnish folk harp played with crystal-like resonance by Grey. The simplicity of the music does not hide its charm and beauty, and Grey's original compositions give full play to the possibilities of this exquisite instrument. The effect is clear, evocative, and dramatic. **New Age Meditation**

Stefan Grossman

Live Shanachie
Shining Shadows Shanachie
*Stefan Grossman and John
  Renbourne* Kicking Mule
The Three Kingdoms
  Shanachie
Under the Volcano
  Kicking Mule

Grossman is an American guitarist whose love of Irish airs and jigs comes through on each of the Shanachie releases. His collaboration with

NATIVE AMERICAN/INDIGENOUS MUSIC

by R. Carlos Nakai*

Nakai is a recording artist with numerous albums to his credit, a concert performer, philosopher, and lecturer. He composes for the Native American flute and participates in an international collaboration, called Atlantic Crossing, with Anima Musica at West Germany.

Music is vital in the sacred and social worlds of Native American peoples, functioning beyond pleasure or entertainment to preserve the integrity of the oral tradition. Accompaniment is provided by rattles, drums, and group chorus, depending upon the context and form of the musical presentation. The kinds of songs, their placement in a ceremony, and the textural form—meaningful words or vocalized sounds—reflect the world views of various tribes. Duple meter (patterns of two drum beats throughout) percussion patterns, a wide variety of tempo, and dynamic accents contribute to the distinctive quality of tribal music. Three areas of music can be distinguished: sacred/ceremonial songs, social songs, and personal vocal and instrumental music.

BILL DENNY, JR.

BROOK MEDICINE EAGLE

MICHAEL HARNER

KEVIN LOCKE

TOM MAUCHAHTY-WARE

R. CARLOS NAKAI

NATIVE AMERICAN CHURCH

NATIVE AMERICAN MUSIC

A. PAUL ORTEGA

CORNELL PEWEWARDY

JOHN RAINER, JR.

*Artist listing compiled by Patti Jean Birosik.

guitarist Renbourn shows another side of him: The album, *Stefan Grossman and John Renbourn,* fuses folk, jazz, and ethnic musical influences to yield some colorful and visionary instrumental guitar duets, combining technical brillance with emotional depth. **New Age World**

Srila Gurudeva

Songs of Harmony New World
Songs of the Soul New World

Songs of Harmony is a pleasing blend of Indian vocals and acoustic instrumentation. Gurudeva's voice is sublime, and the violin, viola, cello, bass, and oboe are played with feeling and mastery by members of the orchestra of La Scala Theatre in Milan. *Songs of the Soul* complements the previous recording by presenting traditional "kirtan" or divine hymns in a more classical Asian musical setting. There is a dancelike lyrical quality to the melodies as well as the occasional voices of children, which help to convey pictures of innocence and joy. **New Age East/West**

Gyume Tibetan Monks

Tantric Harmonies Spirit

The monks of Gyume Tantric College have developed their unique "one voice chording" approach to singing over the last five hundred years. The ability of each monk to chant three notes at once lends incredible resonance and power to this ancient musical tradition. Stimulating the root chakra with bass notes, repetitive and hypnotic tones build into a peak, transcendent aural experience. *Tantric Harmonies* is the first effort ever to capture their sacred mantric prayers of purification and protection on tape. The monks currently live in a monastery in India, having fled Tibet after the Chinese invasion in 1959. According to Spirit Music, most of the proceeds from *Tantric Harmonies* go directly to benefit the Gyume monks. **New Age Meditation, New Age Vocal**

H

The Habibiyya

If Man but Knew Island

The Habibiyya create New Age World music, combining two shakuhachi (Japanese wooden) flutes, koto, and mandola for music straight from the heart. The group members are Western Sufis whose vocal and instrumental performances of Eastern-influenced songs make for spiritual and uplifting listening. The music itself is hypnotic and almost Zen-like in its more tranquil sections. **New Age World**

Paul Halley

Callings (w/P. Winter
  Consort) Living Music
Canyon (w/P. Winter
  Consort) Living Music
Concert for the Earth (w/P.
  Winter Consort) Living Music
Missa Gaia (w/P. Winter
  Consort) Living Music
Nightwatch Gramavision
Pianosong Living Music

Sun Singer (w/P. Winter
  Consort) Living Music

Sure to dazzle New Age Solo instrumental fans, Halley's *Pianosong* features fine improvisational, classically inspired romantic fantasies. Combining pop sensibilities with spiritual values, Halley's open, melodic pieces stimulate the imagination with colorful aural portrayals of places and people. Halley has also been a member of the Paul Winter Consort since 1980 and can be heard on those releases as well. **New Age Solo, New Age Traditional**

Steven Halpern

Among Friends Halpern Sounds
Ancient Echoes (w/Kelly) Sound
  Rx
Birthways (w/Shawn
  Phillips) Halpern Sounds
Comfort Zone Sound Rx
Connections (w/Horn) Halpern
  Sounds
Corridors of Time Hear and Now
Crystal Suite Sound Rx

Dawn (w/Emerald Web) Sound Rx
Eastern Peace Halpern Sounds
Egypt Hear and Now
Eventide Halpern Sounds
Hear to Eternity Hear and Now
Lifetide Halpern Sounds
*Lullabies and Sweet
  Dreams* Sound Rx
Music for Meetings Sound Rx
Music for Sound Health Halpern
  Sounds
Natural Light (w/Dallas
  Smith) Sound Rx
New Age Blues Sound Rx
Newsound (w/D. Smith) Hear and
  Now
Prelude Halpern Sounds
Recollections (w/Kobialka) Sound
  Rx
Rhythms of Vision Sound Rx
Rings of Saturn Hear and Now
Shared Visions (w/Eugene
  Friesen) Halpern Sounds
Soft Focus Halpern Sounds
Spectrum Suite Sound Rx
Starborn Suite Halpern Sounds
Threshold (w/D. Smith) Sound Rx
Timeless Sound Rx
Whisper on the Wind Halpern
  Sounds

Halpern is an internationally acclaimed multi-instrumentalist, recording artist, composer, producer, author, and public speaker, as well as one of the founding fathers of the modern New Age movement. As a composer he has pioneered a whole new vocabulary of composition and performance, one that extracts higher harmonics from the notes to create "etheric" sounds, subtle symphonies, in the overtones. "Silence and space are vital components of my music," Halpern states. In 1965 he was the first New Age musician to study the effects of music on people, actually conducting tests to document the positive healing aspects of sound on individuals' health. Prior to Windham Hill's entry into the marketplace, Halpern actively marketed his antifrantic music recordings to alternative venues, such as health-food stores, bookstores, and yoga centers, effectively paving the way for today's New Age music boom. Working tirelessly to promote the New Age and its music, Halpern created a record company, appeared on television and radio, conducted workshops and seminars, lectured and acted as an inspiration to and collaborator with many of today's top names in New Age music as well as the general public. His efforts have expanded with the recent release of *Summer Wind,* an antifrantic music video, as well as his popular book, *Sound Health.* With more than forty-five albums to his credit, Halpern's first love is "to open up that space within myself where I can hear the music most clearly, where I become the instrument of the instrument, and there is no duality." Already a classic in its field, *Spectrum Suite* fulfills this promise as it effortlessly uplifts and "tunes your human instrument." This soundscape features solo electric piano on side one, then adds the natural sounds of humpback whale, mockingbird, and a lake on side two. Another classic, *Crystal Suite,* deftly links the seven chakras (energy centers within the human body) with the colors of the rainbow and seven musical resonating tones, while mixing electric piano, synthesizers, and the extraordinary Atlantean Quartz Crystal Temple Bowls. *Connections* is a duet with Paul Horn, whose "golden flute" has never sounded better than on this sensual, gently rhythmic album, great for dancing or romancing. For New Age headphone enthusiasts, *Rhythms of Vision* is solo grand piano recorded in three-dimension holophonic sound, placing the listener right on the piano bench with Halpern. This revolutionary recording process is extremely well suited to the intimate and expressive tracks as well as the uplifting and energizing selections. Halpern is a New Age incarnation of da Vinci's "Universal Man." **New Age Sound Health, New Age Traditional**

Peter Michael Hamel

Bardo Kuckuck
Colours of Time Kuckuck
Dharana (w/Between) Wergo
Let It Play Celestial Harmonies
Nada Celestial Harmonies
Transition Kuckuck
The Voice of Silence Wergo

Let It Play is a compilation of pieces by keyboard whiz Hamel for piano, organ, and electronic keyboards, some of which were previously released on Kuckuck Records. Hamel's compositional style is influenced by a musical philosophy based on the thinking of Swiss philosopher Jean Gebser, Hamel's own studies of Tibetan and Indian cultures, and his interest in the interrelationship between music and human consciousness. Some of his compositions seek to integrate the different effects Eastern and Western music

have on the psyche (as discussed in Hamel's book, *Through Music to the Self,* London: Compton Press, 1976), but most of them are meditative and spiritual. *The Voice of Silence* features Indian-inspired chanting for a tantric feel, while *Colours of Time* is more meditative and features organ and synthesizer music. *Nada* is an album of metaphysical synthesizer instrumentals, a great space music soundtrack to your inward journeys. Hamel collaborates with the group Between on *Dharana,* a delicate and haunting New Age World music album that utilizes a full symphony orchestra. **New Age East/West**

Jan Hammer

The First Seven Days Nemperor

Keyboardist/synthesist extraordinaire Hammer is currently known for his innovative, exciting, and dramatic scores for the television series "Miami Vice"; but he has also performed with Jeff Beck, John Abercrombie, and a host of others since the early seventies. His early solo album, *The First Seven Days,* foreshadows the composer he would become. It's a fairly consistent instrumental effort that runs through a variety of emotions, textures, and audio colors. Based on rhythmic rock patterns, it shares the kind of majestic vision that has propelled Yanni and Kitaro into the limelight. **New Age Electronic**

Bennett Hammond

Walking on Air Shanachie

In his liner notes for *Walking on Air,* Hammond comes across as modest about his more-than-respectable talent on acoustic guitar. Combining original with traditional material—plus a wonderful New Age-ish cover of George Harrison's "Here Comes the Sun"—the release is steeped in folk tradition yet performed with contemporary flair. *Walking on Air* is bright, cheerful, and well suited for active listening. Guest artist Lorraine Lee's dulcimer performance on two cuts is magic to hear, a perfect counterpoint to Hammond's guitar. **New Age Folk**

Harmonic Choir
(See David Hykes)

Michael Harner

Didjeridu for the Shamanic Journey Foundation for Shamanic Studies
Drumming for the Shamanic Journey Foundation for Shamanic Studies
Singing Journey for Shamanic Voyaging Foundation for Shamanic Studies

These tapes are intended for use with high-quality stereo headphones as an aid to shamanic journeying as instructed in Michael Harner's book, *The Way of the Shaman* (New York: Bantam, 1982), rather than for casual or meditative listening. *Didjeridu* features the incredible sound of the aboriginal Australian didjeridu (an ancient hollow tube drone) accompanied by click sticks to carry the listener into an extended dreamtime journey. *Singing* is inspired by the singing-journey method of the last of the traditional European shamans among the Laplanders of northern Scandinavia. *Drumming* includes a women's chorus to provide gentle support for the shamanic journeyer. **New Age Native American, New Age Space**

Lou Harrison

La Koro Sutro (The Heart Sutra) New Albion

For fifty years Harrison has been in the vanguard of contemporary American composers, an innovator, juxtaposing and synthesizing musical dialects from virtually every corner of the world. To create the truly lovely New Age Vocal *La Koro Sutro,* he has gathered many distinguished musicians as well as the chorus and chamber chorus of the University of California at Berkeley. The Esperanto title means *The Heart Sutra,* one of the most used and profound of Buddhist sutras, revealing the heart of divine wisdom. The vision that unfolds in *La Koro Sutro,* a work for chorus and gamelan, is a tribute to his virtuosity. **New Age East/ West, New Age Vocal**

Michael Harrison

In Flight Fortuna
Piano One (sampler) Windham Hill

A trip to India during his teenage years introduced Harrison to the "just" (or pure) intonation tuning of Eastern music. When he returned he found his beloved piano "sounded out of tune." Studying the physics of music brought him to an understanding of the equal-tempered or Western piano style but little satisfaction. After a meeting with famed pianist La Monte Young and an apprenticeship as a student tuner, Harrison found a solution to his problem—he invented a new instrument, the Harmonic Piano, "that sounded right." His debut release, *In Flight*, finds him successfully balancing a strong drive to remold the keyboard's acoustic potential with an equally deep appreciation for graceful simple melodies. The result is a pleasant mix of powerfully rhythmic and touchingly evocative solo piano pieces. "When I've seen something, heard something, or felt something that really nourished me, gave me new insight, or made me realize for one moment what being human is about," he says, "that's what I hope to give people through my music." **New Age Solo**

Don Harriss

Elevations Sonic Atmospheres

Refreshingly upbeat and gently energizing, Harriss's debut release, *Elevations,* uses electronic and acoustic keyboards, guitar, and percussion, to create dreamy, fully orchestrated suites. The warm, melodic compositions show hints of Asian and African rhythms, making for a fantasy-laden aural excursion. **New Age Electronic**

Jon Hassell

Aka/Darbari/Jaka Editions EG
Dream Theory in Malaya (w/B. Eno) Editions EG
Earthquake Island Tomato
Possible Musics (w/B. Eno) Editions EG
Power Spot ECM
Vernal Equinox Lovely Music

Hassell is a virtuoso trumpet player with an intense interest in both world music and fusion. His truly transcendent collaboration with Brian Eno, *Possible Musics,* blends Eastern, Western, and African forms through a variety of electronic and acoustic instruments. Other Hassell releases such as *Power Spot* and *Dream Theory in Malaya* reflect his studies with Indian vocalist Pandit Pran Nath; on these, Hassell's trumpet is fluid, warm, and human. Percussive influences from the Aka pygmy tribe of Central Africa are felt on *Aka/Darbari/Jaka.* **New Age World**

David Hayes

Sunbathing in Leningrad Gold Castle

Van Morrison's band leader for fifteen years, Hayes has released a solo record that is both challenging and soothing, featuring rhythmic twelve-string guitar lines, subtle melodies, and deft synthesizer colorings. Celtic folk music, jazz, and blues influences blend seamlessly in this New Age instrumental offering, evoking a radiant tranquility. As Hayes says, "I hope the music makes people feel good and perhaps cleansed a bit." New Age Jazz

Hearts of Space Records

Arabesque Sampler Hearts of Space
Cruisers 1.0 Compilation Hearts of Space
Starflight One Compilation Hearts of Space

Hearts of Space Records specializes in high-quality contemporary space music. *Starflight One* features the music of Steve Roach, Tim Clark, Kevin Braheny, and Michael Amerlan on ten visionary, intrepid voyages through inner galaxies. The synthesizer-based electronic compositions are alternately serene, emotional, and quietly inspiring. *Arabesque* is an exotic journey, contemporary space music inspired by the musical traditions of the Middle East and composed by Al Gromer Khan, Drachir Ztiworoh, Danna and Clement, Shah, Minoo Javan, and Light Rain. New Age Space

Daniel Hecht

Sampler '81 Windham Hill
Willow Windham Hill

Hecht performs sensitive, melodic, and lyrical six- and twelve-string acoustic guitar selections on *Willow*. His spacious style allows each note to take on a life of its own, resonating then blending with the next, to create a rich tapestry of sound. New Age Solo

78

Michael Hedges

Aerial Boundaries Windham Hill
Breakfast in the Field Windham Hill
Evening with Windham Hill Live Windham Hill
Live on the Double Planet Windham Hill
Sampler '82 Windham Hill
Sampler '84 Windham Hill
The Shape of The Land (w/Ackerman and Aaberg) Windham Hill
Watching My Life Go By Windham Hill

Hedges is a solo acoustic guitarist as well as a singer/songwriter. *Live on the Double Planet* amply exhibits his roots: from pop, dance, and mellow jazz instrumentals to vocal renderings of such songs as Bob Dylan's "All Along the Watchtower" and the Beatles' "Come Together." His two-handed guitar stylings on his original instrumental compositions fire the rich visionary music with rhythmic energy. New Age Pop, New Age Solo

Danny Heines

Aqua Touch Silver Wave

Featuring guest appearances by Paul McCandless and Eugene Friesen, *Aqua Touch* showcases the talents of innovative guitarist Heines, whose New Age sensitivity is sparked with jazz and thick passionate rhythms and melodies. Merging sax, conga, cello, and percussion, Heines creates a rich musical collage. He preserves the ethereal textures usually associated with traditional New Age music but adds Latin American and African rhythms, often articulated with percussive string slapping techniques. The songs themselves are well composed and performed with spirit and style—very accessible and pleasurable listening. New Age World

Rudy Helm
(See Music for Progressive Relaxation)

Nancy Hennings
(See Henry Wolff)

Barbara Higbie
(See Darol Anger)

Max Highstein

The Healer's Touch Search for Serenity
Healing Waterfall Search for Serenity
Touch the Sky Search for Serenity
12 Cosmic Healers Search for Serenity

The Healer's Touch reveals the soothing power of music through a warm cascade of richly textured melody. Synthesizer, flute, oboe, horn, clarinet, and cello create gently uplifting background or foreground music suitable for relaxing, reading, or other inwardly directed pursuits. *Touch the Sky* is a more colorful array of tempos and moods featuring piano, winds, cello, bass, and percussion. This music soars! Highstein is

also involved with the Inner Directions Series of guided reveries. *Healing Waterfall* is narrated by Jill Andre, while *12 Cosmic Healers* has narration by Leigh Taylor-Young. Both are excellent examples of music-accompanied visualizations. New Age Sound Health

Steve Hillage

Rainbow Dome Music
  (w./Miquette Giràudy) Virgin

Hillage comes from a progressive rock background, but his solo records fit more snugly into the New Age Space music category. On *Rainbow Dome Music* his electric guitar blends with Giràudy's synthesizers, electronics, and Tibetan bells to create an aural galactic journey that ranges from ethereal to majestically celestial in tone. Full of interesting textures, evocative arrangements, and subtle shadings, Hillage's compositions are well suited to headphone enjoyment. New Age Space

Hiroshima

Another Place Epic
Go Epic
Third Generation Epic

The group Hiroshima performs primarily instrumental jazz enhanced with pop, funk, and assorted Eastern sounds. On the New Age Jazz release *Go* they mix koto, sax, flute, keyboards, synthesizer, and other instruments into a highly successful East Meets West style flavored by commercial pop. The result is closer to the languid, creamy, and silken textures common to New Age music than to the harder jazz/r&b/fusion of their previous albums. Extremely accessible, the album should have special appeal for the novice New Age Jazz listener. **New Age East/ West, New Age Jazz**

Hadley Hockensmith

Heartsongs Meadowlark

Hockensmith is a classic New Age instrumental guitarist. His compositions draw on his jazz and gospel roots as well as the pop stylings from his numerous sessions with such artists as Neil Diamond, David Gates (ex-Bread), and Michael McDonald. The selections on *Heartsongs* are bright, sunny, touchingly melodic, undefeatedly cheerful gems, imbued with a childlike innocence. **New Age Solo**

Michael Hoenig

Departure from the Northern Wasteland Warner Bros./Kuckuck
Xcept One Cinema

On *Xcept One* electronic pioneer Hoenig (formerly of Tangerine Dream) has created one of the most even blendings of New Age and electronic music to date. His selections range from quiet introspective soundscapes to dramatic, cinematic technological compositions exploring the relationship of mathematical progression and musical inspiration. "The music is conceived as several loops of intervals that modulate each other to create new loops of different lengths in shifting patterns," states Hoenig. The result is rather complicated, atmospheric, evolutionary music, shifting through a rich palette of moods and textures. Hoenig's 1977 release, *Departure from the Northern Wasteland,* takes a more compositional approach, basing each track on a mood and working within a single tonal center and a basic rhythmic pulse. Long considered an electronic music classic, it has just been re-released on Kuckuck and can now be enjoyed again. **New Age Electronic**

Mic Holwin

Starting to Remember Life Style

Holwin works with microcomputer-controlled synthesizers, yielding cinematic or "visual tone poems" for the ears. As she says, "My music is visual. When people hear it they turn to me when it's over and tell me what they saw." In addition to keyboards she plays bass, guitar, and saxophone and is a working partner in Synesthetics, a New York audio/ video studio. "I walk into the studio with nothing precomposed, but as soon as my fingers touch a keyboard, I lock in. It's there. *Starting to Remember* is channeled, focused energy." This is excellent space music. **New Age Space**

Paul Horn

China Kuckuck
Concert for Baba Inside
Dream Machine Mushroom
Heart to Heart Golden Flute

Inside the Cathedral Kuckuck
Inside the Great Pyramid Kuckuck
*Inside the Magic of
  Findhorn* Golden Flute/Global
  Pacific
*Inside the Powers of
  Nature* Golden Flute/Global
  Pacific
Inside the Taj Mahal Epic
Jupiter 8 Golden Flute/Global
  Pacific
Live from Russia Golden
  Flute/Global Pacific
Nexus Epic
Paul Horn in Concert Golden
  Flute/Global Pacific
Paul Horn in India World Pacific
Paul Horn in Kashmir World
  Pacific
The Peace Album Kuckuck
Sketches Golden Flute/Global
  Pacific
Traveler Golden Flute/Global
  Pacific
Visions Epic

In 1960, when Horn was still playing jazz, a seventy-year-old woman gave him a psychic reading predicting the rise of a new kind of music. According to Horn, she said, "The purpose of this music will be to raise the level of awareness on the planet. It will be uplifting to the spirit and have the power to raise the vibration of mankind." In that vein, *Traveler* is a seminal New Age work. It unburdens the spirit, making the listener feel calm, relaxed, centered, and full of inner peace. Blending sitar, tablas, Chinese bamboo flute, and a European string orchestra with synthesizer, the album is an aural record of travel between widely disparate countries and cultures. Tempos change to reflect specific moods and ambiences, taking the listener on a well-paced trip around the world with many opportunities for enlightenment and self-awareness. Horn is also a pioneering flutist, having recorded in some of the world's most famous "power" spots such as inside the Great Pyramid and at Findhorn, the Scottish New Age community. In 1968 he recorded the classic solo flute album *Inside the Taj Mahal.* His instrument sounds alternately eerie, sweet, and richly resonant; the single notes seem to hang by an invisible thread as they sustain within the echoing chamber. Much of Horn's music is improvised, drawing upon immediate inspiration and location, so his records sound fresh and alive. **New Age Solo, New Age Traditional**

Garry Hughes

Sacred Cities Jem

Hughes brings a European perspective to his New Age electronic music. The compositions on *Sacred Cities* use a wide variety of synthesizers, computers, and other state-of-the-art technologies to simulate urban environments. The result is hauntingly etheric, mysterious, and surprisingly spiritual music, anchored by an earthiness achieved through the use of unusual percussion instruments—metal oil drums, kitchen utensils, and the demolition of a Ford Cortina automobile—as well as environmental sounds. This is not space music but richly melodic electronic music that is vibrant and alive. **New Age Electronic**

NEW AGE POP MUSIC

by Lucky Clark*

Clark is a freelance writer, music critic, graphic artist, and photographer who previously served as a radio show host for the Maine Public Radio System, where he helped pioneer New Age music airplay.

New Age Pop is a tight, effortless meld of jazz, folk, rock, and classical-influenced New Age music, both ballad oriented and up-tempo in nature. It is usually very melodic, often interweaving acoustic and electronic instruments into a sonic quilt that subtly stimulates the listener. The music has depth, using harmony, melody, and simple key modulations rather than creating space-like sounds. Of all New Age subgenres, New Age Pop is the most energetic and accessible.

CARLOS ALOMAR   RAY CHESER

BRUCE BECVAR   RON COOLEY

CHECKFIELD   GEORGE CRINER

*Artist listing compiled by Patti Jean Birosik.

Les Hurdle and Thor Baldursson

The Melody of Life New World
The Secret Melody New World
The Ultimate Melody New World

Multi-instrumentalists Hurdle and Baldursson construct elegant melodies of tender tones to create a calm, nurturing environment. *The Melody of Life* features a sensitive, deeply meditative pan pipe that seems to hover through the music, adding a peaceful, lingering quality. *The Ultimate Melody* is a bit more "active," yet with its even percussion and sustained melody, it creates the perfect ambience for intimate or inwardly directed pursuits. This is deeply sensual music. **New Age Traditional**

Craig Huxley (Hundley)

Genesis Project Sonic Atmospheres

Huxley has been a successful composer and producer of movie soundtracks for many years, but his double album, *Genesis Project,* demonstrates two very different influences. The first record features dramatic contemporary rhythms of modern jazz fusion drawn directly from his expe-

DAVID DARLING

LARRY DAVID

JORDAN DE LA SIERRA

RICHARD DEL MAESTRO

DURUTTI COLUMN

PAUL EDWARDS

ADAM GEIGER

PAUL GREAVER

MICHAEL HEDGES

JEFF JOHNSON

RADHIKA MILLER

RANDY MORRISS

NIGHTENGALE RECORDS

RAY PLATT

JEAN-LUC PONTY

PRIVATE MUSIC RECORDS

LEWIS ROSS

RYUICHI SAKAMOTO

MASAHIDE SAKUMA

EBERHARD SCHOENER

SHADOWFAX

BILLY SMILEY

LIZ STORY

VOYAGER

JOHN WEIDER

TIM WEISBERG

GHEORGIE ZAMFIR

rience with film, especially the *Star Trek* movies. Dream music is featured on the second record, inviting the listener into a private mystical world. The lush synthesized textures create a delicate but complex soundscape—a world of microtones and newly awakening harmonies. **New Age Progressive**

Lucia Hwong

House of Sleeping Beauties Private Music
Secret Luminescence Private Music

Hwong explores the realm of feminine eroticism, painting expansive, multitextural portraits laced with gentle, almost pastoral images. Modern synthesizer technology blends seamlessly with ancient Chinese stringed instruments on *Secret Luminescence.* The haunting imagery is doubled when Hwong mixes in the sound of her own slow, deep breathing on one of the tracks, an especially sensual effect if heard through headphones. Celtic harpist Alan Stivell guests on this release, mixing his gently evocative strings with Hwong's own soft-toned lute. **New Age East/West**

David Hykes and the Harmonic Choir

Current Circulation Celestial Harmonies
Harmonic Meetings Celestial Harmonies
Hearing Solar Winds Celestial Harmonies

With *Hearing Solar Winds* and *Current Circulation,* Hykes introduced a new sound to the industrialized West: the captivatingly exotic *hoomi* or "throat singing" of traditional Eastern music. Each vocalist simultaneously sings a sustained fundamental tone and as many as seven harmonic overtones, so a small number of harmonic chanters can sound like dozens. On *Harmonic Meetings,* Hykes has integrated droning tamboura and percussion on several tracks to accompany the singers and has incorporated a text of non-denominational sacred words carefully selected for their vibrational qualities. Musically, the Harmonic Choir's prismatic vocal lines slowly ascend and descend, sometimes contracting to an enharmonic point where they beat like Tibetan bells. This is the ultimate in ethereal "music." **New Age East/West, New Age Vocal**

I

Iasos

Angelic Music Iasos
*Birds for Morning and
   Evening* Iasos
Crystal Love Iasos
Elixer Iasos
Essence of Spring Iasos
Throne Realms and Lagoons Iasos

One of the first digital recordings by a New Age pioneer, *Elixir* is considered a traditional New Age classic, built of lush layers of warm synthesized sound. On *Crystal Love,* a composition of love and longing, dazzling instrumental passages of shimmering sound elevate the listener's consciousness and evoke powerful mental pictures of bliss. *Throne Realms and Lagoons* is part of Iasos's Vibrational Elements series. On it Iasos creates an ambience of calm to gently induce mental relaxation and bodily rest. Another release in this same series, *Birds for Morning and Evening,* uses natural and electronic sounds to achieve the soothing effect that birds and their songs create. Iasos combines the organic with the electronic for joyous and inspired New Age music that heals, enlightens, and entertains. **New Age Electronic, New Age Space, New Age Traditional**

Incarnation

*Interpretations of the
   Season* Meadowlark

Incarnation is not a group but a collection of new and established artists on a sampler that continues in the rich tradition of Meadowlark Records's *Music for Your Personal Retreat* album. This is New Age music for more quiet moments, reflecting the special spirit of the year-end holiday season. Combining classical, folk, and jazz influences, artists Richard Souther (Douglas Trowbridge), Amy Shreve, John Michael Talbot, and Billy Smiley are totally diverse but experienced and inspirational instrumentalists who bring craft, joy, and love to each of these positively pleasant selections. **New Age Traditional**

85

Innovative Communications Records

New Age Music Sampler
Innovative Communication

Jean-Michel Jarre, Tangerine Dream, and Klaus Schulze are a few of the top names in electronic music that are featured on this Innovative Communication Records sampler. This is music of dreams, to relax and float to, beautiful melodies played by some of the best composers of the genre. The sampler is a great introduction to electronic music for the traditional New Age music fan. **New Age Electronic**

Inti-Illimani

Flight of the Condor BBC
(soundtrack)
Imagination Redwood
Palimpsesto Redwood

Sometimes serene, sometimes soaring, the music of Inti-Illimani draws on many traditions. Guitars, panpipes, Andean flute, mandolin, violin, harp, and the Argentine bombo drum are among the sixteen instruments that blend together on *Imagination,* an album inspired by folk art. *Palimpsesto* offers vocals and instrumentals in folklorico style, blending contemporary and classical rhythms. **New Age World**

Invincible Records

Incredible Invincible
Sampler Invincible
Sampler Vol. 1 Invincible

Incredible Invincible Sampler offers the latest in New Age fusion sounds, along with some solo harp and acoustic guitar selections that will knock your socks off. This surefire collection is powered by the talents of Kim Robertson (Crimson Series), Mosaic, Mila, and ten other artists. *Sampler Vol. 1* features one full hour of "invincible sounds," ranging from New Age Traditional to New Age Jazz, that serve as a great introduction to the music of Peter Kater, Jim Scott, Radiance, Kim Robertson, and others. **New Age East/West, New Age Jazz**

Mark Isham

Castalia Virgin
Film Music Windham Hill
Sampler 84 Windham Hill
Sampler 86 Windham Hill
Steadfast Tin Soldier Windham Hill
Vapor Drawings Windham Hill
Winter's Solstice Windham Hill

Albums released under the band name Group 87 were wonderful but largely ignored because they were too progressive for their time. By now, though, soundtrack stylist Isham has gained a following through his mesmerizing instrument pairings on numerous film scores. (You might remember the violin and electronics on *The Moderns,* bassoon and synthesizer on *Never Cry Wolf,* and trumpet with synthesizer on *Trouble in Mind.*) Isham's New Age work is no less inspired, as best demonstrated on his solo albums listed above. Using a minimalist technique and combining acoustic elements with state-of-the-art electronics, Isham dishes up aural imagery that is at times shimmering, at other times moody and melancholy. **New Age Progressive**

Isle of Skye

Isle of Skye Sound Sphere

Isle of Skye is a multilayered synthesizer work, the result of experiments by composer Dr. Jeffrey Thompson on stimulation of alpha and theta waves in the brain. According to Thompson, different brain wave patterns are coincident with different states of mind: alpha waves with pleasant relaxation, tranquility, and well-being; theta waves with states of reflective creativity, intuitive leaps, and imaginative inspiration. *Isle of Skye*'s marriage of science and music ranges from warm and healing to beautiful, uplifting, and spiritual sounds. **New Age Sound Health**

Itchy Fingers

Quark Venture/Virgin

Itchy Fingers is a quartet of saxophone players, and a quark is, theoretically, the smallest subatomic particle known to science. Can you guess we're talking about experimental music here? These musicians bring a wide range of influences to this album, from big band and free-form jazz to classical and Irish traditional music. Besides saxophones, *Quark* features bass, drums, and as special guest jazz great McCoy Tyner sitting in on piano. The result is energetic and bright, avoiding the overly intellectual. This New Age experimental offering may not be suitable for meditative purposes, but it is definitely a winner for more outwardly directed quiet pursuits and casual listening. **New Age Progressive**

Akira Itoh

Inner Light of Life
King

Synthesist Itoh creates sensuous, shimmering washes of sound on *Inner Light of Life*. The release is light, bright, and airy with an ethereal overtone that makes for easy listening. The spacious, ambient quality of the compositions makes Itoh's music perfect for meditation, relaxation, and spiritual voyaging. **New Age Meditation**

J

Jade Warrior

Floating World Island
Kites Island
Waves Island

As one of the seminal seventies progressive rock bands, Jade Warrior actually created what is now termed New Age Space or New Age Jazz fusion music. Combining synthesizer, guitar, percussion, and other instruments, the group creates moving layers of subtly shifting sound and futurist soundscapes. The music is stimulating and inspiring rather than meditative or soothing, and extremely well suited to headphone journeying. On *Kites,* a variety of influences can be heard including jazz, Asian, and experimental rock, yet the record remains interesting and accessible rather than disjointed or harsh. New Age Space

Jansen/Barbieri

Worlds in a Small Room Virgin Music

On *Worlds in a Small Room,* Steve Jansen and Richard Barbieri create moody, somewhat dark and mysterious electronic sounds that border on space music. A variety of synthesizers and acoustic instruments are used to evoke these tone poems, at times majestic and compelling, at other times subtle and insinuating. Most of the compositions are instrumental, with a simple vocal piece added to the eclectic brew. New Age Electronic

Jean-Michel Jarre

The Cage Polydor
The Concerts in China Polydor
Equinoxe Polydor
The Essential Jean-Michel Jarre Polydor
Magnetic Fields Polydor
Music for Supermarkets (not available)
Oxygene Polydor
Rendez-vous Polydor
Zoolook Polydor

The work of European synthesist Jarre has been a profound influence on most popular synthesizer-based bands today. Jarre's pop-rock album, *Oxygene,* rocketed to the top of the charts in 1976 and led to the worldwide acceptance of popular electronic music, synthesizers, and cutting edge technology. *Oxygene* offers vocal and instrumental selections that feature densely textured synthesizer arrangements and percolating percussion suitable for dancing. As the first Westerner to have his music broadcast on radio in the People's Republic of China, Jarre was later to tour there and record a double live album, *The Concerts in China.* Including some of Jarre's greatest hits, it features a special composition for a thirty-four-piece Chinese orchestra using two-string lutes, violins, Chinese lutes, and flutes. The sound is intriguingly visual, exotic, and lovely to hear. His next album, *Music for Supermarkets,* was recorded in the usual way, but Jarre—after pressing only one record—had all the printing and lacquering machinery destroyed. The single disc was then auctioned off for charity. *Rendez-vous* features a special musical theme: the history of Houston, Texas, in three movements—rural space, urban space, outer space. The synthesist sculpts each section into a separate but linked sonic overview complete with both passionate and pastoral highlights. The best introduction to Jarre's work is *The Essential Jean-Michel Jarre* compilation, which concentrates on upbeat, chakra-stimulating instrumentals performed on the computers and synthesizers of that era. Fans of Yanni and Vangelis will enjoy the detailed articulation and rich aural majesty of *The Essential*'s progressive synthesizer arrangements. **New Age Electronic, New Age Progressive**

Alap Jetzer

Boundless Aum Edition
Eternity's Sunrise Vital Body
Rising Beyond Vital Body
The Source of Music Vital Body
Towards the Golden Shore Aum
  Edition

Jetzer is well known for his arrangements of Sri Chinmoy's compositions on *Eternity's Sunrise, The Source of Music,* and *Towards the Golden Shore. On Rising Beyond,* part of the Art Of Relaxation series by Vital Body and another collaboration between Chinmoy and Jetzer, the moods are exquisitely serene and the melodies permeated with joy. *Boundless* features Jetzer's own compositions, which he performs on acoustic and electric guitars, synthesizer, Irish harp, tamboura, and the Indian bowed instrument, the esraj. Blissfully radiant, this music emerges like golden sunlight on a lazy summer day while his textural and uplifting compositions are warm, healing, and heartfelt. This is traditional New Age music at its consciousness-raising finest. **New Age Traditional, New Age World**

Eddie Jobson

Theme of Secrets Private Music
World of Private Music
  Sampler Private Music

On *Theme of Secrets* former Roxy Music synthesist Jobson explores cinematic and atmospheric computer-electronic music. The music is startling and evocative visionary space music that places equal emphasis on sound and silence, sensitivity and synergy. Jobson has performed on more than thirty rock and progressive music albums to date, and this one-man show is impressive, enlightening, and fun. **New Age Electronic**

Eric Johnson

Tones Warner Bros.

Johnson plays guitar the way Michelangelo painted ceilings: with a colorful vibrancy that's more real than life. *Tones* is a riveting, mostly instrumental guitar debut that also offers two vocal/guitar showcases penned by Johnson. Fans of hauntingly beautiful, mentally stimulating, and soul-soothing music would do well to let the "tones" of Eric Johnson's guitar flow effortlessly onto their turntables. **New Age Solo**

Jeff Johnson

The Awakening
  (w/Simpson) Ark
Born of Water (w/Eugene
  Friesen) Ark
The Face of the Deep Ark
Fallen Splendor Ark
Icons Ark
*Meadowlark Keyboard
  Sampler* Meadowlark
*No Shadow of
  Turning* Meadowlark
Shadow Play Ark
Through the Door Ark

Synthesist Johnson describes *No Shadow of Turning* as "representing my heart and a deeper exploration of a musical style that's very accessible to anyone. This is the kind of album that allows people to create quiet for themselves, within themselves." Johnson's music is ethereal and contemplative, combining elements of rock, jazz, and classical music with his unique palette of tones via keyboards, studio effects, and ambient sounds. Some cuts feature poetic lyrics that reflect Johnson's interest in art history as well as his personal travel abroad. *Icons* is more cerebral, featuring suitably complicated keyboard arrangements and sonic effects. **New Age Pop**

Alex Jones and Friends

*Angels of Color and
  Sound* Eastern Gate
Awake and Dreaming Eastern
  Gate
Awaker of Hearts Eastern Gate
*Haunts of Harmonic
  Breath* Eastern Gate
Imagination's Door Eastern Gate
Infinite Directions Eastern Gate
Inside the Hollow Eastern Gate
Kali's Dream Eastern Gate
Lokas Eastern Gate
Peace Offering Eastern Gate
Pranava Eastern Gate

Pianist Jones and friends Doug Cutler, Larry David, Heidemarie Garbe, and others create some of the most uplifting and inspired recordings around. *Kali's Dream* features joyful piano melodies while *Awake and Dreaming* is a mellow blend of devotional piano and synthesizer

NEW AGE PROGRESSIVE MUSIC

by Lee Abrams*

Abrams is a New Age radio programming consultant, as well as the founder of Cinema Records and Radio Lisa.

New Age Progressive music mixes the excitement and vision of progressive and experimental music with the sensitivity and warmth of the New Age. Largely created through state-of-the-art technology and a battery of electronic instruments, the music is cinematic in scope with a feeling of momentum. Though it lacks the airy feel of most New Age Space music, New Age Progressive music delivers symphonic, sometimes psychedelic crescendos that shake the listener's perception of reality. It is ideal for headphone listening.

AMERICAN GRAMAPHONE   PETER BAUMANN

   RECORDS   AMIN BHATIA

PETE BARDENS   MICHAEL BROOK

*Artist listing compiled by Patti Jean Birosik.

melodies. *Lokas* offers celestial piano works that flow gently and slowly; and *Inside the Hollow* is the solo instrumental background tape from the guided visualization *Infinite Directions*, which aids explorations of inner consciousness. A truly inspirational New Age Vocal tape, *Awaker of Hearts* features devotional songs ranging from joyful, uplifting tunes to deeply meditative chants. In addition, Jones has made available three guided meditations, *Angels of Color and Sound,* the above-mentioned *Infinite Directions,* and *Imagination's Door* as well as two books, *Seven Mansions of Color* and *Creative Thought Remedies.* **New Age East/West, New Age Vocal**

Michael Jones

After the Rain (w/Darling, Rumbel) Narada Lotus
Amber (w/Darling) Narada Lotus
The Narada Collection Narada Three Label
Pianoscapes Narada Lotus
Sampler #1 Narada Lotus
Sampler #2 Narada Lotus
Sampler #3 Narada Lotus
Seascapes Narada Lotus
Solstice (w/Lanz) Narada Lotus

GAVIN BRYARS

BARRY CLEVELAND

CUSCO

PAUL DRESHER

BRIAN ENO

EXCHANGE

FRANCISCO

GEIST

PATRICK GLEESON

CRAIG HUXLEY

MARK ISHAM

ITCHY FINGERS

JEAN-MICHEL JARRE

DANIEL LENTZ

ALVIN LUCIER

MANNHEIM STEAMROLLER

MICHAEL MANRING

PATRICK MORAZ

PATRICK O'HEARN

MICHAEL OLDFIELD

PLANT MUSIC

ROGER REYNOLDS

KLAUS SCHULZE

DIETER SCHUTZ

MICHAEL SHRIEVE

THILO VON WESTERNHAGEN

DARRYL WAY

YANNI

Sunscapes
   Narada Lotus
Wind and Whispers
   Sona Gaia
Windsong Antiquity

Jones's acoustic piano work bridges the classical and the contemporary, uniting the styles into sensitive, light-filled music brimming with lyrical energy. "When I record, I hope to convey the serenity I experience as I play. . . . Music is a medium of suggestion and inspiration. I hope I create music that enhances the quality of life," explains Jones. The introverted, calming, and gentle moods of *Pianoscapes* have made it one of the most popular albums in New Age acoustic music. "Initially music was my meditation. I played to balance myself and ground my energy while managing a busy schedule. It was also how I brought myself into harmony with nature while living in the middle of a large city." Jones's work with fellow pianist Lanz on *Solstice* yields a quietly engaging album that is tranquil, elegant, and intimately evocative. Its lovely melodies flow gently and create the atmosphere of a warm embrace. **New Age Solo, New Age Traditional**

Lou Judson

Sonoma Surf
  Intuitive Audio

No instruments are played on *Sonoma Surf;* rather, Judson captures the powerful, compelling, and ultimately relaxing music of the sea. Soft and gentle waves subtly caress your ears and soothe your mind, quieting the body and brain for a peaceful night of rest. The sound of the ocean has long been known as a therapeutic agent and detensifier; Judson's release is ample demonstration that what the ancients knew is true. **New Age Environmental**

K

Nancee Kahler

The Gathering Nebula

With acoustic piano and synthesizer, plus supporting ensemble members on bass, drums, and guitar, Kahler has created a fine New Age Jazz debut album. Her keyboard solos have a friendly, egoless quality; her sublime melodies are given sensitive readings by the ensemble players. The album is a journey through loosely structured song forms that are colorful, vibrant, and evocative. Good casual listening. **New Age Jazz**

Ariel Kalma and Richard Tintl

Music for Dream and Love Eurock Dist.

This album, from synthesists Kalma and Tintl, is stimulating yet soothing. Combining environmental sounds recorded in the jungles of Borneo with breathtakingly beautiful electronic arrangements, the cut "Osmose" is like a phantasmal tropical paradise. **New Age Environmental**

Kano (Don Campbell)

Runes Spirit Music

The album's cover is adorned with the ancient Viking rune symbols, but the principal instrument on this release is the contemporary organlike synthesizer. Drums, wood blocks, flute, finger cymbals, and metallophone provide a quiet, meditative background for relaxation, channeling, or other inwardly directed pursuits. This somewhat repetitive trance music effectively enhances harmonic attunement and chakra balancing while providing a soothing, ambient background. **New Age Meditation**

Karma

Ionospheres New World

Ionospheres is ambient New Age music that combines solid instrumentation and effects for a light, refreshing style. Exploring nature through a gentle mix of synthesizer, bird song, and organic earth sounds, Karma creates a warm and sensual sonic tapestry that evokes feelings of renewal and well-being—perfect for unwinding or meditation. New Age Environmental, New Age Meditation

Peter Kater

Anthem Nebula
Coming Home Invincible
*The Fool and the
   Hummingbird* Silver Wave
For Christmas Silver Wave
Gateway Sona Gaia
Spirit Optimism
Two Hearts Optimism

Composer/pianist Kater developed the theme of *The Fool and the Hummingbird* from an encounter he had in the mountains of Colorado. The story is beautifully conveyed through moving ensemble pieces for sax, flute, synthesizer, bass, drums, and piano. *Two Hearts* ranges from solo piano pieces to three-piece New Age Jazz tunes, while *Spirit* is Kater's first album of solo piano works. Improvising a progression or melody, Kater's inspirational compositions evoke a range of emotions from joyous to reflective. Kater's music also can be heard on Broadway, on film soundtracks, and on several PBS television specials. Actor Robert Redford says, "I can appreciate Kater's technical ability—but it's the content of his songs that I really ad-

mire." New Age Jazz, New Age Solo

Bibi Bhani Kaur

A Gift to Be Simple
   Invincible
My Crosswinds Invincible

The voice is the oldest musical instrument. Bhani's beautiful voice delivers songs inspired by spiritual traditions but set to New Age music influenced by folk, jazz, and pop. On *A Gift to Be Simple,* homespun folk songs with a cozy guitar accompaniment speak of simple devotion with touching and uplifting lyrics. *My Crosswinds* offers warm acoustic guitar and sweet vocals of poems written by sages of centuries past while they were in the ecstasy of union with the divine. New Age East/West, New Age Vocal

Sat Kartar Kaur

Domain of Shiva Invincible
*Healing Sounds of the Ancients
   #9* Invincible
*Healing Sounds of the Ancients
   #10* Invincible
*Healing Sounds of the Ancients
   #11* Invincible
Spirit in Blossom Invincible

On *Spirit in Blossom* two ancient ragas describe the flowering of the meditative mind, the experience of the soul touched by the divine, and the longing for this sacred bond. Kaur's vocal line is unforgettable, balanced, and drawn to a fine point by the blend of synthesizers, percussion, tamboura, and mandolin. *Domain of Shiva* is an etheric dancelike piece that showcases Kaur's exotic voice and amazing range. New Age East/West, New Age Vocal

Singh Kaur

Crimson #1
  (w/Robertson) Invincible
Crimson #2
  (w/Robertson) Invincible
Crimson #3
  (w/Robertson) Invincible
Crimson #4
  (w/Robertson) Invincible
Crimson #5
  (w/Robertson) Invincible
Crimson #6
  (w/Robertson) Invincible
*Songs of the Lord's
  Love* Invincible

The Crimson series blends Kaur's crystal-pure voice with Kim Robertson's Celtic harp and other instrumentation to forge a new kind of spiritual meditation music. *Crimson #1* is the most instrumentally rich of the series, featuring French horns and plucked strings underlying the vocals and harp. *Crimson #2* offers a root sound current, the repetition of which eradicates tension and conflict. The music is stately and baroque-influenced, executed with oboe and flutes and steady percussion. *Crimson #5* is subtitled "Mender of Hearts." It's a love song to the infinite, aimed at healing and reawakening joy and enthusiasm for life. New Age East/West, New Age Vocal

Brian Keane

Snowfalls Flying Fish
Suleyman the Magnificent
  Celestial Harmonies/Kuckuck

A virtuoso guitarist, Keane created *Suleyman* as the soundtrack for the film of the same name, focusing on the life of the great sultan who ruled the Ottoman empire from 1520 to 1566. His was a golden age of art and architecture, and Keane's music reflects the riches of this era. The album features original and traditional Turkish melodies blending Keane's impressive guitar with such exotic instruments, as the tanbur (long-necked lute), daire (drum), and the kanun (plucked box zither). The compositions are so magical, intense, and powerful that you feel you could actually reach out and touch the hem of a swirling dancer's robe. New Age World

Georgia Kelly

Ancient Echoes
  (w/Halpern) Sound Rx
Big Sur Tapestry (w/Lloyd) Pacific Arts
Birds of Paradise Heru/Global Pacific
Eros and Logos Heru/Global Pacific
Fresh Impressions
  (w/Kindler) Global Pacific
Harp and Soul (w/Lloyd and Richard Hardy) Heru/Global Pacific
In a Chord (w/Huxley) Global Pacific

Rainbow Butterfly Heru/Global
  Pacific
Seapeace Heru/Global Pacific
The Sound of Spirit Heru/Global
  Pacific
Tarashanti Heru/Global Pacific
Woman Spirit
  Heru/Global Pacific

Georgia Kelly is largely responsible for the modern resurgence in popularity of harp music. Historically the harp has been a symbol of peace and serenity, figuring predominantly in the myths and stories of ancient times. A classically trained musician and composer, Kelly has invoked this tradition to create music that positively affects the mind, body, and spirit. To this end she formed her own record label, Heru, as well as provided the musical background on two albums of guided meditation—*Woman Spirit* with Hallie Iglehart and *Rainbow Butterfly* with Dr. Emmett Miller. Kelly's New Age classic recording *Seapeace* is a collection of musical meditations and etudes for solo harp that blend Eastern and Western musical idioms, using natural sounds and violin to bring out the tidal motion of the melody. *Eros and Logos,* inspired by Kelly's deep interest in Jungian psychology, mythology, and dance, examines the eternal struggle between reason and emotion. Kelly's music has also gained recognition for its therapeutic effects and is used extensively in hospitals and mental health facilities. This is music that inspires the heart and provides the mind with a peaceful place to rest. **New Age Solo, New Age Traditional**

David Kessner

(See Music for Progressive Relaxation)

Liv Singh Khalsa and Sat Want Kaur Khalsa

Music of the Spheres Guru Ram
  Das Recordings

One of the great undiscovered New Age classics, *Music of the Spheres* is pure meditation music. Its bells, tamboura, guitar, harmonium, flute, and recorder evoke serenity; its cyclic dronelike sound calms your mind and centers your spirit while propelling you deeper and deeper into the alpha state. *Music of the Spheres* can aid concentration for both the beginner and experienced meditator. **New Age Meditation**

Al Gromer Khan

Cai and Roses Isis
Divan I Khas Beyond
Sounds of the New Age
  Sampler Isis
The Voyage Beyond
  Sampler Beyond

Khan studied sitar for ten years with Imrat Khan, the younger brother of Sufi leader Pir Vilayat Khan. He is the first European musician to be honored with the Khan title, presented for his extraordinary mastery of the instrument. *Divan I Khas* is a Sufi-influenced mixture of Northern Indian sitar sounds and Western electronic avant-garde music. At times aerial and ethereal, at other times densely lush and vibrant, the compositions are ultimately serene, intricately beautiful, and transcendent. This is radiantly positive music. **New Age East/ West**

and recorded with Oregon, Vasant Rai, Ravi Shankar, and Dave Brubeck, among others. **New Age Traditional**

Bob Kindler

The Fruits of Our Labors (compilation) Global Pacific
Music from the Matrix Global Pacific
Music from the Matrix II Global Pacific
Music from the Matrix III Global Pacific
Wingspan Global Pacific

Although he is proficient on guitar and other stringed instruments, New Age pioneer Kindler is best known for his hauntingly lovely cello playing, as superbly demonstrated on *Waters of Life,* part of his *Music from the Matrix* series exploring space, earth, water, fire, and air. As he explains, "Everyone likes the well-known 'mello cello' midrange sound that resonates in the heart, but . . . I have spent a lot of effort to cross over into other areas and adapt the cello to other musical forces, [such as] Indian modes for ragas, contemporary modes for jazz and fusion . . . [and] bringing back some of the improvisation that used to be part of the classical mode." Several tracks on *Waters of Life* are relaxing, meditative, and lyrically textured with a heart-touching devotional rather than cerebral sound. "I feel all artistic expression originates from a higher source and is given to human beings to bring beauty and inspiration to the world," Kindler adds. Kindler has performed

Steve Kindler

Automatic Writing Global Pacific
Dolphin Smiles (w/Bell) Global Pacific
Fresh Impressions (w/Kelly) Global Pacific
The Fruits of Our Labors (compilation) Global Pacific

Imagine windsurfing, sailing, and swimming in clear blue water where friendly dolphins and whales frolic beneath the surface. Now listen to the acoustic blend of New Age Jazz and classical instrumental music of violinist Kindler and guitarist Teja Bell on *Dolphin Smiles.* Kindler shares his inspiration for this release: "I wrote [it] after hearing Jacques Cousteau tell about diving to the bottom of the ocean and seeing a perfect circle of dolphins standing up with their tails touching the sand like they were meditating." The fluid melody lines on the record are developed through a close interplay between violin and guitar, creating rich textures and lush, sparkling soundscapes. A former member of the influential Mahavishnu Orchestra, Kindler says of group founder John McLaughlin, "[He] is a tremendous artist and major influence on my life, music, and spiritual outlook. I began meditation and learned that music is a spiritual pathway that takes concentration and mind control just like meditation." Kindler has also performed and recorded with Cat Stevens, Jeff Beck, and Jan Hammer, among others, including, briefly, Shadowfax. *Automatic Writing* is stunningly realized New Age Pop, radiantly performed on violin, guitar, and synthesizer. The album is a montage of musical impressions that successfully balance the ethereal and the earthy. New Age Traditional

Ben Tavera King

Border Crossing (as Los
  Jazztecs) Folklorico
Desert Dreams Global Pacific
The Fruits of Our Labors
  (compilation) Global Pacific
Southwestern Scenarios
  Terra/Vanguard

The music of guitarist King is a timeless, impressionistic trip through the American Southwest. "I think people relate to the spaciousness," King says. "I go for a spare, minimalist sound that is different from most Latin music where the notes are close together. Things are far apart in the desert, and that wide-open feeling comes across in my songs." On the New Age fusion release *Desert Dreams,* saxophone fills out the guitar, bass, and percussion lineup. Songs range from Hopi-influenced melodies to more mystic impressions, "like the dreamy feeling you get on a hot day when you think you are seeing something but it's not really there," as King describes it. New Age Jazz

Osamu Kitajima

Benzaiten Antilles
Masterless Samurai Headfirst

Osa-Mu Island
The Source CBS

An accomplished guitarist, kotoist, percussionist, and synthesist, Kitajima stresses style and simplicity on *The Source.* The music is thoughtful, introspective, and spacious. Kitajima's articulate performances yield beautiful melodies that calm the mind and ease the body. *Benzaiten* and *Osa-Mu* are excellent space music journeys that fuse Eastern mysticism with Western pop sensibility. New Age Space

Kitaro (Masanori Takahashi)

Asia Geffen
Astral Voyage Geffen
Full Moon Story Geffen
India Geffen
Ki Gramavision/Kuckuck
Kitaro in Person
  Gramavision/Kuckuck
The Light of the Spirit Geffen
Millennia Geffen
My Best Gramavision/Kuckuck
Oasis Gramavision/Kuckuck
Silk Road I Gramavision/Kuckuck
Silk Road II Gramavision/Kuckuck
Silver Cloud Geffen
Tenku Geffen
Towards the West Geffen
Tunhuang Gramavision/Kuckuck

Kitaro is a multi-instrumentalist, a composer, and one of the foremost exponents of New Age music. Although his style defies categorization, it features elements of romantic Western classical, traditional acoustic, and electronic music as well as sounds derived directly from nature. His records have sold tens of millions of copies worldwide and fans have attributed healing powers to his music. The *Silk Road* releases have become New Age classics, using both modern and traditional instruments to evoke the period, more than two thousand years ago, when trade between the East and West began, reminding the listener that spiritual ideals were exchanged along with material goods. *Tunhuang* features Kitaro on various synthesizers, guitar, sitar, santool, drums, Irish harp, and wind chimes, among other instruments, creating a gentle web of wonder. *The Light of the Spirit* (co-produced by the Grateful Dead's Mickey Hart) continues the meditation and reflection on childhood that Kitaro began on *Tenku,* and explores his visions of life, death, and rebirth, the harmonies and tensions of the created and creative universe. A practicing Buddhist and reported devotee of Bhagwan Shree Rajneesh, Kitaro states, "I was always a universalist in my outlook." His reverence for the natural world and its beauty is in evidence on his recordings; of his twenty-four-track home recording studio he says, "I open up the windows when I record and let everything in—the air, the sounds of birds and rustling leaves. Nature informs the music, and the music travels outdoors to inform nature." What drives Kitaro is a vision of world peace: "People create [wars], people who have a war within themselves. I want to create music that eases the war within. . . . Music has a transformative capacity. You can change [your] karma through music." **New Age East/West, New Age Traditional**

Daniel Kobialka

Afternoon of a Fawn Li-Sem
Coral Seas Li-Sem
Daniel Kobialka Performs Li-Sem
Dream Passage Li-Sem
Fragrances of a Dream Li-Sem
Going Home Li-Sem
Journeys in Time Li-Sem
Mind Dance Li-Sem
Moon-glow Li-Sem
Path of Joy Li-Sem
Softness of a Moment Li-Sem
Sun-space Li-Sem
Timeless Motion Li-Sem

Violinist/composer Kobialka creates classically inspired tone poems that evoke a sense of peace and are well suited for massage or meditation. Most selections are introduced by strings and enhanced by synthesizers so that the long, flowing instrumental phrases create a serene, nurturing atmosphere to help reduce stress. On *Timeless Motion,* Kobialka uses the theme from *Pachelbel's Canon* to create an extended-listening meditation piece. The repetitive melody is gently hypnotic, aiding concentration through sustained violin phrasing and a synthesizer foundation. Kobialka's other releases also feature New Age instrumental reworkings of classical masterpieces by composers such as Bach, Dvorak, Vivaldi, Beethoven, and Debussy. **New Age Traditional**

Masayuki Koga

Autumn Mist Fortuna
Beyond Time and Space Fortuna
The Distant Cry of Deer Fortuna
Moon at Dawn Fortuna

RELATED ARTISTS OF INTEREST

by P. J. Birosik

It became apparent during the compilation of this book that while some artists and groups were responsible, in part, for the development of New Age music's various subgenres, they themselves more accurately belonged to several other fields of music such as new classical, experimental, American folk, minimalism, ethnic, and jazz.

These innovative and influential artists have recorded many albums that I would recommend to fans who want to expand their listening habits beyond the New Age. Some of the releases are challenging, based on intellectual concepts rather than heartfelt inspiration; other releases feature invigorating, kinetic arrangements, faithful deliveries of traditional ethnic standards, or contemporary soft-jazz stylings.

Here are some artists New Age fans might well enjoy.

THOMAS ALMQVIST	HAROLD BUDD
LAURIE ANDERSON	DAVID BYRNE
ROBERT ASHLEY	JOHN CAGE
ADRIAN BELEW	LARRY CARLTON
THOMAS BELLINO	JOEL CHADABE
DAVID BENOIT	NICHOLAS COLLINS
GEORGE BENSON	CHICK COREA
BETWEEN	MILES DAVIS
LESTER BOWIE	STUART DEMPSTER
ANTHONY BRAXTON	TOR DIETRICHSON

Shakuhachi flute master Koga has devoted his life to bringing the beauty and mystery of his instrument to the Western world. Having spent years studying the traditional compositions for the bamboo flute, Koga decided to experiment with both jazz and free-form styles. "There are differences in timing, melody, scale, or dynamics," he reflects, "but the essence of any kind of music—Japanese, Western, classical, or rock—is the human element." On *Autumn Mist* with guitarist Douglas Hensley, Koga brings the vibrancy of the shakuhachi to a collection of baroque

WILLIAM DUCKWORTH	SEIGEN ONO
GLEN DUNCAN	PRESTON REED
KIMBALL DYKES	SUN RA
ELEMENTS	STEVE REICH
JOHN FAHEY	TERRY RILEY
ROBERT FRIPP	DAVID SANBORN
JAMES GALWAY	PHAROAH SANDERS
PHILIP GLASS	STEPHEN SCOTT
KEITH JARRETT	RICHARD STOLZMAN
KING CRIMSON	MORTON SUBOTNICK
LEO KOTTKE	L. SUBRAMANIAM
KRAFTWERK	DAVID SYLVIAN
KRONOS QUARTET	TANGERINE DREAM
MAHAVISHNU ORCHESTRA	DAVID TUDOR
DAVID MANN	GENE TYRANNY
HUGH MASEKELA	DAVID VAN TIEGHEM
WIM MERTONS	GLEN VELEZ
CHARLES MINGUS	ROBIN WILLIAMSON
STEPHEN MONTAGUE	YELLOWJACKETS
GORDON MUMMA	LA MONTE YOUNG
PANDIT PRAN NATH	

and more contemporary Western classical selections. Other albums feature classic and contemporary Japanese compositions spanning more than three centuries by both Koga and Tomoko Sunazaki, renowned master of the koto. The works leave the listener uplifted and filled with a deep calming sense of peace. **New Age East/West**

Jonathan Kramer

Gong with the Wind (w/Dean Evenson and D'Rachael)
Soundings of the Planet

Starry Night Soundings of the Planet

Tree O2 (w/Dean Evenson and Verdeaux) Soundings of the Planet

Whistling Wood Hearts (w/Dean Evenson and D'Rachael) Soundings of the Planet

Cellist Kramer's classical background enhances the moving compositions he performs with other Soundings of the Planet artists. On *Starry Night* Kramer extends the tonal range of his instrument from deep bass to clear high sounds, blending effortlessly with the flute and autoharp. Compositionally, Kramer's work has world music influences, the product of his study in Banaras, India, and later performances in the Soviet Union with Dean and Dudley Evenson. Kramer's cello sound strikes a harmonious balance between solo and ensemble performance. **New Age Traditional**

John Robert Krause

Heart of the Flower Living Waters

Heart of the Flower, Krause's debut release, communicates the music of the spheres—fine synthesized orchestral space sounds. Incorporating state-of-the-art digital synthesis with a superb sense of the ethereal, this deep, colorful work takes the listener on a healing journey. **New Age Space**

Van Krueger

Musical Fantasies for Relaxation Krueger/Backroads

Krueger creates synthesizer-based sounds that gently perch between New Age Space music and Meditation music. There is a refreshingly buoyant quality to most of the material on *Musical Fantasies for Relaxation*, yet the selections remain both smooth and fluid. The electronics are warmed up with piano and flute. Designed to inspire mental imaging, the music lifts and soars. **New Age Meditation, New Age Space**

Steve Kujala

Fresh Flute CBS

Former member of Auracle and Chick Corea's band, Kujala has created wonderful new music for the flute. Jazz great Bob James says, "This music has so much positive energy that it's impossible to be in a bad mood after listening to it. It is overflowing with beautiful melodies." Kujala achieves his dazzling sound through some surprising innovations, including a "slide" flute technique and a "126-track flute orchestra." He also plays piccolo on *Fresh Flute* while a virtual orchestra of other instruments adds spice to his lovely New Age instrumental compositions. **New Age Jazz**

L

Jean-Pierre Labreche

Sadhana Chacra Alternative
Yi-King Chacra Alternative
Yi-King Vol. II Chacra Alternative

Yi-King is music for relaxation inspired by the Chinese *Book Of Changes (I Ching)*. *Yi-King Vol. II,* its sequel, mingles calming nature sounds with soft, flowing synthesized music and enchanting feminine vocals. Both albums are superb examples of the transcendent style of New Age music that is warm, nurturing, intimate, and transformational. **New Age Electronic**

David Lange

Return of the Comet Hearts of Space

Return of the Comet offers interstellar harmonics with warm-sounding strings, bells, and rich bass, allowing for relaxing listening. Using cutting-edge electronic technology, Lange creates space music of unearthly di-mensions without losing the human quality. **New Age Space**

David Lanz

Cristofori's Dream Narada Lotus
Desert Vision (w/Speer) Narada Equinox
Heartsounds Narada Lotus
Narada Sampler I Narada
Narada Sampler II Narada
Natural States (w/Speer) Narada Equinox
Nightfall Narada Lotus
Solstice (w/Michael Jones) Narada Lotus
Woodlands (w/Rumbel and Tingstad) Narada Lotus

Lanz is one of the most popular New Age pianists. *Cristofori's Dream,* inspired by the eighteenth-century Italian harpsichord builder who is credited with inventing the piano, topped the debut New Age music chart in *Billboard* magazine and held that position for more than fifteen weeks. Featured on that album is a piano-Hammond B-3 organ duet of

"Whiter Shade of Pale," a hit for sixties group Procol Harem that is sweetly sentimental without being cloying. Lanz's classical influences, sensitive touch, and deft arrangements on both this cut and on his original compositions make *Cristofori's Dream* a must for keyboard lovers. Lanz's audio and video partnership with Paul Speer has also put him into the limelight. On *Natural States* and *Desert Vision,* Lanz's piano is a perfect counterpoint to Speer's guitar virtuosity. Both records aim to reflect the full spectrum of nature's beauty, from idyllic, calm sonic passages to powerful rhythmic storms, by maximizing the interplay between both instruments yet making good use of silence and sustain. For a slower, more inwardly directed listening experience, try *Heartsounds,* a soulful collection of original solo piano pieces that are intimate, peaceful, and somewhat romantic. **New Age Traditional**

Laraaji (Edward Larry Gordon aka Swami Nadananda)

Celestial Realms (w/Lyghte) Spirit Music
Celestial Vibrations Spirit Music
Day of Radiance (w/B. Eno) Editions EG
Essence/Universe Audion

Performing primarily on the Electronic Mode Zither, a musical instrument he developed from midseventies experiments with the open-tuned autoharp, Laraaji creates highly inspirational music. In 1975, while practicing "deep self-meditation discipline," he says he received a major musical vision during which he heard, felt, and realized the eternal, simultaneous *I AM* as an all-encompassing harmonic sound. Since that transcendental event, his life and mode of artistic expression have become more and more the reflection of celestial awareness. On *Celestial Realms* Laraaji joins Lyghte (Jonathan Goldman) to create some of the best sustained trance music around, using zither, bells, synthesizer, and guitar to initiate an epic galactic journey filled with supercharged light imagery. **New Age Meditation, New Age Sound Health**

David Larkin

Concert Journey Antiquity
Earthlight Sona Gaia
Moments Empowered Sona Gaia
O'Cean Sona Gaia
Summer Savory Sona Gaia
To the Essence of a Candle Antiquity

On *Earthlight* multi-instrumentalist Larkin examines man's ability to see the light of Earth from outer space as well as his ability to see the light within himself and others. Flute, panpipes, recorder, hammered dulcimer, synthesizers, guitar, and percussion as well as the sounds of nature—including the wind, ocean, and crickets—intertwine to evoke the vision of a world in harmony. Larkin especially shines on flute; and the album *O'Cean*—in particular his duet with the ocean and humpback whales—highlights his improvisational style and technical brillance. "I use tones as colors to create the feeling I'm trying to express. . . . I treat all instruments that I play the same way, they are extensions of my feelings. The synthesizer, for instance, I use to create a vast wash for a landscape of sound. I walk, gallop, trot, slide, dance over the landscape as the feelings lead me," explains Larkin. On his debut release, *To the Essence of a Candle,* his hypnotic solo flute sounds were composed to coincide with the movements of a flame. **New Age Traditional**

Grey Larsen
(See Malcolm Dalglish)

Yusef Lateef

Little Symphony Atlantic

Multi-instrumentalist Lateef has been a jazz innovator since he began his musical career more than four decades ago. He was one of the first modern musicians to introduce Asian scales and meters into his work. Then, surprisingly, in 1987 this respected jazz musician won a Grammy Award for Best New Age Recording with *Little Symphony.* The album is all grace, subtlety, and elegance, crossing the border between jazz and New Age Jazz. Along with such conventional instruments as saxophones, flutes, and keyboards, Lateef spices his compositions with the exotic shannie, gourdophone, and kalangu. **New Age Jazz**

Latitude

40 Degrees North
  Life Style
Latitude
  Life Style

40 Degrees North features sensual instrumental ballads, Latin fusion rhythms, and virtuoso progressive instrumental music performed on synthesizers and guitars by the talented composing and performing duo Ben Verdery and Craig Peyton. Their debut release, *Latitude,* demonstrates a certain synergy in the memorable textures and subtle rhythms of the instrumentation. Peyton says, "Ben's formed his whole career around melody, and I've done the same with rhythm tracks." Peyton was exploring jazz fusion and r&b while Verdery was performing classical guitar when they began writing together and laying the foundation for *Latitude.* The result is memorable. **New Age Jazz**

Gail Laughton

Harps of the Ancient Temples Laurel

Laughton's inspired performances on *Harps of the Ancient Temples* should be enjoyed immensely by fans of both Georgia Kelly and Patrick Ball, among others. The harp is one of the most ancient instruments, and Laughton's emotive playing techniques evoke the spirits of centuries-old harpists as well as their lovely music. The shimmering, ethereal quality of the harp sings out under her loving care. **New Age Solo**

Teresa Lawlor

Moods Green Linnet

On *Moods* Lawlor captures the haunting beauty and deep emotional qualities of the Irish harp. The album features traditional compositions that range in feeling from joyful simplicity to bittersweet poignancy. Viola, violin, cello, guitar, bouzouki, and keyboards are used to offset the crystal-clear resonance of Lawlor's harps. This is heart-lifting, visionary music. **New Age World**

Gabriel Lee

Impressions (w/Slepian) Narada
  Lotus
Narada Sampler 1 Narada
Seasons (w/Slepian) Narada Lotus

Guitarist Lee uses nature's subtle changes as his premise on *Seasons*. His compositions are based on strong melodic themes that progress and evolve, executed with the polished blend of classical and Spanish influences that mark Lee's style. Don Slepian adds masterfully restrained and lovely synthesizer complements on this album, and the result is a pensive, introspective vision. On *Impressions,* once again teamed with Slepian, Lee explores new tonal territory. This album leads the listener through a relaxing impressionistic sequence of dances and dreams. **New Age Traditional**

Jonathon Lee

Dreamworld Jondi
A Thousand Moods New World

A Thousand Moods is an environmental music album that combines the lyrical richness of Lee's grand piano with the sounds of the Earth—oceans, streams, wind, and rain. Perfect for meditation, yoga, or massage. **New Age Meditation**

Riley Lee

Oriental Sunrise Sona Gaia
Satori Sona Gaia

Lee is one of the first non-Japanese artists to be awarded the "Dai Shihan" (grand master) rank for his sensitive and compelling mastery of the shakuhachi flute; he also performs on yokobue (transverse flute) and taiko festival drums. His recordings have been highly praised for their exquisite, graceful interpretations of Japanese traditional standards as well as for his own contemporary improvisational pieces. As Lee puts it, "The shakuhachi is an instrument that makes the player want to create inspiring music. An old shakuhachi-playing Zen master once said that the tone is the most important thing when playing the shakuhachi. The pitches, melodies, and techniques are secondary. The tone one produces on the flute refect one's character, one's life." **New Age East/West**

Edith Leicester
(See Shawna Culotta)

Daniel Lentz

Missa Umbrarum New Albion

Missa Umbrarum (Mass of Shadows) is a New Age experimental symphony for voices with wineglasses, drums, bells, and rasps. The result is reminiscent of Gregorian chants, with ethereal voices floating softly upward toward never-ending spires in some imaginary chapel. The wineglasses are tapped, rubbed, and struck to make them sing, wail, or percussively crack in a mind-boggling blend of exotic sounds. It's not easy to figure out how the rasps fit in, but most listeners should enjoy this very unusual yet accessible album. **New Age Progressive**

Frank Lentz

Unstroken Fonix

Created with sitar, tabla, synthesizer, acoustic guitar, and flute, *Unstroken* envelops the listener with its celestial themes and melodic tones. Unusual textures combine with soothing washes of sound to gently stimulate the imagination while relaxing the body. **New Age Meditation**

Randall Leonard
(See Jerry Florence)

Joaquin Lievano

It Takes Two CBS
One Mind Global Pacific
Saudade (w/Masayoshi Takanaka) Narada

The name Lievano is synonymous with fluid, expressive, and soaring guitar playing; and his music is an amalgam of Latin, rock, jazz, and classical sounds. On *Saudade* Lievano teams up with Masayoshi Takanaka, one of Japan's hottest guitarists, for an inspired and incendiary performance, New Age Jazz music at its boiling point. **New Age Jazz**

Life Style Records

Sampler Vol. 1 Life Style

Life Style is a label dedicated to offering an overview of today's contemporary music. While heavy on the New Age Jazz and electronic subgenres, the tracks featured on this sampler also include environmental and traditional New Age music. Highlighted artists are Latitude, Mic Holwin, Dieter Schutz, Thilo Von Westernhagen and Band, Robert Bearns and Ron Dexter (Golden Voyage), Serge Blenner, and Robert Schroeder. **New Age Electronic, New Age Jazz**

Charles Lloyd

Big Sur Tapestry (w/Kelly) Pacific Arts
Pathless Path Unity

On *Big Sur Tapestry* flutist Lloyd is joined by harpist nonpareil Georgia Kelly to evoke the beauty and power of the majestic California coastline. At times peacefully expressive, at other times airy and ethereal, the music reflects the serenity of the big trees, the lushness of the verdant foliage, the spiritual as well as the sensual. *Pathless Path* mixes Asian and jazz influences into a spacious, antifrenetic offering suitable for reverie

NEW AGE SOLO INSTRUMENTAL MUSIC

by Shel Kagan*

Kagan has produced a dozen albums, is the former editor of Circus *magazine, and has more than 127 feature articles to his credit in various publications.*

New Age Solo Instrumentals serve to slow down the mind and thus can aid relaxation or meditation. The music, which often consists of long tones and is at times almost harmonically structureless, acts as a blank canvas on which the listener can impose personal "mind pictures." Utilizing a single instrument such as piano, guitar, harp, or bamboo flute, New Age Solo instrumentals mirror the pulse of a universal harmonic note, a "feeling tone" or fundamental frequency; it is not entirely a music for entertainment, arousal, or intellectual stimulation but is music that touches the heart. Without lyrics or dense instrumental layers to concentrate on, the mind is directed inward. While some artists' styles and techniques have symphonic or classical forms, New Age Solo instrumentalists also display new directions in composition and execution that set them apart from more historically bound forms of delivery.

PHILIP AABERG	ROBBIE BASHO
MARCUS ALLEN	CELESTIAL HARMONIES
CHRISTOFER ASHBY	RECORDS

*Artist listing compiled by Patti Jean Birosik.

and quiet activity. **New Age Traditional**

Annie Locke

Living Earth Search for Serenity
Portraits Search for Serenity

Inspired by crystals, synthesist Locke creates glistening, vibrant music for the spirit on *Living Earth*. Her gentle, flowing piano and harp-like synthesizer sounds soothe the stress and tension of everyday life. At her home in London, Locke works with individual clients to create musical "portraits" designed to inspire and "help them get where they want to go." *Portraits* is a collection of these musical consultations. **New Age Traditional**

CHANDRESH

JIM CHAPPELL

GEORGE CROMARTY

GINO D'AURI

ALEX DE GRASSI

JOHN DOAN

RICK ERLIEN

EDWARD GERHARD

CHRIS GLASSFIELD

PAUL GREAVER

PAUL HALLEY

LOU HARRISON

MICHAEL HARRISON

DANIEL HECHT

MICHAEL HEDGES

HADLEY HOCKENSMITH

PAUL HORN

ERIC JOHNSON

MICHAEL JONES

PETER KATER

GEORGIA KELLY

GAIL LAUGHTON

ALLAUDIN MATHIEU

CLARE MISSEN

JAMES NEWTON

JOHN NILSEN

PRIVATE MUSIC RECORDS

VLADISLAV SENDECKI

BOLA SETE

RICHARD SOUTHER

WILL TUTTLE

VILAS

ANDREAS VOLLENWEIDER

MARY WATKINS

PHIL WELLS

GEORGE WINSTON

SYLVIA WOODS

DENNY ZEITLIN

Kevin Locke

Lakota Wiikijo Olowan Canyon
Lakota Wiikijo Olowan Vol. II
Canyon
Love Songs of the Lakota
Canyon

For the Lakota Indian the flute is the sound of the wind: it gives voice to the beauty of the land, trees, and water. *Lakota Wiikijo Olowan* features the tribe's traditional flute music, which is soft, melodic, and almost dreamlike in its beauty and simplicity. Featured are love songs, the Lakota national anthem, and the chief's honor song. Volume II offers vocal and instrumental selections incorporating chant, rattles, and drumming. These are hauntingly serene and evocative albums recorded at

Storm Mountain in the sacred Black Hills of South Dakota. New Age Native American

Rosie Lovejoy and Charley Thweatt

Angelight Music
   Sampler Angelight
Heavenly Angels Angelight
I Claim a Miracle Angelight
Life on the Planet Is Fun Angelight
Wings to My Heart Angelight
You Are Light Angelight

Singer-songwriter Lovejoy is fast becoming one of the leading creators of original New Age music for children; the delightful songs feature simple, upbeat melodies and sing-along, positive-consciousness lyrics. Thweatt's gentle but strong voice and the guitar/keyboard instrumentation quickly captivates children and adults alike. A good introduction to the duo's music is the *Angelight Music Sampler*. New Age Vocal

Alvin Lucier

I Am Sitting in a Room Lovely
   Music
Music for Solo Performer Lovely
   Music
*Music on a Long Thin
   Wire* Lovely Music
Sferics Lovely Music
*Still and Moving Lines of
   Silence* Lovely Music

Lucier is an aural experimenter, constantly pushing back the boundaries between art-noise and music, using a wide array of instruments, voices, and technological effects. One of his more successful projects is *Music on a Long Thin Wire*. Perfect for patient people, the "music" is created by oscillating an eighty-foot wire through various minute gradations of pitch and timbre. This takes place very slowly, allowing first the ears and then the mind to relax and flow with the almost imperceptible alterations in sound. For those bored with normal meditation tapes, this might prove an interesting and useful focusing device leading to inner concentration and physical relaxation. New Age Meditation, New Age Progressive

Lyghte (Jonathan Goldman)

Celestial Realms (w/Laraaji) Spirit
   Music
Crystal Resonance Spirit Music
Windows of Sound (w/Michael
   Noll) Spirit Music

A light, ethereal beauty suffuses *Windows of Sound*, which was composed to help deepen the relaxed and self-healing state of mind. The music is performed by Lyghte, Michael Noll, and Laraaji on synthesizers and electronic guitars with unusual vocalizations and special sonic effects. The subtle "almost felt rather than heard" background resonates with the "singing" of quartz crytal meditations while dominant chimes and bell tones ring out clearly. The liner notes explain that side one was created in the key of F, believed by the Chinese to be the fundamental tone of the Earth, while side two is in the key of C, "which many scientists . . . believe to be a resonant harmonic of the ionosphere." In addition, both sides contain drones that are pulsed at sixty beats per minute, which is conducive to creating an alpha state, as well as resonating and balancing the chakras. It should be noted that *Window of Sound* contains two guided meditations and is based on the book of the same name by Dr. Randall Baer and Vicki Baer. *Crystal Resonance* features Lyghte's solo work on synthesizers, electric guitars, and Tibetan bells with overtone chanting, further developing his authority in the therapeutic use of sound and music. **New Age Sound Health**

Ray Lynch

Deep Breakfast Music West
The Sky of Mind Music West
Truth Is Only Profound Music West

One of the best-selling New Age Space music albums ever, *Deep Breakfast* strikes a balance between emotional lyricism and pure fun through Lynch's fine synthesizer orchestrations. Along with the synthesizer, Lynch blends piano, flute, and viola, weaving classical influences and contemporary sounds. *The Sky of Mind* features radiant compositions on synthesizer, Tibetan bells, acoustic instruments, and voices. Lynch's music is balanced, meticulous in detail, and extremely emotional all at once. A childhood pianist, Lynch switched to classical guitar after hearing the works of the extraordinary Andrés Segovia. As he explains, "I was just blown away. I was literally lying on the floor weeping." During a profitable career as a solo composer/performer and member of the Renaissance Quartet, Lynch had, as he calls it, a "personal and spiritual crisis. I was standing in my front yard and suddenly felt as though I was on the edge of an abyss looking down into a black hole. I was looking at death and knew my life had come to a dead end." He then set out for California and began a period of intense spiritual study and personal growth. Experimenting with a little Arp synthesizer, Lynch felt he "could more easily and economically create music which can approximate the size and dense textures of orchestral sound." The resulting albums are a deeply emotional musical journey. **New Age Traditional**

Cecil Lytle

Keys of Life Celestial Harmonies
Seekers of the Truth Celestial Harmonies

On the double-album release, *Seekers of the Truth,* pianist Lytle presents a profound performance of the visionary music of G. I. Gurdjieff/Thomas de Hartmann. Attracted by eccentric and offbeat music, Lytle says, "I have a nondenominational approach," and his impressive history illustrates that fact: classical, blues, jazz, gospel, and avant-garde as well as theatrical music fit into Lytle's style. The nineteen-part *Seekers of the Truth*

113

was arranged by Gurdjieff's protégé, de Hartmann, while three other selections were arranged in the style of de Hartmann by Lytle himself. Through his grounded understanding and delicate, profound performance, Lytle helps illuminate Gurdjieff's mysticism. **New Age East/West**

Magical Strings

Above the Tower Flying Fish
Glass Horse Magical Strings
On the Burren Flying Fish
Spring Tide Flying Fish

Magical Strings is actually Philip and Pam Boulding, who perform energetic arrangements of Celtic music as well as their own compelling original compositions. On wire- and nylon-strung harps, hammered dulcimers, field organ, and pennywhistles, they create warm, graceful music. *Above the Tower* was produced by Michael O'Domhnaill and is comprised primarily of Magical String's own sweetly poetic, ethereal, and evocative pieces. **New Age World**

Reed Maidenberg

Poppies Rhythmythology Music

Electronic and acoustic instruments together create melodic sound paintings on *Poppies,* from quiet moods to upbeat rhythms, all inspired by the beauty and mystery of nature. Maidenberg adds, "As nature revels in diversity, so the music reflects many moods and feelings. It is [my] hope that this record will convey a peaceful yet vital appreciation of Earth's fragile beauty and further the awareness of ecological concerns." Maidenberg succeeds on a grand scale: his blend of synthesizer, guitar, percussion, pan flute, and ocarina are vibrant and soul-filling. **New Age Traditional**

Maitreya
(See Michael and Maloah Stillwater)

Malaysian Pale

Nature's Fantasies Fortuna

Nature's Fantasies is a boldly conceived collection of electronic tone poems that project a quick series of images from around the world: emerald green jungles, the Serengeti Plain, wind over the tundra, Brazilian sunsets, and tranquil Japanese gardens. Says group member Manfred Saul, "If Mother Nature were to describe her own creations, hopefully she would express things the way we wrote them." Drawing on Western and non-Western rhythms and scales, Malaysian Pale explores these cinematic soundscapes through synthesizers, programmable drum machines, electric guitar, and bass. Leaning toward the romantic, the group looks for sounds that delicately capture the images of life, Earth, and space. Says Saul, "You discover these sounds, adapt them musically, and find that there is a beautiful harmony between everything." Group member Steve Mecca adds, "Whereas pop music tends to be more formularized, this music is accidental and methodical." **New Age Electronic, New Age World**

Mannheim Steamroller

Christmas American Gramaphone
Classical Gas (w/Mason Williams) American Gramaphone
Fresh Aire American Gramaphone
Fresh Aire II American Gramaphone
Fresh Aire III American Gramaphone
Fresh Aire IV American Gramaphone
Fresh Aire V American Gramaphone
Fresh Aire VI American Gramaphone
Interludes American Gramaphone
Mannheim Steamroller Christmas American Gramaphone

Saving the Wildlife American Gramaphone
(Plus two excellent video samplers)

Mannheim Steamroller creates an intriguing blend of new classical, environmental, and New Age music. Each recording in the *Fresh Aire* series is based on a different theme, but all are magnificent, complex, and detailed, recordings that deserve to be played on the best state-of-the-art sound system you can afford. Their production is impeccable and the compositions stunning; extensive liner notes detail the themes of the music. Dramatic and inspired, *Fresh Aire VI* takes listeners across legendary seas to the enchanted, timeless world of ancient Greece. Subtitled *Impressions of Greek Mythology*, this record evokes the power of the ocean as the source of all life; one selection depicts two dolphins holding a conversation in Poseidon's watery depths, while another tells the story of Helios, who mounts a chariot pulled by four winged horses to take up the sun each morning. The spirits, gods, and heroes of this era are conjured up by the eighty-piece London Symphony and the thirty-voice choir of the Cambridge Singers in addition to core Mannheim Steamroller members. On *Classical Gas* the group joins forces with guitarist extraordinaire Mason Williams to rearrange and re-record the title track, one of the most popular instrumentals of the last two decades. *Fresh Aire I* is more baroque; *II* reflects medieval influences; *III* is characterized by renaissance melodies that flow into contemporary sounds; and *IV* features twentieth-century avant-garde music. One of the best-sellers in New Age music today, Mannheim Steamroller mystifies and entertains through a deep, ethereal expression that offers more than meets the ear. **New Age Progressive, New Age Traditional**

Michael Manring

Unusual Weather Windham Hill

Manring is a fretless bassist who has appeared on many of the Windham Hill recording sessions. His debut release, *Unusual Weather,* offers an emotional yet subtle musical palette of bass, piano, cello, flute, percussion, and wordless vocals. Ranging from delicately intricate to thunderously powerful, this eclectic offering is great for headphone or casual listening. **New Age Progressive**

Robert Margouleff

Caldara Kama Sutra
Tonto's Expanding Head Band (w/Cecil) Embryo

Featuring one of the most outstanding examples of visionary cover art, *Tonto's Expanding Head Band* was a pioneering effort of seventies electronic/space music. One track was even freely adapted to become the theme for the popular television series, "The Six-Million-Dollar Man"; and the remaining selections range from soothing instrumental ballads to roller-coaster progressive sound experiments. An underground college favorite, this release still holds up well and should be enjoyed by fans of Steve Roach, Tangerine Dream, and Manuel Gottsching. *Caldara* is another unusual gem that weaves rich sonic tapestries by combining electronic and acoustic instrumentation into a spiritual/space adventure. **New Age Electronic**

Ingram Marshall

Fog Tropes New Albion
The Fragility Cycles New Music
   Distribution Service

Fog Tropes is an extraordinarily calm and mellow piece that eases the listener into a quietly introspective mood. Marshall mixes synthesizer, piano, Indonesian flute, fog horns, and mandolin with ambient sounds to create a work of almost limitless depth, ideal for meditation or inwardly directed mental pursuits. **New Age Meditation**

Mike Marshall
(See Darol Anger)

Allaudin Mathieu

Available Light Windham Hill
In the Wind Cold Mountain
Piano Sampler Windham Hill
Second Nature Vital Body
Streaming Wisdom Cold Mountain

Part of Vital Body's "Art Of Relaxation" series, Mathieu's delightful piano release is a refreshing, impressionistic look at nature from a man who writes, "I live in a valley of exquisite beauty, and I look at it 365 days a year. This is all I do, and somehow it turns into music." His solo piano compositions are by turns delicate, fluid, and evocative; as Mathieu puts it, "The grass is green by nature; by second nature it becomes flowing chords. Likewise the patterns of trees and shrubs become a finished composition." Mathieu's background includes writing music for Stan Kenton and Duke Ellington, studying with Pandit Pran Nath and Terry Riley, and directing the Sufi Choir. **New Age Solo**

Ian Matthews

Walking a Changing Line Windham hill

One of the original members of the seminal folk-rock group Fairport Convention, Matthews is a music industry veteran. In the early seventies he headed the groups Matthews Southern Comfort and Plainsong, then created a series of solo rock albums. Now, with *Walking a Changing Line,* Matthews offers consciousness-oriented New Age Pop vocals. The songs were penned by Jules Shear and have a slightly impromptu feel while remaining warm, intimate, and straight from the heart. Swirling synthesizer lines ably support Matthews's pleasant vocal stylings. **New Age Vocal**

Tom Mauchahty-Ware

Flute Songs of the Kiowa and Comanche Canyon
Tradition and Contemporary Indian Flute Canyon

An acclaimed Kiowa-Comanche Indian flutist, Mauchahty-Ware tells us that originally the flute was used for courting. On *Flute Songs of the Kiowa and Comanche* some of the cuts are traditional courting songs while others have been transcribed for flute from traditional vocal songs, including the "Kiowa Flag Song," which is a patriotic song to honor the United States flag and the nation itself. Mauchahty-Ware is a master of his instrument. The sounds flow, bend, sustain, and float effortlessly, making the ancient melodies seem surprisingly contemporary and fresh. **New Age Native American**

Lyle Mays

Lyle Mays Geffen

Mays is a keyboardist and co-composer for the Pat Metheny Group. After eight albums with the band and numerous other contributing projects, Mays has delivered his first solo album, *Lyle Mays.* The release blends the sonorities of Mays's various keyboards ("but all my solos are on the acoustic piano," he notes) and melds jazzy improvisation with elements of other musical cultures, such as Scots-Irish folk music and Japanese scales. The centerpiece of *Lyle Mays* is a beautiful three-part piece that is fourteen minutes long. Called "Alaskan Suite," this inspired multitextured song evokes the magnificience and overwhelming spaciousness of that state. New Age Jazz fans will be well pleased with *Lyle Mays.* **New Age Jazz**

118

Susan Mazer

The Fire in the Rose Rising
   Sun/Narada
Inner Rhythms (w/Smith) Music
   West
Lifetide (w/Smith and
   Halpern) Gramavision/Polygram
Summit (w/Smith) Pro Jazz

Mazer was one of the first artists to apply modern electronic technology to the amplification of the concert grand harp—fourteen years before the popularity of Vollenweider. A classically trained musician, she blends pop and jazz stylings on *Inner Rhythms,* a compilation of New Age Jazz improvisations by Mazer and Lyricon wind synthesist Dallas Smith. High-energy, low-stress selections are the hallmark of Mazer and Smith who blend unusual time signatures and cool jazz influences into melodic fire. As Mazer says, "Our music should create a blank canvas for the listener to fill with his own picture using his own imagination, rather than we as artists trying to get across a specific picture. What we are giving is our aesthetic joy in making music." **New Age Jazz**

James McCarty
(See Stairway)

Sam McClellan

Life Patterns Spirit Music
Music of the Five Elements Spirit
   Records
*Music of the Five Elements Vol.
   II* Spirit Music

*Music of the Five Elements Vol.
   III* Spirit Music

McClellan creates gently grounded music that endeavors to balance the chakras and to lead the listener into a positive, peaceful state of equilibrium. Referencing the ancient Chinese concept of the elements (fire, water, wood, metal, and earth), he uses his experience as an acupressurist to create a musical acupressure session utilizing the sounds of piano, guitar, zither, Chinese flute, and synthesizer. The initial release in the series, *Music of the Five Elements,* has useful liner notes, including a chart connecting the five elements of the yogic/vedic chakras to the Chinese elements. There is also a section on "Music and Healing" of which McClellan, like Steven Halpern and a few others, is a pioneer. As a vehicle of personal transformation, the entire series is excellent for yoga or healing contexts. **New Age Sound Health**

Dennis McCorkle
(See Larry Snyder)

James McElroy

All Day, All Night Invincible
Mystique Invincible

McElroy's woodwinds—alto flute, C-flute, and soprano sax—blend perfectly with piano, guitar, and percussion on *Mystique.* The record spans many musical moods but is well suited to reflection and meditation. On *All Day, All Night,* McElroy adds African percussion to the mix to create some unusual and exciting rhythms. New Age Traditional

Tom McFarland

Just Got In from Portland Flying Heart
Travelling with the Blues Arhoolie

McFarland discovered the blues in the volatile sixties but over the years he has come to concentrate on fluid, heartfelt guitar instrumentals. McFarland's New Age Folk styling on *Just Got In from Portland* reflects the voices of nature through tasteful picking and strumming as well as lovely melody lines. Moving, tender, and uplifting, his music tells lyrical stories without words. New Age Folk

Randy Mead
(See David Michael)

Meadowlark Records

Keyboard Sampler 1987 Meadowlark
Sampler 1985: Music for Your Personal Retreat Meadowlark
Sampler 1986 Meadowlark

In 1985 the Meadowlark line was launched with a sampler defining the label's musical philosophy. *Music for Your Personal Retreat,* an all-instrumental release, features gentle folk and jazz-inspired selections from John Michael Talbot, Douglas Trowbridge, Justo Almario, Richard Souther, and Jeff Johnson. The end product is meditative and inspirational, ethereal and eclectic. New Age Folk, New Age Jazz

Megabyte

Powerplay Innovative Communication

Powerplay is energy-flow music; the sensual sounds are performed by a band of studio musicians who create exciting poetry inspired by such artists as Yellow, Art of Noise, Alan Parsons, and Vangelis. Unique and specially created sounds sparkle like pure crystals merging with deep soft tones, lush melodic lines, and exotic percussive patterns. Slip on the headphones and sink into this music. New Age Electronic

Kim Menzer

Skywalks Fonix
Ways Fonix

Menzer's calm, quietly inspiring flute work is perfect for relaxation, meditation, or massage. On *Ways,* Menzer superbly demonstrates the character and nuance of silver and wooden flutes as well as pan pipes. Guitar and flute gently entwine in flowing harmony on *Skywalks,* guiding the listener on an uplifting aural journey through the air. New Age Meditation, New Age Traditional

Peter Mergener and Michael Weisser (aka Software)

Beam-scape Innovative Communications
Best Of Innovative Communications
Chip-Meditation Innovative Communications

Electronic Universe Innovative
Communications
Night-Light Innovative
Communications
Phancyful-Fire Innovative
Communications
Syn-Code Life-in-Concert
Innovative Communications

Software is a team made up of German science-fiction author Weisser and synthesist Mergener that creates mysteriously beautiful electronic music. The sound is carried more by melody and harmony than by harsh, obviously technical experiments. On *Phancyful-Fire* the two orchestrate fragile movements interwoven with sequences of whispering voices describing the interaction of modern science and our environment. On *Night-Light,* saxophone and guitar join the complex electronic mix to add a warm, flowing sensation. This is electronic space music for those who have been afraid of this subgenre of New Age music as well as for those who have already discovered that electronic music can reflect human feeling as well as technical sophistication. **New Age Electronic**

Pat Metheny

American Garage ECM
As Falls Wichita, So Falls Wichita Falls ECM
Bright Size Life ECM
80/81 ECM
First Circle ECM
New Chataugua ECM
Offramp ECM
Pat Metheny Group ECM
Rejoicing ECM
Song X Geffen

Still Life Geffen
Travels ECM
Watercolors ECM

Virtuoso guitarist/guitar synthesist Metheny has performed and/or recorded with most of the interesting musicians of the past two decades, including Eberhard Weber, Jack DeJohnette, Joni Mitchell, Lyle Mays, Jaco Pastorius, and Ornette Coleman. With keyboardist Mays, his frequent writing partner in the Pat Metheny group, he has won many music awards. *New Chataugua* is a departure from the sizzling jazz fusion music that made Metheny's reputation. It is a New Age-inspired pastoral air performed on acoustic guitar, electric six- and twelve-strings, fifteen-string harp guitar, and electric bass. *Offramp* is by turns coolly futuristic (featuring Metheny's guitar synthesizer for the first time on vinyl) and buoyantly optimistic. Metheny describes *Offramp* as "probably the most diverse [recording] within itself." The Grammy-winning *First Circle* is reportedly Metheny's own favorite, offering a seamless blend of the well-honed Metheny group fusion and the airy sonorities of Brazilian popular music plus some vocals from Pedro Aznar. A jazz critic's favorite as well as a fusion crossover success, the Pat Metheny group has long been in the foreground of instrumental music. **New Age Jazz**

David Michael and Randy Mead

Petals in the Stream Fortuna

NEW AGE SOUND HEALTH MUSIC

by Jonathan Goldman*

Goldman is president of Spirit Music Records, the founder of Sound Healers Association, and (under the name Lyghte) a recording artist. He also teaches seminars and workshops on the therapeutic uses at sound and music throughout the world.

New Age Sound Health music is specifically created as a tool for health and wellness. The use of specific frequencies, scales, intervals, and chants to alter consciousness was well known in the ancient mystery schools of Egypt and Greece, and has only emerged recently in the West. Some releases consciously deal with the relationship among keynotes, colors, and the chakras. Others combine vowel sounds, rhythmic pulses, drones, and different scales to resonate and affect the physical body, as well as the etheric energy field. The music can be executed with acoustic instruments such as guitar, piano, or woodwinds, or with synthesizers. New Age Sound Health music can either facilitate brain activity for accelerated learning or entrain the listener to very slow brain waves, taking them to deep places in the consciousness for meditation.

*Artist listing compiled by Patti Jean Birosik.

The light, lyrical voices of Celtic harp, flute, zither, and recorder blend with strings, synthesizers, and guitar on this graceful record from Michael and Mead, co-performers since 1973. *Petals in the Stream* combines elements of renaissance, baroque, impressionist, and ethnic traditional influences for wistful and delicately reassuring sound. Mead is also known to the New Age listening audience as a member of the group Ancient Future. **New Age Traditional**

Jamie Michaels

Bouquet Innersong

Singer/songwriter/guitarist Michaels brings a decidedly spiritual element to the gentle songs on *Bouquet*. "I made this album very carefully," says Michaels, "for the kind of person who lights a candle, sits down, and really listens to the music." Synthesist Steve Roach and other stellar New Age musicians guest on the album. This is intimate, romantic, folk-inspired music that vibrates with

ANUGAMA	LYGHTE
DON CAMPBELL	SAM MCCLELLAN
SKY CANYON	MIRAGE
DAVID CASPER	MU-PSYCH RECORDS
DAVID COLLETT	MUSIC FOR PROGRESSIVE
TERENCE DOLPH	RELAXATION
ELEVATION EXPRESS	NATOPUS
DANIEL EMMANUEL	SPIRIT MUSIC RECORDS
ROGER ENO	DAVID SUN
KAY GARDNER	PAUL SUTIN
STEVEN HALPERN	PAUL TEMPLE
MAX HIGHSTEIN	MICHAEL UYTTEBROEK
ISLE OF SKYE	ARDEN WILKEN
LARAAJI	BETH YORK

sincere but quiet intensity. **New Age Vocal**

Stephan Micus

Behind Eleven Deserts Wind
Implosions Japo
Ocean ECM
Sambodhi Music
  (w/Deuter) Chidvilas
Till the End of Time Japo
Twilight Fields ECM

Micus has studied the traditional instruments of Morocco, Japan, India, and other countries, and his compositions use these devices in fresh new ways. He blends guitar, flute, sitar, shakuhachi, gagku no sho (Japanese mouth organ), suling (Balinese flute), Uillean pipes, and other instruments into rich, textural music that is punctuated with haunting, reverberated tones. *Sambodhi Music,* his collaboration with electronic composer Chaitanya Hari Deuter, is especially dazzling, with exquisite melodies delicately arranged in a shimmering, harmonious balance. **New Age World**

Mila (Mila Gilbert)

*Like the Wind as a
  River* Invincible
Night Jasmine in June Invincible
Sky Without End Invincible

"Music is a very powerful medium of expression and communication. More than the notes, it is a tangible expression of the artist's frame of mind and clarity of spirit," says guitarist Mila. His philosophy and vision come through in both the beautiful compositions and the eloquent fingering technique displayed on *Night Jasmine in June*. Mila creates deceptively simple songs with a purity of line and a masterly diversity of melody. "I think my Filipino heritage accounts for my affinity with island music and the pace of life island cultures usually have—really laid back," he adds. Incorporating eight years of study and performing experience in India with more Americanized modes of style, Mila's mini-concertos for guitar rarely last longer than four or five minutes yet evoke a wealth of mental imagery that is lush, texturally rich, and abundantly positive. **New Age East/West**

Billy Miller

Wind and Wood Turquoise

Miller appears at renaissance fairs all over the United States selling the flutes he handcrafts and plays. *Wind and Wood* is filled with his warm, flowing flute melodies enhanced with mandolin, acoustic and bass guitar, bouzouki, and pennywhistle. Starting from simplicity, many of the compositions gain texture and vibrancy as they meander melodically. Sweetly innocent, *Wind and Wood* is ultimately gentle music. **New Age Folk**

Radhika Miller

The Lark's Bride (w/E.
  Friesen) RMM
Lotus Love Call RMM
Sunlit Reverie RMM
Within the Wind RMM

The Lark's Bride offers majestic renaissance and traditional melodies. Special guest Eugene Friesen adds cello, double bass, and voice to Miller's lyrical and stirring flute while piano and harp add color and vibrancy. *Lotus Love Call* features gentle, peaceful flute with keyboards and natural sounds in a balanced program of classical selections and original compositions by Miller. *Within the Wind* combines flute with exotic world instruments. *Sunlit Reverie* weaves flutes, harp, piano, and the sounds of nature to create peaceful, lovely melodies. **New Age Pop**

Mind over Matter

Music for Paradise Innovative
  Communications

If heaven had a soundtrack, this might be it. Mind over Matter creates shimmering, swirling layers of computerized electronic instruments designed to evoke emotion rather than to enhance meditation. The group holds that "paradise" is not an unreachable island of the blessed on another world but a quiet place to be discovered within oneself. New Age Electronic

Mirage (Jon Coe and Steve Winfield)

Crystal Silence Spirit Music

Crystal Silence consists of two long pieces centered around the key of G, which, according to the artists, is supposed to facilitate openness and an awareness of the connections among all living things. The release relies heavily on synthesized sounds to create an atmosphere for meditation, using a few simple, recurring themes—effective, trancelike music. Coe is a skilled keyboardist and guitar player who also writes New Age music criticism for several Boston newspapers. Keyboardist/saxophonist Winfield has several solo albums out on Narada Records, works independently with musicians in the areas of stress reduction and holistic Western health care, and is a teacher of Hawaiian Huna spiritual practice. **New Age Sound Health**

Clare Missen

Earth Child New World
Sea Child New World

Pianist Missen composes and performs New Age instrumentals that incorporate her jazz and classical training. Nature-connectedness is a frequent theme; the listener is encouraged to "join with" the ocean, the earth, the wind, and the rain. The records alternate between quietly inspiring and hauntingly beautiful solo pieces. **New Age Solo**

Bruce Mitchell

Hidden Pathways Narada Mystique

In his own words, Mitchell creates "music that unites all timbral possibilities and styles in a warm and healing environment, a music that inspires and uplifts people." On *Hidden Pathways* computer-music consultant Mitchell performs on keyboards, guitar, flute, saxophone, harp, and percussion, imbuing his music with a variegated richness that reflects his personal interest in philosophy, ancient history, and world religions. Subtly spiritual, overtly joyous, *Hidden Pathways* is a scintillating symphony. **New Age Electronic**

Dieter Moebius
(See Cluster)

Karma Moffett

Himalayan Bowls I Pathways
Himalayan Bowls II Pathways
Kallash Pathways
Sitting Still Within/Without Pathways

Moffett's recordings are not so much music, defined in the narrow sense, as a rich, meditative atmosphere of sound created by gently resonanting Tibetan bells. *Sitting Still Within/Without* features a single low resonance bell on side A that is struck only occasionally to allow the full tone and vibrations to be heard fully. The sounds of nature—birds, a stream—can also be heard in the background. Side B features multiple bells as well as chimes. *Himalayan Bowls II* offers long tusk horns combined with bells and gongs to recall the ancient spiritual culture of Tibet. Those familiar with meditation bowls will enjoy the resultant sounds, surely unlike anything else on Earth. New listeners will find that the bowl-shaped bells will enhance quiet reflection as well as deeper meditative states. **New Age Meditation**

Clara Mondshine

Memorymetropolis Innovative Communications

Mondshine creates lovely music for meditation featuring subtle Asian and Indian influences that ease the listener into a relaxation or dream state. Her synthesizers are programmed to meld tabla sounds with flowing lyrical melodies similar to those of Klaus Schulze or Tangerine Dream, combining Western music and Eastern rhythms. This is inspirational and evocative electronic music. **New Age Space**

Jack Montgomery
(See Sandy Smith)

Tom Moore
(See Voyager)

Patrick Moraz

Coexistence PVC
Flags (w/Bill Bruford) Editions EG
Future Memories PVC

Future Memories II PVC
Human Interface Cinema
Music For Piano & Drums (w/Bill Bruford) Editions EG
Patrick Moraz Atlantic
Time Code Passport

Classically trained keyboardist Moraz has created twelve solo albums and thirty-five soundtracks. In the early seventies he worked with Dr. Robert Moog to develop the Polymoog synthesizer, then did a progressive rock stint, performing and recording with the Moody Blues and Yes. *Human Interface* is a welcome offering that bridges the gap between technology and intuitive creativity. As Moraz relates, he works with synthesizers and other electronic music gear "for weeks on end, writing, composing, and editing, choosing the right moment between . . . the poetry of creation and the prose of fabrication." The result is a galactic soundscape of dense aural layers accented by bright notes—perfect for midnight headphone journeys. **New Age Progressive**

Randy Morriss

Circle of Stone Allegro
Conversations with Myself Allegro
Desert Dreams Allegro
Lifeline Allegro
Pieces of the Sky Allegro
Randy Morriss Allegro
Shambhala Allegro

Morriss is a multi-instrumentalist who blends innovative arrangements with soaringly romantic melodies, moving beyond the quiet sounds of New Age Traditional music into the direction of New Age Pop. *Conversations with Myself* and *Pieces of the Sky* feature spontaneous piano solos; *Circle of Stone,* chronicling a year in the life of Stonehenge, approaches New Age Jazz. Its thirteen tracks are appropriately eclectic, ranging from spirited Irish/Celtic folk dances to progressive fusion highlighted by saxophone solos. **New Age Pop**

Mosaic (Doug and Matt Brody)

Form and Illusion Invincible
Invisible Landscapes
   Invincible
New Blue Invincible

Having created a new kind of high-energy electronic music while still in high school (as demonstrated on *Form and Illusion*), Doug and Matt Brody have now embraced New Age Jazz, moving it up an octave in sheer electronic excitement. The duo blends the full range of synthesized and sampled electronic keyboards with the soulful sound of sax. On *New Blue* many instrumental lines interweave to form a complex tapestry of sounds; then suddenly a particular passage will resolve into a single solo line. On *Invisible Landscapes* Mosaic takes the listener on a hypnotic journey inspired by Italo Calvino's book, *Invisible Cities.* The groups states, "It is our goal to entrap the audience both sonically and musically but still leave them room to move freely within the atmosphere." **New Age Electronic, New Age Jazz**

Alphonse Mouzon

Early Spring Optimism

For more than ten years Mouzon has been a prominent jazz fusion artist—a drummer of incredible energy, a talented writer, and a keyboardist. A charter member of Weather Report, Mouzon has also worked with artists such as George Benson, Al DiMeola, Eric Clapton, and John Klemmer. On *Early Spring* he demonstrates a lighter, more spacious and upbeat personal vision. "A lot of feeling, effort, and thought went into this album. Every song is special and personal to me," explains Mouzon. Leaning more toward New Age Jazz than traditional jazz, *Early Spring* features Mouzon's original acoustic piano as well as a tight, polished ensemble sound. **New Age Jazz**

Mu-Psych Music Records

Floating Deeper
   Sampler Mu-Psych
Good Feelings Sampler Mu-Psych

Floating Deeper is a compilation of soothing, relaxing, meditation-enhancing, and mind-quieting performances by the Ghostwriters, Fred Wackenhut, Zavijava Orchestra, Rocco Notte, and Richard Bush. The music was specifically created to induce positive emotional responses and balanced energy states in listeners, elevating them above stress. The same artists are featured on *Good Feelings,* a sampler of uplifting, and tension-reducing performances. The music is buoyant and scintillating, predominantly featuring synthesizers and other electronic equipment but also offering guitar, piano, and other organic instrument accents. **New Age Sound Health**

Music for Progressive Relaxation

Earthbeat Yvonne
Gentle Harmony Yvonne
Innerlight Yvonne

Rudy Helm and David Kessner create highly effective, relaxing, and therapeutic New Age music designed to increase "sound health." Combining guitar, synthesizer, and piano with the sounds of nature on *Innerlight* and *Earthbeat,* they create ambient rather than intrusive music that soothes frayed nerves like a hot bath or a warm glass of milk. **New Age Sound Health**

Music West Records

Anthology Music West

Embracing New Age Jazz, Pop, and World music influences, *Anthology* is an eclectic overview of the styles of Music West's artists. Pop-space master Ray Lynch, jazz fusion duo Susan Mazer and Dallas Smith, plus Jim Chappell, Kenneth Nash, and Teja Bell are featured. Each track is a unique, self-contained gem, basically upbeat and cheery in tone. *Anthology* serves as a good introduction to the works of some of the most popular New Age musicians today. **New Age Jazz, New Age Traditional**

Robert Aeolus Myers
(See Aeolus)

N

David Naegele

Dawning of the New Age Valley
  of the Sun
Dreamscapes Valley of the Sun
Dreams of Atlantis Valley
  of the Sun
Journeys out of Body Valley
  of the Sun
Temple in the Forest Valley
  of the Sun

Naegele is a multi-instrumentalist who draws inspiration from his own personal out-of-body experiences to create New Age Traditional music. Using synthesizers, he develops ethereal, abstract, and contemplative motifs with bell-like tones that induce expanded states of consciousness. On *Journeys out of Body*, Naegele encourages the listener to experience the peace and timelessness of imaginary places through electronic resonance and almost-infinitely-sustained notes. *Dreamscapes* creates a warm, nurturing ambience utilizing synthesizer and natural effects. Naegele says, "[I will] hopefully bring the listener into closer communion with their inner selves and that deep nostalgia for Oneness and inner peace." **New Age Traditional**

R. Carlos Nakai

Changes Canyon
Cycles Canyon
Earth Spirit Canyon
Jackalope Canyon
Journeys Canyon
Native American Flute
  Music Canyon
Sundance Season Celestial
  Harmonies
Weavings Canyon

The leader in Native American flute recordings and performances, Navajo-Ute Indian Nakai creates music that powerfully evokes the expansiveness and color of the American Southwest. *Changes* offers tender, gentle, and emotional solo flute originals. *Cycles* combines flute and synthesizer to evoke the more spiritual realms of the region. *Jackalope* is a bit of a departure, an innovative blend of Native American music with New Age Jazz. High spirited and energetic, the music vibrates with intensity. *Sundance Season* focuses on the sun dance ritual that honors man's relationship with Mother Earth. "Tribal dancers in the ritual are encouraged," he explains, "to concentrate on their reasons for dancing and the orderliness of life." Nakai's original melodies on this release blend his inspired flute playing with vocal chanting, drumming, and the lonely sound of the eagle bone whistle. **New Age Native American**

Neil Nappe

July Audion

Guitarist/synthesist Nappe was given his first electric guitar at age six and reportedly "immediately began trying to make it sound like something else." At first he created his own complex electronic gadgetry, then embraced the commercially available guitar-synthesizers in his search for a personal sound. This spirit of innovation and dedication is expressed on *July*. Like the month, this album ranges from blissfully calm to sizzling hot, and his basic six-string sounds like anything else but. Experimental without being overly electronic or cold, Nappe's densely textural compositions evoke the best of space music and warm up potentially sterile techno-pop. This is intelligent music. **New Age Space**

Narada Records

Narada Collection Narada
Sampler 1 Narada

Sampler 2 Narada
Sampler 3 Narada

Narada Collection marks the first time that a major New Age music label has offered three primary styles of New Age music on one record, with New Age acoustic, New Age Jazz fusion, and New Age Electronic artists providing insight into their respective areas. Narada Lotus's acoustic artists include Spencer Brewer, John Doan, Michael Jones, and Tingstad/Rumbel/Lanz. Narada Equinox's jazz fusion artists include David Lanz, Paul Speer, and Friedemann. Electronic artists on Narada Mystique include David Arkenstone, Peter Buffet, and Bruce Mitchell. **New Age Electronic, New Age Jazz, New Age Traditional**

Kenneth Nash

Mister Ears Music West
Music from a Far Away Place Music West

Nash creates lyrical, superbly syncopated sounds that fuse jazz, pop, and Afro-Caribbean elements. A respected pioneer in the use of percussion instruments, Nash has contributed to more than two hundred forty albums in the last twenty years. Of *Music from a Far Away Place,* he says, "[This record] is the culmination of a lot of work and desire—kind of a dream into reality on wax. What I'm doing is taking my musical influences: classical, Cuban, African, jazz, pop, and funk, and expressing them within the melodic language I've developed." The music moves, flows, and bends gracefully, an aural illustration of his belief that "music is born in the movement of dancers." New Age Jazz

Native American Church of North America

Bright Morning Star Songs Canyon
Chants Vol. 1 Canyon
Chants Vol. 2 Canyon
Chants Vol. 3 Canyon
Kiowa Peyote Songs Canyon
Peyote Canyon
Peyote Chants Canyon
Peyote Healing Chants Canyon

Peyote is a collection of peyote rite chants from the Kiowa, Cheyenne, Cherokee, Bannock, Paiute, and Omaha tribal regions. The album features fast-paced, powerful chanting accompanied by rattles and drums as appropriate to the sacred peyote ceremonies. Not recommended for casual listening, Peyote does convey the spirit of the rituals through original native language renditions of each song. This is serious vision-inducing vocal music. New Age Native American

Native American Music (various)

The Song of the Indian Canyon

The Song of the Indian is a well rounded compilation of various tribal chants and songs featuring performers such as Ed Lee Natay, the Oglala Sioux Singers, and Fred Romero with the Taos Singers. The music encompasses Navajo, Apache, Zuni, Sioux, Taos, Hopi, and Chey-

enne traditional vocal selections, most of which are of a medium to medium-fast tempo and delivered in the native tribal language. This album is a good introduction to the variety of subjects and styles of Native American music. New Age Native American

Natopus

Transition Valley of the Sun

In Latin, nato means "birth" or "to create" while opus means "song" or "melody." Originally created to be used in a Lamaze birthing environment, the mellow, extremely soothing New Age music of Natopus is one of the best anti-stress forces around. New Age Sound Health

Nature Recordings

Dawn and Dusk in the Ventana
  Wilderness Tape Masters
Mountain Stream Tape Masters
The Sea Tape Masters
Thunderstorm in Big Sur Tape
  Masters

These offerings are strictly ambient sounds of birds, waves, streams, crickets, and so forth, unaccompanied by instruments. Although not exactly music, these "nature sound tracks" are growing increasingly popular as de-intensifiers, stress fighters, and background for meditation. Dawn and Dusk in the Ventana Wilderness features bird song in the mountains on side one, with crickets, cicadas, and frogs by a mountain pond on side two. New Age Environmental

John Kaizan Neptune

Dance for the One in Six Fortuna
West of Somewhere Milestone

Shakuhachi flute master and New Age Jazz composer Neptune combines the textures and colors of world music in the vivid fusion release *Dance for the One in Six.* Combining Indian raga, American jazz, and Japanese traditional music into a flowing, cohesive whole, Neptune's innovative compositions still leave each instrument room to breathe. His sensuous and haunting flute tones move smoothly and gracefully among the sounds of tamboura, piano, guitar, tabla, sitar, and bass in a seamless merging of East Meets West. *Dance for the One in Six* is upbeat, dynamic, and exotic. Neptune says, "Music is like a tree: traditional music forms the roots, and we've got to protect and feed them, but if there are no leaves, then the tree isn't alive. I guess you could say I'm the green stuff." New Age East/West, New Age Jazz

Antonio Newton

Novaphonia Novaphonic
Novastreams Novaphonic

Newton's *Novaphonia* features instrumental compositions using computer-assisted synthesizer and other electronic gear in combination with the "Novaphonic Sound of Quintal/Quartal Harmony" system based on Newton's discovery of more than twelve hundred new chords. Newton's powerful music crosses the boundary between electronic and space music; the compositions are by turns majestic, spacious, cinematic, and galactic. As he says, "New Age music contains a level of artistry and communication that causes one's mind to explore greater inner potential freely. A level of enlightenment that carries [from the composer] to the listener is also present, as it is projected from the internal attunement of the artist on higher levels of awareness, which are universal and harmonious to the universe at large." New Age Space

James Newton

African Flower MBN
Axum ECM
Echo Canyon Kuckuck
In Venice Kuckuck
I've Known Rivers Gramavision
James Newton Gramavision

On *Echo Canyon,* New Age Jazz flutist Newton has created an improvisational soundscape inspired by red and orange hills baking under the hot New Mexico sun. He combines the elemental forces of wind, rain, sun, and gravity with the recording process; as co-producer Stephen Hill writes, "At seven-thousand-feet elevation, sound travels one foot in a thousandth of a second. If you clap your hands, you will hear two distinct echoes from the left and right about a quarter-second and half-second after the original sound, followed by an enormous cloud of reverberation as the impulse diffuses to the farthest reaches of the canyon. It is an intoxicating, amazingly beautiful sound environment." Recorded under a full moon, Newton's plaintive and inspired solo flute melodies combine with the sound of crickets, native birds, and little rock slides for a perfect blending of spirit and nature. **New Age Jazz, New Age Solo**

Eduardo Niebla and Antonio Forcione

Celebration Venture/Virgin

Celebration intermingles the two acoustic guitars of Niebla and Forcione, mixing Spanish and Italian influences to expand the horizons of New Age Jazz. A yin/yanglike tension keeps the seven duets superbly balanced. This is melodic, accessible New Age Jazz for those who have previously avoided the intellectual and dissonant styles of mainstream jazz artists. **New Age Jazz**

Night Ark

Moments Novus/RCA
Picture Novus/RCA

While many New Age fusion groups struggle to reconcile disparate musical styles, Night Ark revels in them. Their work is a celebration rather than a clash of styles, meshing Middle Eastern, classical, jazz, and pop into a resonant whole. Group founder Ara Dinkjian performs on many exotic instruments including the oud (lute), cumbus (resembles a fretless banjo), canoon (seventy-eight-string zither), saz (six-string long-necked lute), and Portuguese mandolin, adding color and texture to the ensemble's more traditional instrumentation. *Moments* features

one outstandingly emotional and poignant song, "Offering," which Dinkjian wrote for a dying friend. Based on a timeless Middle Eastern melody, it is especially life-affirming. **New Age Jazz, New Age World**

Nightengale Records

Celebration Sampler III Nightengale
Meditation Sampler II Nightengale
Sampler I Nightengale

Nightengale Records' artists combine for two totally different but satisfying listening experiences. *Meditation Sampler II* features quiet, peace-inducing music, while *Celebration Sampler III* is upbeat, playful dance music performed with a light and delicate touch. The original Nightengale *Sampler I* features some of the best pieces from artists Karunesh, Kamal, Luna, Anugama, Prabohi, and Chandresh. **New Age Meditation, New Age Pop**

John Nilsen

Blue Pacific Magic Wing
October in September Eagle
Sea of Inspiration Eagle
Transparencies Eagle

Nilsen's solo piano outings are effortlessly fluid, colorful, and vibrant sounds that promote relaxation, health, and a sense of peace. While similar to George Winston's acoustic piano pieces, Nilsen says his music "breaks too many rules to be classical and is more melodic than jazz. My music is like water the way it flows along." **New Age Solo**

NEW AGE SPACE MUSIC

by Anna Turner*

For thirteen years Turner co-produced America's first weekly New Age radio program, "Music from the Hearts of Space," heard on 225 stations.

New Age Space music carries visions in its notes; it is transcendent inner and outer space music that opens, allows, and creates space. Though born of electronics, it is harmonic, beautiful, and emotionally compelling. Almost all of its composers use synthesizers, sometimes exclusively, which can sustain notes timelessly or produce wholly new sounds. Space music moves; the balance between the rhythm track and melody line determines a great deal of the imagery, altitude, and impact of a particular piece. Works often feature stately galactic processions and high-powered space drives, or float into realms of subtle, chimed voices and languidly dissolving chords. At its best and most essential, this music speaks to our present moment, to the great allegory of moving out beyond our boundaries into space, and reflexively, to the unprecedented adventures of the psyche that await within.

WILLIAM BENT	CELESTIAL ODYSSEYS
AMIN BHATIA	CRYSTAL
KEVIN BRAHENY	MYCHAEL DANNA AND TIM
THOM BRENNAN	CLEMENT
RICHARD BURMER	PETER DAVISON
BUTTIGIEG	CONSTANCE DEMBY

*Artist listing compiled by Patti Jean Birosik.

Neil Norman

Music from the 21st Century GNP
   Crescendo
Not of This Earth
   GNP Crescendo

Guitarist/synthesist Norman is both a composer/performer and the mastermind behind the compilation and release of several progressive space and New Age electronic albums. *Music from the 21st Century* features music by Steve Roach, Alex Cima, Tangerine Dream, and others—a great introduction to otherworldly soundscapes. Norman's own original album, *Not of This Earth,*

DOUBLE FANTASY

BRIAN ENO

FRANCO FALSINI

MORTON FELDMAN

FRANCISCO

EDGAR FROESE

MICHEL GENEST

MIQUETTE GIRAUDY AND
   STEVE HILLAGE

PATRICK GLEESON

MANUEL GOTTSCHING

MICHAEL HARNER

HEARTS OF SPACE RECORDS

STEVE HILLAGE

MIC HOLWIN

IASOS

MARK ISHAM

JADE WARRIOR

KITARO

JOHN ROBERT KRAUSE

VAN KRUEGER

DAVID LANGE

RAY LYNCH

CLARA MONDSHINE

NEIL NAPPE

ANTONIO NEWTON

NEIL NORMAN

DAVID PARSONS

P'COCK

ANTHONY PHILLIPS

STEVE ROACH

MASAHIDE SAKUMA

KLAUS SCHULZE

ANDY SHAPIRO

LARRY SNYDER AND DENNIS
   MCCORKLE

MICHAEL STEARNS

GREG STEWART

IAN TESCEE

VANGELIS

STOMU YAMASHTA

uses many types of effects-treated guitars to create intense sonic expressions. As he puts it, *"Guitar Player* magazine noted the absence of any normal-sounding guitars."* Norman's creations range from pure fun to serious astral-journey music. **New Age Space**

No Strings Attached

Dulcimer Dimensions Turquoise
Isles of Langerhans Turquoise
Just Another Hammer Dulcimer Band Enessay
Take 5 Turquoise
Traditional Music of the Future Turquoise

No Strings Attached is a versatile four-piece string band whose instruments include two hammered dulcimers, mandolin, guitar, bass, harmonica, bouzouki, pennywhistle, flute, bowed psaltery, kalimba, and synthesizer. The group is one of the pioneers in the world of New Age music, expanding the concept of folk and traditional music with their innovative original compositions and unique arrangements of the Irish ballads called planxties, acoustic jazz, old-time fiddle tunes, and southern Appalachian dance tunes. *Traditional Music of the Future* is an evenly textured yet ear-catching all-instrumental release that shimmers, bounces, and shines. Hammered dulcimer fans as well as devotees of contemporary swing or traditional folk will like No Strings Attached. **New Age Folk**

Rocco Notte and Richard Bush

Elysian Fields
Mu-Psych

Notte and Bush create traditional New Age music that relaxes, centers, and uplifts, the perfect accompaniment to meditation or quiet contemplation. *Elysian Fields* is gently invigorating and subtly melodic, its music rising on soft rhythmic currents. Pianist Notte is schooled in both classical and jazz traditions but ultimately transcends both, while Bush commands a complicated array of electronic sound processing equipment that creates broad swashes of audio color. Bush also contributes some ethereal vocals to *Elysian Fields*. **New Age Traditional**

Gerald O'Brien
(See Exchange)

Mark O'Connor

False Dawn Rounder
Mark O'Connor Rounder
Markology Rounder
Meaning Of Warner Bros.
On the Rampage Rounder
Picking in the Wind Rounder
Stay Tuned Columbia
*Stone from Which the Arch Was
   Made* Warner Bros.

Meaning Of is an eclectic, all-instrumental effort that crosses all musical boundaries while fitting firmly into the New Age Folk subgenre. A true wizard of strings, O'Connor plays the guitar, the mandolin, and the dobro, but the fiddle is his forte. "Basically my approach is to not make the acoustic instruments sound wimpy next to the huge sound of the electronic things. I try to fuse them together in a format that's basically a pop rhythmic base while borrowing elements of classical, jazz, country, folk, and various ethnic influences," he explains. The album is upbeat, uncomplicated, and enjoyable. New Age Folk

Michael O'Domhnaill
(See Billy Oskay)

Patrick O'Hearn

Ancient Dreams Private Music
Between Two Worlds Private
   Music
*World of Private Music
   Sampler* Private Music
*World of Private Music Sampler
   II* Private Music

Known to rock fans for bass and synthesizer performances with his former group Missing Persons, O'Hearn is also one of the premier New Age Progressive composers. His impressionistic music ranges from undulating oceanic rhythms to pointedly multiethnic-influenced melodies to colorful vast washes of synthesizer experiments. Mysterious, lush, and rhythmic, *Between Two Worlds* extends the sonic borders delineated by the multi-instrumentalist's *Ancient Dreams* album. "[It's] a more melodic album than *Ancient Dreams . . .* a little more organic. *Ancient Dreams* has a spacious sound while *Between Two Worlds* places greater emphasis on compositions." One of the reasons for the organic feel of *Between Two Worlds* is ceramic percussionist Brian Ransom. Marrying ceramics with drum skins and strings, Ransom adds fascinating rhythmic patterns and percussive textures. O'Hearn fuses the diverse dialectics of pop, jazz, classical, and world music into an intensely personal language. **New Age Progressive**

Michael Oldfield

Boxed Virgin
Crises Virgin
Discovery Virgin
Exposed Virgin
Five Miles Out Virgin
Hergest Ridge Virgin
Incantations Virgin
Islands Virgin
Ommadawn Virgin
Orchestral Tubular Bells Virgin
Platinum Virgin
QE2 Virgin
Tubular Bells Virgin

From his auspicious debut, *Tubular Bells* (also known as the theme for the film *The Exorcist*), to his latest release, *Islands,* Oldfield has continued to explore the question of personal transition. *Tubular Bells* is an instrumental record that weaves hypnotic tone poems with vocal effects, orchestral arrangements, and of course, those incredible tubular bells. Oldfield's fifty-minute composition floats and dips and bobs and rises to a transcendent crescendo, leaving the listener breathless and blissed. *Islands* is unusual in that side one features Oldfield's instrumentals while side two showcases six rock/pop compositions with vocals by Bonnie Tyler and Max Bacon, among others. **New Age Progressive**

Om

The Eternal Om Valley of the Sun

Using the latest in electronic technology, *The Eternal Om* offers synthesized pitches from human voices all intoning the word *Om* together at the prescribed vibrations, backed by an almost subliminal choir. Soothing, uplifting, and spiritually inspiring, this record is ideal for meditation, concentration, or chanting. **New Age Meditation**

Oman and Shanti

Holy Messengers Songs for a Small Planet
Inner Love Songs for a Small Planet
Let Me Remember Songs for a Small Planet
Touch the Rainbow Songs for a Small Planet
We Are Home Songs for a Small Planet
You Are Light Songs for a Small Planet

In 1975 Oman and Shanti made a conscious decision to sing only songs that would celebrate life. *Let Me Remember* and *Holy Messengers* feature inspiring and prayerful songs using principles and quoted text from *A Course in Miracles* (Tiburon, Calif.: Foundation for Inner Peace, 1975), one of the most popular New Age books. Their vocal magic dances through the music with simplicity and grace. *You Are Light* is an uplifting and pleasurable blend of the voices of Oman, Shanti, and guest vocalist Charley Thweatt. Music on the releases features synthesizers, cello, violin, flutes, piano, and harp. **New Age Vocal**

Seigen Ono
(See Seigen)

On Wings of Sound
(See Dr. Robert Gass)

Rudiger Oppermann
Journey to Harpistan Fortuna

An exotic original, German harpist Oppermann combines Celtic traditional sounds with the music of non-Western cultures, including those of China, Zimbabwe, Mozambique, Turkey, and Indonesia. This is spirited and bright music for those who love rich, resonant strings. **New Age World**

Oregon
Crossing ECM
Distant Hills Polydor
Ecotopia ECM
Friends Vanguard
In Concert Vanguard
In Performance Elektra
Music of Another Present Era Vanguard
Oregon ECM
Our First Record Vanguard
Out of the Woods Elektra
Roots in the Sky Elektra
Violin Vanguard
Winter Light Vanguard

Oregon has long been considered a seminal New Age Jazz fusion band and currently consists of Ralph Towner, Paul McCandless, Glen Moore, and Trilock Gurtu; founding member and brilliant percussionist Collin Walcott died in an unfortunate accident in 1984 after a lengthy and successful recording career. Oregon is an improvisational band that draws on jazz, classical, Indian, and African influences, blending them into a nonfrenetic, melodic style as best demonstrated on their live album, *In Performance.* The four members play more than fifty different instruments and create an infinite range of sonic colors, amply demonstrated on *Oregon;* stimulating without becoming overbearing, the music lifts the soul and moves the feet. In 1969 Moore, Towner, and Walcott were hired as members of the Paul Winter Consort, where they met McCandless. The inspired chemistry worked and they decided to form Oregon. The resulting vinyl magic has been pleasuring listeners for years with no signs of slowing down or becoming repetitive. **New Age Jazz**

A. Paul Ortega

The Blessing Ways Canyon
Three Worlds Canyon
Two Worlds Canyon

The Blessing Ways is a contemporary expression of the Native American tradition, with guitar and flute as featured instruments. Burch composed the songs in her native language (Navajo) and sings of her people, of Mother Earth, and "Grandmother Ways." Ortega composed additional songs in English as well as in Navajo, singing the prayers of the Indian world as well as discussing the importance of the flute and "Grandfather." This is an unusual and satisfying album. **New Age Native American**

Susan Osborn

Susan Living Music

Osborn is a talented vocalist and frequent guest performer with the Paul Winter Consort. Her solo debut *Susan* contains nine pop-ballad–based original compositions combining warm tones, eloquent phrasing, and intimate songwriting skills—plus a surprising cover of Al Jolson's classic "Sonny Boy." With her husband, David Densmore, Osborn created and presents the Seeds of Singing workshops held across the United States. **New Age Vocal**

Billy Oskay and Michael O'Domhnaill

Nightnoise Windham Hill

Acoustic multi-instrumentalists Oskay and O'Domhnaill are renowned for their renditions of traditional Celtic music. *Nightnoise* is an album of their original pieces performed on violin, violas, guitars, pennywhistles, pianos, and harmoniums. *Nightnoise* acknowledges their traditional roots but moves beyond the Celtic music genre. This is heart music with imagination and soul. **New Age World**

P

Vangelis Parathanassiou

(See Vangelis)

David Parsons

Sounds of the Mothership
  Fortuna
Tibetan Plateau Fortuna

Parson's music is like a message from another galaxy. On *Sounds of the Mothership* he mixes birdcalls, waterfalls, synthesizers, and classical Indian instruments to create a naturally meditative sound experience. On *Tibetan Plateau* the listener is set upon a journey through plateaus both earthy and celestial, evoking deep feelings of mystery and awe. This is delicate electronic music, enhanced with traditional Indian instrumentation of sitar and tabla. **New Age Space**

Maggi Payne

Crystal Lovely Music

Flutist Payne uses synthesizers, digital delays, and other electronic gear to experiment with sound and create accessible, colorful, and oftentimes emotional music. Her compositions on *Crystal* are clear and vibrant, bordering on space music yet sweetly melodic and easy on the ears. **New Age Electronic**

P'Cock

In'Cognito Innovative
  Communications
The Prophet Innovative
  Communications

If you like early Genesis or Pink Floyd, P'Cock is a group for you. Mixing the delicate tonalities of New Age Space music with symphonic rock elements, P'Cock travels beyond progressive into a new galactic dimension of sound. Creating phantasmal images through computer-controlled synthesizers and other high-end electronic gear, *In'Cognito* is perfect for armchair space travelers. **New Age Space**

Peak

Ebondazzar Innovative
  Communications

Australia is home not only to some great contemporary rock bands but also to the fine electronic synthesizer duo, Peak. *Ebondazzar* features very emotional, warm, innovative music influenced by Tangerine Dream, King Crimson, and Michael Oldfield. Fusing Australian rhythmic directness with sophisticated European arrangements, Peak has created an album full of dynamic high-tech instrumentals. This is accessible electronic music that can easily convince the most traditional listener that electronic space music is not created by soulless machines. **New Age Electronic**

Penguin Cafe Orchestra

Broadcasting from Home
  Editions EG
*Music from the Penguin
  Cafe* Editions EG
Penguin Cafe Orchestra
  Editions EG
*Penguin Cafe Orchestra
  Mini-Album* Editions EG
Signs of Life Editions EG

On *Signs of Life,* Penguin Cafe Orchestra creates sweetly textured New Age sounds that are reminiscent of chamber music but with a totally contemporary feel. Combining cello, violin, viola, percussion, synthesizer, piano, ukelele, and a host of other instruments, the orchestra's compositions by multi-instrumentalist Simon Jeffes draw on equally eclectic classi-

cal, traditional, and folk influences. Some songs are meditative and calming in nature while others inspire the body to sway and feet to move to an uplifting, sunny rhythm. **New Age Traditional**

Frank Perry

Deep Peace Kuckuck
New Atlantis Kuckuck

New Atlantis was inspired by Sir Francis Bacon, a personal hero for multi-instrumentalist Perry. From the opening note—a single clear bell tone that resonates and decays to calm and focus the mind on the music—Perry creates a "ritual dance of light woven according to the One will" and dedicated to "beings of the abstract mystical sound." The repeated striking of richly resonant bells and chimes in a slow, deliberate pattern creates all sorts of interesting harmonics and overtones that are useful for meditation. **New Age Traditional**

Robin Petrie
(See Danny Carnahan)

Cornel Pewewardy

Flute and Prayer Songs Canyon

Comanche/Kiowa songs from Oklahoma are featured on Pewewardy's flute release. The tone is overwhelmingly spiritual, and Pewewardy's performance is appropriately soulful, inspiring, and uplifting. *Flute and Prayer Songs* also offers three Kiowa church hymns with voice only (a capella, with no musical instruments) that are incredibly moving. Native American flute has long been regarded as an instrument of exceptional purity and emotion. As performed here, its power to raise consciousness is amply demonstrated. **New Age Native American**

Craig Peyton
(See Latitude)

Anthony Phillips

Antiques PVC
Back to the Pavillion PVC
A Catch at the Tables PVC
The Geese and the Ghost PVC
Ivory Moon PVC
1984 Passport
Private Parts and Pieces PVC
Slow Waves, Soft Stars Audion
Twelve PVC
Wise After the Event Audion

A founding member of Genesis, synthesist Phillips has recorded a series of very personal, atmospheric records since leaving the group in 1970, including *The Geese and the Ghost,* which features guest performers Phil Collins and Mike Rutherford. In a New Age vein, *Ivory Moon* is an emotional collection of solo piano pieces, while *Slow Waves, Soft Stars* is a lush space music release perfectly suited for mental voyaging. Utilizing various synthesizers, guitars, and percussion, the latter record combines both compositions and improvisations with a respect for dynamic, spacious arrangements that give equal weight to sound and silence. **New Age Space**

Shawn Phillips

Faces A&M
Transcendence RCA

Since the seventies Phillips has been making what is now termed New Age Vocal music. His expressive lyrical voice is the perfect vehicle for pop-based tunes that address spirituality in a gentle, indirect fashion while maintaining an upbeat, melodic feel. **New Age Vocal**

Judith Pintar

Changes like the Moon Sona Gaia
Secrets from the Stone Sona Gaia

Pintar is a modern-day harpist and storyteller whose roots are in the myth and folklore of ancient cultures. Inspired by seventh-century bard Taliesen, Pintar undertook a quest to Scotland and Wales to discover the craftsman who made her first harp. She says, "The harp appealed to me romantically because of its traditional link with the spoken word. To this end I compose music that is visual and emotional, music that tells stories as well as accompanies stories." *Secrets from the Stone* combines lap, Welsh, Tara, and Gothic harps with voice, telling stories that are partly traditional and partly Pintar's own creation. The music is poignant, ethereal, and achingly beautiful in spots. Pintar brings an ancient oral tradition to the New Age. **New Age Folk**

143

Plant Music

The Secret Music of Plants
New World

The Secret Music of Plants guarantees you will never look at a plant the same way again. This is not music to be played for plants but rather an amazing recording produced entirely *of* plants. The selected plants emit incredible tones and pure musical notes that are in perfect harmony, whether as a solo by a philodendron or as a lush, vibrant tapestry produced of a variety of flora. Recorded using a complex variety of microphones and electronic gear, these mysterious and beautiful sounds are somewhat reminiscent of the whale songs. How wonderful to contemplate that plants also have a capacity for vocalizing joy. **New Age Progressive**

Ray Platt

Dancical Magical Land Paradise Boutique
D. M. Z. Paradise Boutique
Fields of View Paradise Boutique
Sculpture Splash Paradise Boutique

Multi-instrumentalist Platt explains his music: "The intent of my explorations with sound is to create movement; to take listeners to the edge, to arouse those parts of them that may still be sleeping. [My music] allows for an exploration through image, feeling, and subtle yet active contemplation. I have evoked a palette of moods that are both relaxing and challenging, yet not confrontational or difficult for the ears." On the New Age Pop release *Fields of View,* Platt performs all instruments and shares his affinity for Native American-like chanting, African rhythms, and South American flute and percussion sounds. The overall effect is calming but stimulating to the imagination. **New Age Pop**

David Pomerantz

It's in Every One of Us Arista

Singer/songwriter Pomerantz has created what is probably the best-known and loved New Age Vocal song to date, "It's in Every One of Us," the title track on his positive-consciousness album. His gentle ballads and uplifting pop-based melodies speak of love, peace, spirituality, earth connectedness, and human potential without sounding preachy or heavy-handed. **New Age Vocal**

Sanford Ponder

Etosha Private Music
Tigers Are Brave Private Music
World of Private Music
    Sampler Private Music

Tigers Are Brave combines synthesized and natural sounds for a light and dreamy feel, enhanced by guest Jerry Goodman's majestic violin. The title track opens with a shimmering, lush Asian mood, slowly builds with the introduction of percussion and piano, and peaks with the inspired interplay between Ponder's keyboards and Goodman's violin. Ponder is a whiz at creating rich, sophisticated textures that evoke a sense of peace. As he says, "All my life I have been searching for a larger or better, more complete experience of existence. My music is a reflection of and a crystallization into tangible form the working out of my journey." New Age Traditional

Jean-Luc Ponty

Aurora Atlantic
Civilized Evil Atlantic
Cosmic Messenger Atlantic
Enigmatic Oceans Atlantic
Fables Atlantic
The Gift of Time Columbia
Imaginary Voyage Atlantic
Individual Choice Atlantic
Jean-Luc Experience Pausa
Live Atlantic
Mystical Adventures Atlantic
Open Mind Atlantic
Sonata Erotica ICT
Taste of Passion Atlantic
Upon the Wings of Music Atlantic

For more than fifteen years virtuoso electric violinist Ponty, formerly a member of John McLaughlin's Mahavishnu Orchestra, has created beautiful New Age music that alternates between symphonic pop and space-jazz instrumentals. *Imaginary Voyage* is an excellent example of how Ponty develops an aural theme; the music is visionary, developed through a tight ensemble sound featuring synthesizer, percussion, and bass. Ponty's violin sweeps and soars, guiding the listener on an inward pilgrimage of self-discovery; the range of tones he achieves is impressive. On *The Gift of Time* Ponty plays the Zeta electric violin with a Synclavier synthesizer as well as a variety of keyboard instruments. The music ranges from the quietly atmospheric to jubilant. New Age Jazz, New Age Pop

Popul Vuh

Affenstunde Innovative Communications
Hosanna Mantra Celestial Harmonies
In the Gardens of Pharaoh/Aguirre Celestial Harmonies
Sacred Songs of Solomon United Artists
Sohne des Lichts (compilation) Celestial Harmonies

The group Popul Vuh mixes ancient and contemporary instruments and sounds. In *Hosanna Mantra* piano, guitar, violin, tamboura, and synthesizer join other acoustic and electronic instruments and an ethereal female vocal track to yield hypnotic, cyclical selections. *Sohne des Lichts* is a rather introverted selection of songs that are atmospheric and spacious, featuring piano, guitar, and percussion. Earlier work by the group is more in the New Age Electronic and Space music subgenres, like *Affenstunde* which is an extended altered-state vehicle performed on synthesizer, guitar, and percussion. New Age World

Private Music Records

Piano One Sampler Private Music
Piano Two Sampler Private Music
World of Private Music Sampler Private Music
World of Private Music Sampler II Private Music

Piano One features four acclaimed musicians interpreting their individual poetry on this familiar and beloved instrument. Ryuichi Sakamoto, Eddie Jobson, Joachim Kuhn, and Eric Watson demonstrate different influences and stylistic tendencies, from classical to rock, jazz to progressive. *Piano Two* is equally successful, featuring Yanni, Suzanne Ciani, Michael Riesman, and Joachim Kuhn performing expressive, elegant, and inspiring acoustic piano compositions. **New Age Solo**

Chris Proctor

Delicate Dance Flying Fish
Runoff Kicking Mule

New Age acoustic music connoisseurs have already discovered Proctor, but for novice fans who are only just venturing beyond synthesizers, his six- and twelve-string acoustic guitars should be a real eye opener. Proctor's style ranges from dreamy melodic ballads to up-tempo jams that have his fingers racing across the fretboard. Combining traditional American folk with Irish and classical influences, his original compositions are fluid, richly textured, and very easy to enjoy. **New Age Folk**

Pushkar

Ding Fonix
Inner Harvest Chidvilas

Pushkar's albums are gently caressing, sweetly melodic, and artfully arranged. They mix dancing guitar, tinkling wind chimes, bamboo flutes, pennywhistles, bouzouki, synthesizer, and other instruments, all played by Pushkar himself. *Inner Harvest* is wonderful for inward focusing, meditation, or other quiet activities. **New Age East/West**

R

Ali Jihad Racy

Ancient Egypt
Pathways

Inspired by the Tutankhamen exhibit as well as the Egyptian *Book of the Dead,* Racy's meditative music features such traditional Middle Eastern instruments as the nay, oud, and buzuq. Drones, strings, and pentatonic scales create an exotic feel, evoking the time of the pharaohs. New Age World

Radha Krshna Temple

Radha Krshna Temple,
London Apple

Produced by George Harrison, the Radha Krshna Temple ensemble creates contemporary musical mantras that are based on traditional Indian cyclic chanting. The inspired blending of voices resonate through and open the chakras. New Age Meditation, New Age Vocal

Radiance

Inverness Invincible
Lake unto Clouds Invincible
A Song for the Earth
Invincible

The members of Radiance (Jim Scott, David Darling, Nancy Rumbel, and Jim Saporito) traverse a range of sounds from orchestral to jazz to folk. Radiance's compositions have words, some tell stories without words. On the compelling album *A Song for the Earth,* the group incorporates the vibrant rhythms of Africa, Brazil, the Caribbean, and Asia into a series of hymns for the earth, expressing mankind's role in the great design. New Age World

Elaine Radigue

Jetsun Mila Lovely Music
Mila's Journey Inspired by a Dream Lovely Music
Songs of Milarepa
Lovely Music

Jetsun Mila is inspired by the life of Milarepa, a great yogi and poet of Tibet who lived in the eleventh century. Through her music, Radigue illustrates how in one lifetime amazing deeds can be accomplished through ascetic practices and spiritual endeavors. Radigue's inspired electronic compositions are reminiscent in tone of the works of Morton Subotnick, Rhys Chatham, and others; the scope of this project—the evocation of the one hundred thousand songs of the Tibetan master Milarepa—is vast. The music itself is minimalistic; it almost forces the listener to slow down, to be patient, and to observe subtle changes. Sometimes so soft as to be imagined rather than heard, the notes begin to rise, coalesce, and form new musical identities that cycle through repetitive drones, hypnotizing rhythms, and unusual textures. **New Age Electronic**

John Rainer, Jr.

Songs of the Indian Flute Seven Arrows Music

Rainer is from Taos Pueblo, New Mexico, and the collection of traditional Indian songs and original compositions on his *Songs of the Indian Flute* is an absolute must for anyone who has fallen under the spell of this magical and hypnotic instrument. Some selections on the album are solo flute compositions, while others have drum, voice, or guitar accompaniment. The very smooth, mellow sound of Rainer's instrument lulls the listener into a receptive spiritual state. **New Age Native American**

Swami Kriya Ramananda

Hymn to a New Age Satsaya
In the Garden Satsaya
Song of the Golden Lotus Satsaya

On *Song of the Golden Lotus* Ramananda blends synthesizer, flute, and cello into an inspired mystical atmosphere, ideal for deep meditation or trance work. A monk of the Self Realization Fellowship, Ramananda is well acquainted with the beneficial effects of meditation and is able to guide the novice as well as experienced meditator into deeper, more blissful states. **New Age Meditation**

Ravi
(See Tsumi)

Giles Reaves

Wunjo MCA

Reaves's debut, *Wunjo,* is an eclectic mix, blending melodic New Age Pop music with more intense space music. Some of the tracks display a mythical Nordic influence as their titles suggest: "Odin (The Unknowable)" and the Viking rune called "Sowelu (Wholeness)." This is computer-based synthesizer music, but the effect is intimate and relaxing. **New Age Electronic**

Don Reeve

Nature's Way Soundings of the Planet

Multi-instrumentalist Reeve shines on guitar, mandolin, and flute while merging his interest in Indian music with a Western heritage. As he explains, "[I] am impressed by the perfect unity of melody and rhythm in Indian music," and the music he creates is a fusion of that subtle Eastern grace with the intensity of contemporary sound. **New Age East/West**

Vini Reilly
(See Durutti Column)

John Renbourn

The Black Balloon Kicking Mule
Live (w/Grossman) Shanachie
The Nine Maidens Flying Fish
*Stefan Grossman and John
  Renbourn* Kicking Mule
The Three Kingdoms Shanachie
Under the Volcano Kicking Mule

Switching between acoustic and electric guitars, Renbourn explores jazzy improvisations as well as traditional Irish dance tunes on *The Black Balloon*. This New Age fusion release also features flute and percussion, but it is Renbourn's special guitar style that weaves the distinctly diverse selections into a listenable whole. Recorded live in concert with guitarist Stefan Grossman, the album *Live* features delicate interplay and shining solos that reveal the nuance of each note played, along with some entertaining introductions and commentaries by the players themselves. **New Age Jazz**

Roger Reynolds

Distant Images Lovely Music
Voicespace Lovely Music

Each side of *Distant Images* features a single instrumental piece that provocatively hangs in the balance between acoustic and mechanistic, executed by guests, pianist Cecil Lytle and violinist Janos Negyesy. The sound is intellectually stimulating rather than heartwarming or nurturing; the piano and violin sound crisp and clear as they go through a musical progression described by composer Reynolds: "I selected four pairs of properties and arranged them sequentially: airy, tenuous, volatile, rigid, continuous, independent, elastic, and cooperative." **New Age Progressive**

The Tony Rice Unit

Backwaters Rounder

Supported ably by his talented backup ensemble, guitarist Rice combines his jazz roots with samba for a global fusion sound. Most of the instrumentals are richly textured, with Rice's guitar cheerfully bouncing over the danceable percussion rhythms. A few tracks are more subtle in tone and suitable for more inwardly directed pursuits. **New Age Jazz**

John Richardson

The Calling New World
Devotion New World
Spirit of the Redman New World

On *Devotion* Richardson pays homage to the indigenous peoples of America and creates chants to the Earth that evolve slowly into simple vocal harmonic lines eulogizing each

NEW AGE TRADITIONAL MUSIC

by Suzanne Doucet*

Doucet is a recording artist, president of Beyond Records, and owner of the Holly-wood retail store Only New Age Music, as well as the founder at the International New Age Music Network and the International New Age Music Conference.

New Age Traditional music distinguishes itself not by style, performance, technique, or personality, but by its nature, which is contemplative rather than entertaining. Ideally it is instrumental and incorporates sacred, meditative, and healing properties. Its structure is based on ancient traditions such as Pythagorean harmonics, and its impact can be found in our society as well as on animals and even plants. Since it transforms the vibrational level of any environment into a relaxing, inspiring, and healing atmosphere, the entire planet has a growing demand for this music, which also evokes intuition, imagination, and altered states of consciousness.

AEOLUS

WILLIAM AURA

TOM BARABAS

ROBERT BEARNS AND RON
　DEXTER

ERIK BERGLUND

BEYOND RECORDS

CHRISTAAL

SUZANNE CIANI

CONSTANCE DEMBY

CHAITANYI HARI DEUTER

SUZANNE DOUCET

D'RACHAEL

DEAN AND DUDLEY EVENSON

EUGENE FRIESEN

KAY GARDNER

GLOBAL PACIFIC RECORDS

STEVE AND DAVID GORDON

PAUL HALLEY

STEVEN HALPERN

PAUL HORN

LES HURDLE AND THOR
　BALDURSSON

IASOS

INCARNATION

ALAP JETZER

MICHAEL JONES

MICHAEL JONES AND DAVID
　DARLING

GEORGIA KELLY

BOB KINDLER

STEVE KINDLER

KITARO

DANIEL KOBIALKA

JONATHAN KRAMER

DAVID LANZ

*Artist listing compiled by Patti Jean Biroski.

DAVID LARKIN

GABRIEL LEE

CHARLES LLOYD

ANNIE LOCKE

RAY LYNCH

REED MAIDENBERG

MANNHEIM STEAMROLLER

JAMES MCELROY

KIM MENZER

DAVID MICHAEL AND RANDY
MEAD

MUSIC WEST RECORDS

DAVID NAEGELE

NARADA RECORDS

ROCCO NOTTE AND RICHARD
BUSH

PENGUIN CAFE ORCHESTRA

FRANK PERRY

SANFORD PONDER

GABRIEL ROTH

JOHN ROTH

KEVIN ROTH

SCHAWKIE ROTH

MIKE ROWLAND

MICHEL RUBINI

NANCY RUMBEL

DAVID SATCHELL

SEARCH FOR SERENITY
RECORDS

JOHN SERGEANT

SHAYLA

AMY SHREVE

ROBERT SLAP

SOUNDINGS OF THE PLANET
RECORDS

PAUL SPEER

CHRIS SPHEERIS

STAIRWAY

IRA STEIN AND RUSSELL
WALDER

DAVID STORRS

TIM STORY

YOSHIO SUZUKI

JOHN MICHAEL TALBOT

MATTIAS THUROW

ERIC TINGSTAD

MICHAEL TREW

TSUMI

UPPER ASTRAL

VALLEY OF THE SUN
RECORDS

VANGELIS

CYRILLE VERDEAUX

ANDREAS VOLLENWEIDER

VOYAGER

TONY WELLS

TIM WHEATER

ANDREW WHITE

ROB WHITESIDES-WOO

ANNE WILLIAMS

WINDHAM HILL RECORDS

GEORGE WINSTON

PAUL WINTER

HENRY WOLFF AND NANCY
HENNINGS

ZAVIJAVA ORCHESTRA

tribe by name. The a capella singing underscored by tribal drum beats is mesmerizing and powerful, unmistakably modern and at the same time ageless. **New Age Vocal**

Kurt Riemann

Electronic Nightworks Innovative Communications

Riemann started experimenting with electronic music at age ten, developing his own instruments and new methods to generate unique and transcendent sounds. On *Electronic Nightworks* he offers warm, dynamic synthesizer music that takes you on a midnight run through the heart of a sleeping city. The majestic, lyrical sweep of synthesizers evokes dream visions and then deposits you gently back in your chair by the end of the record. **New Age Electronic**

Rising Sun Records

The Rising Sun Collection Rising Sun

Mainly focusing on New Age Jazz, *The Rising Sun Collection* is a great introduction to some of the top artists of this subgenre, including Teja Bell, Marcus Allen, Sky Canyon, Dallas Smith, and Bill Nowlin. The compositions are energetic without losing sensitivity or becoming frenetic. Smith's Lyricon wind synthesizer is particularly melodic, and his selections induce subtly rhythmic movement. **New Age Jazz**

Lee Ritenour

Banded Together Elektra
Best Of Epic
Captain Fingers Epic
The Captain's Journey Elektra
Earth Run GRP
Feel the Night Elektra
GRP Digital Sampler Vol. 2 GRP
Harlequin GRP
On the Line Elektra
Rio GRP

A pioneer of the New Age fusion movement and champion of the latest guitar technology, Ritenour creates records that are inspired, melodic, and jazzy. He released the album *Earth Run* in the International Year of Peace, during which he served as a spokesman for the international torch ceremony sponsored by the United Nations. The music ranges from fluid, melodic acoustic guitar compositions to sonic explorations using various guitar synthesizers. Sax sensation Ernie Watts adds to the magic. **New Age Jazz**

Steve Roach

Dreamtime Return Fortuna
Empetus Fortuna
The Leaving Time (w/Michael Schrieve) RCA
Now Fortuna
Quiet Music 1 Fortuna
Quiet Music 2 Fortuna
Quiet Music 3 Fortuna
Structures from Silence Fortuna
Traveller Fortuna
Western Spaces (w/Braheny and Burmer) Innovative Communications

Roach is one of the best visionary electronic composers recording today. His *Quiet Music* series was created to celebrate silence and is the ultimate for musically supported meditation. Each release from the series supports a different theme; for example, on *Quiet Music 1* Roach mixes gentle synthesized sounds with flute to express the riches of nature and the simple innocence of childhood. The more recent *Dreamtime Return* is the culmination of a dream for the artist. Roach explains: "This recording is a documentation of my dreamtime travels over the past three years beginning in Southern California and continuing to Northern Australia . . . with its endless plateaus, gorges, and sandstone escarpments which conceal the sacred and secular sites of times past. It is in this vast continent that the essence of dreamtime still remains and my return continues." Mixing synthesizer with native instruments, such as the didjeridoo (hollow tube drone), the music creates mental images of the majestic rock art galleries and conjures up the mystical spirituality of ancient inhabitants of the outback. The beauty and expansiveness of the American Southwest is celebrated on *Western Spaces,* a collaboration among synthesists Roach, Kevin Braheny, Richard Burmer, and Thom Brennan. With broad washes of sound and crisp electronic flourishes, the musicians encourage you to slip into reverie and feel the heat, see the shimmering mirages, and smell the oncoming thunder when the tape begins to roll. **New Age Electronic, New Age Space**

Sheila Roberts
(See Shayla)

Kim Robertson

Celtic Christmas Invincible
Crimson Vol. 1 Invincible
Crimson Vol. 2 Invincible
Crimson Vol. 3 Invincible
Crimson Vol. 4 Invincible
Crimson Vol. 5 Invincible
Crimson Vol. 6 Invincible
Moonrise Invincible
Water Spirit Invincible
Wind Shadows Invincible

Robertson captures the distinctive harp style of the Irish bards while her work on synthesizer adds depth of sound and feeling. In the *Crimson* series, ancient compositional styles from the East are combined with the latest technological innovations from the West. Guest artist Singh Kaur blends in the most beautiful of all instruments, the human voice. Each release from the *Crimson* series uses specific sound currents repeating over a thirty-one-minute-per-side cycle, which Robertson explains is the brain's cycle for integrating change. Repetition plays an important factor in this series, and Robertson suggests that to experience lasting subtle effects, the tapes should be listened to as background music while working, exercising, or meditating. *Vol. 1* is for inner guidance; the tempo is moderate and the music expansive so the overall sound relaxes and elevates. *Vol. 2* is slow and serene, a musical lullaby. *Vol. 3* features lively percussion, harmoniously balanced between the energetic and relaxed. *Vol. 4*'s strong, steady rhythm inspires the capacity to rise above the challenges of life. **New Age East/West, New Age Meditation, New Age Vocal**

Teed Rockwell
(See Geist)

Hans-Joachim Roedelius

Desert Sky
Gift of the Moment Editions EG
Momenti Felici Venture/Virgin

Roedelius was a founding member of the Zodiak Free Art Center in Berlin in 1968, the club that became the birthplace of some of the most important electronic music groups, including Tangerine Dream, Ashra Temple, and Roedelius's own Kluster. Originally a trio, Kluster was changed to Cluster in the seventies; and the duo of Roedelius and Dieter Moebius released a series of ambient-style electronic music that paved the way for today's New Age Space music. *Momenti Felici* is a stylistically eclectic collection of synthesizer-based music featuring phantasmal images, weirdly beautiful and colorful washes of electronically processed tones, and spectacular and varied special audio effects. If you're tempted to cross the border from New Age into classic electronic music, this is the album to try. (See also Cluster.) **New Age Electronic**

Rohani
(See Shardad)

154

Lewis Ross

A Collection of Favorite Christmas Carols Revere
Mood Soup Revere
Songs, Hymns and Carols Revere
Sounds Familiar Revere

Ross, well known from his work with the New American Guitar Ensemble, was trained as a classical pianist long before he ever touched fingers to strings. On *Mood Soup* he has created original instrumental selections that showcase his penchant for the ivories. The music is atmospheric, emotional, and delicate; Ross's performance style is warm, immediate, and sensitive. The result is a heady brew featuring ethereal ballads and upbeat ditties. **New Age Pop**

Gabriel Roth

Totem Moving Center

This music invokes the spirit of dance both to aid meditation and to fight stress. Roth and his group, the Mirrors, perform on a wide range of electronic and acoustic instruments, including drums, guitar, percussion, harmonica, bass, shakers, flutes, and congas. The music has a slightly Eastern influence and is almost ritualistic in its intensity, sweeping and gliding, passionate and earthy. **New Age Traditional**

John Roth

Seadream Rosewood

Roth's guitar playing on *Seadream* is versatile, sweet, and hot. His recorded performances are well developed with high-tech production touches that enhance but don't consume the pure vitality of his instrument. **New Age Traditional**

Kevin Roth

Voyages Flying Fish

Voyages is an instrumental dulcimer album filled with incredibly lovely melodies and brightly resonant sound. For those who love dulcimer music and those few New Age fans not yet aware of the emotional and spiritual qualities of that instrument, this record is an entirely satisfying introduction. **New Age Traditional**

Schawkie Roth

Fortune Center of Heavenly Music
Heaven on Earth Center of
    Heavenly Music
Ocean Dreams Center of
    Heavenly Music
Rainbow Ray of the Masters
    (w/Debra Conant) Center of
    Heavenly Music
You Are the Ocean Center of
    Heavenly Music

On *Ocean Dreams* Roth skillfully merges flute, harp, cello, and zither with the sounds of the ocean and dancing streams to create an emotionally dynamic range of sound. *Heaven on Earth* is more meditative in style, featuring gently flowing flute, zither, saxophone, and natural sounds. Roth's inspired flute performances are combined with the delicate yet intricate sound of Debra

Conant's harp on *Rainbow Ray of the Masters,* to create beautiful music suitable for relaxation, massage, or gentle reverie. **New Age Environmental, New Age Traditional**

Mike Rowland

The Fairy Ring Antiquity
Silver Wings Antiquity
Solace Antiquity

Rowland's gentle piano melodies, accented by carefully arranged strings, are perfect for massage, yoga, or other quiet pursuits. *The Fairy Ring* is especially soothing, shimmering, and delectably lush. **New Age Traditional**

Michel Rubini

Secret Dreams Gold Castle

Secret Dreams is a very romantic, relaxing release by synthesist Rubini, probably best known for his extensive list of soundtrack credits as well as sessions with such top recording artists as John Lennon, Diana Ross, Barbra Streisand, and Frank Sinatra. The music is a series of improvisations on the Synclavier and features delicate harplike string sounds, shimmering color washes, and rich, resonant guitar tones. Slow, spiraling phrases carry the listener blissfully away from reality. **New Age Traditional**

Nancy Rumbel

Emerald (w/Tingstad and
    Brewer) Narada Lotus

The Gift (w/Tingstad)
  Sona Gaia
Woodlands (w/Tingstad and
  Darling) Narada Lotus

Emerald is an extraordinary collaboration among oboist Rumbel, guitarist Eric Tingstad, and pianist Spencer Brewer. Rumbel's first exposure to the oboe outside of classical music came through performing as a member of the Paul Winter Consort. Of her latest pairing with Tingstad and Brewer on *Emerald,* she says, "Our music is crystalline. It has given me the chance to actually play my instrument. In improvising, the contact with the instrument is direct." (See also Radiance.) **New Age Traditional**

Terry Rypdal

After the Rain ECM
Descendre ECM
Odyssey ECM

Combining classical and jazz influences, Rypdal creates New Age music that is mostly spacious, meditative, and gently invigorating. His electronic guitar is suitably showcased on *Descendre* and supported by his ensemble's synthesizer, horns, and drums. At times the rhythm becomes a bit frenetic, but overall this album is energizing and positive. *After the Rain* evokes watercolor portraits of a rain-washed earth emerging fresh and green through Rypdal's lush instrumental arrangements. **New Age Jazz**

S

G. S. Sachdev

Bansuri Phillips
Full Moon Fortuna
Golden Sun Invincible
Raga Bhupali Unity

Full Moon presents ragas played with passionate detachment by the Indian bamboo flute master Sachdev. He brings original improvisations to the ancient classical music of India yet preserves the purity of this two-thousand-year-old tradition, striving to evoke from the hollow bamboo the divine sound mentioned in the Vedic texts. Because of Indian music's basis in melody, as opposed to Western music's basis in harmony, Sachdev says, "For us the beauty and depth of each note is important. You will find harmony, but as an outcome of melody. When [I] play, my mind is on each note, but when the sounds are there, and the atmosphere, they create a harmony." Since each raga on *Full Moon* is written for a particular time of day, each embodies a particular mood. Sachdev's music is ac-companied only by the drone of the tanpura and swar-peti, allowing the Indian bamboo flute's naturally resonant and lovely voice free range. **New Age World**

Ryuichi Sakamoto

Esparanto School
Neo Geo CBS
Piano One Sampler Private

Founder of the Yellow Magic Orchestra, Sakamoto has been credited with inventing "techno-pop." After the group's demise he collaborated with such artists as Thomas Dolby and David Sylvian, and created absorbing, innovative soundtracks for such films as *Merry Christmas, Mr. Lawrence* and *The Last Emperor*. His solo albums, including *Neo Geo,* are captivating mixes of East and West, traditional and modern, ancient Asian instruments and state-of-the-art computerized synthesizers. "Different equipment can add more extraneous sounds," he points out. "Range on a piano is limited, but the synthesizer has no limit. . . . The computer is my best friend." The album *Neo Geo* manages to sound at once traditional and futuristic, colloquial and cosmopolitan. It's New Age Pop with a Balinese or Polynesian flavor, featuring a vocal track by Iggy Pop. **New Age Pop**

Masahide Sakuma

Lisa Attic

Sukuma's *Lisa* is hypnotic, electro-acoustic music that percolates to an undulating beat. Using repetition and drone to counterpoint his enigmatic melodies, Sakuma uses guitar, synthesizers, strings, and percussion to evoke mysterious, vibrant jungles of sound. This is innerspace music that stimulates the imagination and uplifts the soul. **New Age Pop, New Age Space**

David Samuels
(See Double Image)

Jim Saporito
(See Radiance)

Rahul Sariputra

East Meets West Invincible
Footprints in the Sand Invincible
Music of the Spheres II Invincible

Footprints in the Sand is an appealing East/West fusion created by sitarist Sariputra and tabla player Zakir Hussain (of John McLaughlin's

group Shakti). The percolating tabla drums and reverberating strings of the sitar create a perfect counterpoint. Sariputra "sees raga music as meant for love, compassion, devotion. Raga is the personification of a sentient being. We are [all] sentient beings, meaning full of changing sentiments, sensations, feelings, emotions, passions. Raga displays all these moods. It is like a symphony." **New Age East/West**

David Satchell

Images New World

Satchell's haunting guitar and clear soft melodies evoke images of faraway places. *Images* is a warm and sensual sonic tapestry that is perfect for relaxing. **New Age Traditional**

Somei Satoh

Litania New Albion

Satoh is a minimalist Japanese composer who relishes lyricism as well as repetition in his creations. On *Litania* the music flows in long, unbroken melodic contours over simple harmonic progressions. Satoh's evocative musical language is a fusion of Japanese timbral sensibilities, electronic technology, and nineteenth-century romanticism. As he says, "My music is limited to certain elements of sound, and there are many calm repetitions. I think silence and the prolongation of sound is the same thing in terms of space. More important is whether the space is 'living' or not. Our [Japanese] sense of time and space is different . . . from the West . . . [and] I would like it if the listener could abandon all previous conceptions of time and experience a new sense of time presented in this music as if eternal time can be lived in a single moment." The release features keyboards, violin, percussion, and soprano vocals. **New Age East/West, New Age Electronic**

Karl Schaffner

Birds of Paradise Beyond
Flying Carpet Isis
Many Lives Ago Valley of the Sun
Mountains in the Sea Isis
Music for Friends Beyond
Peace Valley of
  the Sun
Sounds of the New Age
  Sampler Isis
The Voyage Beyond
  Sampler Beyond

After performing with folk groups in the sixties, Schaffner experimented with fusion/rock, r&b, and progressive music. Then a spiritual odyssey led him to India where he studied flute and the sarod (a stringed instrument similar to a slide guitar). *Birds of Paradise* was created in collaboration with German/Japanese guitarist Lothar Takashi Grimm, whose forefathers were the famous Brothers Grimm of childhood tales. Schaffner performs on guitar, bass, and keyboards while Grimm uses guitar synthesizer to create colorful, melodically exciting interplays with Third World influences. **New Age World**

Johannes Schmoelling

Wuivend Riet Life Style

Former Tangerine Dream member Schmoelling uses computers, keyboards, and electronic percussion, but he transcends mere electronic special effects. On *Wuivend Riet* ("wind-blown reeds" in Dutch), in place of the monochromatic, slow-motion stylings usually found on hypnotic trance music releases, he combines the sounds of nature with a melodic electronic-pop base, to develop a miniature world teeming with life. Through each selection on the album you are encouraged to explore this landscape and indulge yourself in gentle reverie. **New Age Electronic**

Eberhard Schoener

Bali Agung Kuckuck
Meditation Kuckuck
Sky Music Kuckuck
Video Magic (w/Sting and Andy
  Summers) Gaia

Violinist/keyboardist Schoener says, "In music one must make no compromises. The moment you try to orient yourself to something, you lose your identity. One must accept the danger of not riding the wave, of not being in fashion, and remain true to oneself." *Video Magic* features pleasant keyboard melodies and unusual synthesizer accents, with the Munich Chamber Opera orchestra, vocalist Sting, and guitarist Andy Summers (of the defunct group Police) guesting on a few cuts. **New Age Pop**

Klaus Schonning

Cyclus Fortuna
Lydglimt Fortuna

Lydglimt means "glimpses of sound" in Danish, and the album translates visions of the natural world into vibrant electronic music. Blending synthesizers, acoustic instruments, and the sounds of nature, Schonning paints shimmering aural portraits. *Cyclus* is a spiraling eight-part suite of musical variations, an electronic/acoustic tribute to the cycles of nature. The music moves like the seasons, echoing Arabian drums, sidewalk cafes, and your own heartbeat. **New Age Electronic**

Robert Schroeder

Brain Voyager Life Style
Harmonic Ascendant Innovative Communications

Composed for a 3-D West German film, *Brain Voyager* is an album to dream by. In an unusual move Schroeder eliminated the drum computer on these tracks, resulting in a less rhythmic but spacious sound balance between acoustic guitars and synthesizers. The music is romantic and intimate. *Harmonic Ascendant* combines acoustic classical guitar and cello with an electronic instrument base for a progressive spirit. **New Age Electronic**

Kristian Schultze

Metronomics Life Style

Metronomics features Schultze's forte: powerful, rhythm-oriented electronic crossover music that fuses jazz, progressive, and synthesized New Age sounds. Achieving a delicate balance between structural programming and improvisational sections, the record is smooth, lively, and vibrant. The album's subtitle is *Handmade and Programmed Music;* this is a clue to the loving care and attention to detail that Schultze lavishes on each composition. **New Age Electronic**

Klaus Schulze

Babel (w/Andreas Grosser) Venture/Virgin
Cyborg Gramavision
Dune Gramavision
Irrlicht Brain
Klaus Schulze Live Brain
Mindphaser Gramavision
Mirage Island
Moondawn Brain
Picture Music Gramavision
Timewind Brain
Trancefer Gramavision
X (Part 1) Gramavision
X (Part 2) Gramavision

First as a member of Tangerine Dream and then as a solo artist, Schulze is one of the founding fathers of New Age Electronic and Space music. *Picture Music* is surreally ethereal, an audio expression of vivid dreams and fantasies. Created by computer-controlled synthesizers and self-built electronic effects, Schulze's never-before-heard sounds propel the listener into a soundscape that is thrilling, spacey, dreamy, and hypnotic by turns. On *Babel* Schulze teams with electronic composer Andreas Grosser to present an atmospheric space music suite. The long instrumental pieces are very relaxing. **New Age Electronic, New Age Progressive**

Dieter Schutz

Voyage Life Style

Dedicated "To Our Good Old Mother Earth," Schutz's *Voyage* offers synthesizer-based compositions that suggest strong visual images; they convey, for example, the wildness of jungle scenery through lush instrumentation or the image of a solitary plant in the middle of a desert by suspending a single musical note in space. Multi-instrumentalist Schutz also incorporates lively percussion accents on several tracks, stimulating in a positive rather than aggressive manner. **New Age Progressive**

Jim Scott

Alone Invincible
First Winds of Autumn Songs for a Small Planet
Lake unto Clouds Invincible
Songs for Kids Songs for a Small Planet

Guitarist and member of the group Radiance, Scott has also worked with the Paul Winter Consort since 1977 and is featured on four of their albums, contributing solo guitar pieces and compositions for chorus and large ensemble. Of his own albums, *Alone* is an emotional, instrumental tone poem embracing the folk heritage of European classicism, exotic rhythmic devices from Latin America and Africa, and delicate accents from Asia. On his all-vocal release, *First Winds of Autumn,* each song is a highly polished gem offering personal and moving lyrics as well as Scott's melodic guitar-based instrumentation. **New Age Vocal, New Age World**

Molly Scott

Honor the Earth Songs for a Small Planet
We Are All One Planet Songs for a Small Planet

Founder of the group Sumitra and a committed activist in the areas of ecology and disarmament, Scott aims to "create music which illumines our connections with the earth and each other." Her voice is a beautiful instrument on her passionate and honest compositions. *Honor the Earth* features Scott and Sumitra in a poetic tapestry of songs for guitar, flute, piano, dulcimer, cello, and other instruments backed by the choir On Wings of Sound. **New Age Vocal**

Tony Scott

Music for Zen Meditation Verve

If any one album could lay claim to have launched the New Age music movement, this one can. Created in 1962, Scott's ethereal blend of clarinet, shakuhachi flute, and koto still sounds as evocative, peaceful, and powerful as ever. The instrumentals promote relief of daily stress and frenetic mental activity, encouraging the listener to focus gently and begin

161

NEW AGE VOCAL MUSIC

by Michael Stillwater*

Stillwater is a recording artist with numerous albums to his credit, a retreat and workshop leader, a humorist, and an author. He is also co-founder of Heavensong, a nondenominational ministry.

New Age Vocal music gives lyrical expression to the philosophy or vision of the New Age. Its musical styles include folk, pop, jazz, and rock. Themes associated with the songs include an expanded sense of personal identity, a recognition of connection with the global family, and a holistic awareness of the planet; an awakened responsibility for one's thoughts, words, actions, and an acknowledgment of the wisdom or divinity in everyone; an emphasis on the healing power in relationships, and a recognition of the wholeness of body, mind, and spirit; and finally, an admission that there is an underlying omnipresent power and intelligence called Love, God, Universal Spirit, and so forth, with an absence of spiritual elitism.

LAURA ALLAN	JAMES DURST AND FERNE
JIM BERENHOLTZ	BORK
CLANNAD	BROOKE MEDICINE EAGLE

*Artist listing compiled by Patti Jean Birosik.

a deep, refreshing meditation. Whether used as an aid to facilitate trance, meditation, massage, or reverie, or enjoyed simply as beautiful spacious music, *Music for Zen Meditation* is a classic. New Age Meditation

Search for Serenity Records

87 Sampler Search for Serenity

This collection of outstanding New Age artists features music that renews, nurtures, and inspires. Dean and Dudley Evenson, Tom Barabas, and others add their special musical perspectives without ego, allowing each musician time to stretch out within the mostly improvisational pieces. Whether performing solo or in ensemble mode, the Search for Serenity artists embody their philosophy of creating "peace through

DEBORAH FIER	SHAWN PHILLIPS
STEPHEN LONGFELLOW FISKE	DAVID POMERANTZ
DR. ROBERT GASS	RADHA KRSHNA TEMPLE
ELIZA GILKYSON	JOHN RICHARDSON
GREGORIAN CHANTS	KIM ROBERTSON
GYUME TIBETAN MONKS	JIM SCOTT
DAVID HYKES	MOLLY SCOTT
ALEX JONES	AZRA SIMONETTI
BIBI BHANI KAUR	AVTAR SINGH AND KULWANT
SAT KARTAR KAUR	SINGH
SINGH KAUR	VIKRAM SINGH
ROSIE LOVEJOY AND CHARLES	DEBBIE SPITZ
THWEATT	MICHAEL STILLWATER
IAN MATTHEWS	MALOAH STILLWATER
JAMIE MICHAELS	LISA THIEL
OMAN AND SHANTI	GLORIA THOMAS
SUSAN OSBORN	MICHAEL TOMLINSON

music" on this lovely record. **New Age Traditional, New Age World**

Seigen (Seigen Ono)

Seigen Innovative Communications

Seigen's self-titled release interweaves a strong sense of Western sound structures such as classical and jazz with the atmospheric improvisations of electronic music. The result-ing music is spacious and intricately textured, utilizing many interesting audio effects within the compositions. Seigen has worked with David Sylvian and Ryuichi Sakamoto, so a New Age Pop influence shows up in the arrangements. **New Age Pop**

Peter Seiler

Flying Frames Innovative Communications

163

Sensitive Touch Innovative
Communications

Seiler creates synthesizer-based
electronic music that ranges from
relaxing to rhythmically driven. *Flying Frames* is made up of musical
travel impressions of landscape,
flights, city life. The mood ranges
from the quiet beauty of the Serengeti Plain to the hectic bustle of life
in Tokyo. Seiler's music is warm, direct, sensuous, and alive, easily accessible to most New Age fans. **New
Age Electronic**

Vladislav Sendecki

Men from Wilnau Antilles/Island
Stuttgart Aria Jazzpoint

Throughout Europe keyboardist
Sendecki is known for his fusion and
straight ahead jazz bands. *Men from
Wilnau,* his solo acoustic piano
album, represents a real departure;
as Sendecki explains, "I felt I needed
to change my attitude. I felt my classical roots coming up again, and I
just went with that feeling." The result is a highly personalized musical
statement that makes dramatic use of
silence. The record is not filled with
conventional delicate meandering
phrases or light-touch flair but rather
with music full of conviction and passion. **New Age Jazz, New Age Solo**

John Sergeant

The Cauldron of Thoth (w/Nicki
Scully) Plumrose Music
The Joy of Being (w/Terry
Cole-Whittaker) Plumrose Music

Music from the Desert Plumrose
Music
Radiant Emotions
(w/Terry Cole-Whittaker)
Plumrose Music
*Ringing Through the Halls of
Heaven* Plumrose Music

Multi-instrumentalist Sergeant creates music that reflects love and commitment to the healing of the planet.
Ringing Through the Halls of Heaven
offers calm, gentle piano and synthesizer pieces that merge the spirit of
Northern California's rivers and redwood trees with the essence of meditation. Each song embodies a different emotional theme, from joy and
wonder to the delicate balance between searching for your path and
knowing you're on it. Sergeant has
also created the instrumental soundtrack for guided reveries featuring
narration by healer/teacher Nicki
Scully and author Terry Cole-Whittaker. **New Age Traditional**

Jonn Serrie

*And the Stars Go with
You* Miramar

Although the title sounds like a
throwaway line from *Star Wars,* Serrie's music is actually synthesized
water, wind, and siren sounds
blended with voice, bass, vibes, and
keyboards for a lush, multitextured
listening experience. Mixing jazz,
progressive, and electronic influences, the music is striking and transcendent, rising from restlessness to
serenity by the completion of the
tape. **New Age Electronic, New
Age Jazz**

164

Bola Sete

From All Sides Fantasy
Incomparable Fantasy
Jungle Suite Dancing Cat
Live at Matador Fantasy
Ocean Lost Lake Arts/Windham
  Hill
Solo Guitar Fantasy
Tour de Force Fantasy
Vol. 1 Takoma

Solo Guitar is a passionately performed New Age amalgam influenced by Brazilian folk, bossa nova, jazz, and classical guitar. Sete's style on the instrumental selections is vibrant and resonant, with colorful imagery that uplifts the spirit. Each note gracefully coalesces with the next until a lush aural texture is created. This album is a must for guitar fans. **New Age Solo, New Age World**

Steve Sexton
(See Exchange)

Shadowfax

Big Song Windham Hill
Dreams of Children
  Windham Hill
*Folk Songs for a Nuclear
  Village* Capitol
Sampler 82 Windham Hill
Sampler 84 Windham Hill
Shadow Dance Windham Hill
Shadowfax Windham Hill
Too Far to Whisper Windham Hill
Watercourse Way Passport/ABC
Winter Solstice Windham Hill
Word from the Village Windham
  Hill

Their name comes from J. R. R. Tolkien's book, *The Lord of the Rings,* and like that work, the group's sources and influences are worldwide. Drawing from classical, rock, folk, and jazz, Shadowfax forges a multitextural sound that ranges from the progressive rock bent of their debut release *Watercourse Way* to the eclectic but more melodic *Too Far to Whisper,* which features two vocal tracks from this largely instrumental band. Keyboards, violin, Lyricon, saxophone, guitar, drums, and other instruments give Shadowfax an especially colorful tonal palette. **New Age Jazz, New Age Pop**

Ravi Shankar

Tana Mana Private Music
(Many other classical Indian
  albums)

For more than thirty years sitarist Shankar has dramatized the beauty of the traditional music of his native India as well as its ability to interact with Western classical and pop styles. In the process he has achieved worldwide stature. "What makes Indian culture unique," he says, "is that it represents a living tradition. Unlike other ancient civilizations—those of Egypt or China, for example—we're not looking at a culture that flourished five thousand years ago but which has no connection with the present. Rather, we have traditions in art, sculpture, painting, dance, and music that go back many centuries yet which have evolved and which are alive to this day." Shankar's numerous East Meets West–style albums have done much to speed this evolution and to expand communication among musicians of all traditions. *Tana Mana* is different from Shankar's previous releases in that it combines traditional Indian instruments and vocals with synthesizers, autoharp, bass, and guitar through collaborations with George Harrison, Patrick O'Hearn, and others. The result is upbeat, spirited music that is heavily rhythmic without losing its playful melodiousness. **New Age East/West**

Shanti
(See Oman and Shanti)

Andy Shapiro

Inner Wings New World
Journey New World
Thoughts and Harmony New World
Wind Woman (w/Simonetti) New World

On *Inner Wings* Shapiro creates smooth, harmonic, synthesizer-based music. The compositions feature deep, resonant bass tones and pure, crystalline highs to accent its swirling currents. This is music that invites you to close your eyes and relax. **New Age Space**

Shardad (Rohani)

Dream Images Serenity

Multi-instrumentalist Shardad's *Dream Images* is rather thematic in concept. Its first song was written a week after the death of his father, and as Shardad says, "his spirit runs all through this album, but he told me to be happy, not sad, after he was gone, so the recording is not melancholy." Rather, the strings, percussion, and keyboard work suggest a celebration of life after death. **New Age World**

Shayla (Sheila Roberts)

Moonflower Yansa
Moonflower Ascending Yansa
Vision Seeker Yansa

Shayla creates New Age Traditional music for a generation that, as she told the *Phoenix Gazette*, "came of age in the sixties searching for inner knowledge. They want to address quality-of-life issues." *Vision Seeker* showcases her keyboard and composition talents while adding subtle percussion techniques that propel the music forward. *Moonflower* and *Moonflower Ascending* are both exclusively keyboard-generated offerings of mood-lifting music inspired by the Arizona landscape, the spiritual teachings of Native American Indians, and ancient mythology. She hopes her music will help listeners "move into the deep recesses of their visions and creativity. The more each of us learns to trust our own inner voices, our creativity and inner strengths, the less we need to employ the tactics of aggression and defense in our dealings with others. The world naturally becomes a more peaceful and productive place." **New Age Traditional**

Amy Shreve

Peace in the Puzzle Meadowlark

Harpist Shreve's debut release, *Peace in the Puzzle,* is meditative and soothing, with a hint of New Age Jazz. "We wanted it to have the ambience of a live recording," she adds, "where the listener would feel as if he or she were right there—something they could put on when they wanted an atmosphere of peace and contentment." Shreve's approach to playing is very emotional, displaying both her innate sensitivity and her technical prowess on the Salvi harp. **New Age Traditional**

Michael Shrieve

Audentity (w/Schulze) Brain
The Big Picture Fortuna
In Suspect Terrain Relativity
The Leaving Time (w/Roach) RCA
Trancefer (w/Schulze) Brain
Transfer Station Blue Fortuna

Shrieve is one of the finest pop drummers in the world, period. Long the driving edge for multi-platinum rock group Santana, Shrieve also contributed to works by Mick Jagger and the Rolling Stones, and expanded techno-pop's horizons with his groups Go and Automatic Man. On *Transfer Station Blue* Shrieve and synthesist Klaus Schulze transcended the previous limitations of electronic music composition by mixing rock, pop, jazz, and classical influences into an inspired release that received rave reviews from both *New Age Journal* and *Billboard* maga-zines. The highly impressionistic rhythmic sound of *Transfer Station Blue* is complex enough to be appreciated in the foreground but gentle enough to be enjoyed as ambient background or "journey" music. *In Suspect Terrain* is an all-percussion solo record centered largely around the Linn drum machine with other acoustic and electronic percussion added in. **New Age Electronic, New Age Progressive**

Richard Shulman

Solo Flight New World

On *Solo Flight* New Age Jazz pianist Shulman combines the disparate elements of traditional jazz, classical, folk, Latin, and Third World music into a distinguished and ecstatic unity. This is more foreground music than background, especially suitable for headphone listening. **New Age Jazz**

Elan Sicroff

Journey to Inaccessible Places Editions EG

Pianist Sicroff has taken a group of nine short pieces of various origins and fused them into a lucid, flowing whole. Some of the instrumentals are Kurdish, others are Armenian, Sayyid, and Eastern Orthodox. One track, "The Bokharian Dervish," was written after a reading of chapter forty-one in *Beelzebub's Tales to His Grandson* in which G. I. Gurdjieff describes Beelzebub's meeting with a dervish who possessed a very high knowledge of the laws of vibrations. Gurdjieff himself refers to the "science of musical vibrations" that would have an objective, tangible, and predictable effect on people. Sicroff delivers particularly inspired interpretations of a number of Gurdjieff/Hartmann pieces, and they do have an uplifting spiritual quality about them that New Age fans are sure to relish. **New Age East/West**

Ben Sidran

On the Cool Side Windham Hill
On the Live Side
   Magenta/Windham Hill

Pianist Sidran is widely recognized as a hit pop songwriter and contemporary jazz artist, but he also creates music that fits comfortably in the category of New Age Jazz with *On the Live Side*. Sidran says his goal with the album was "to use technology, use all the synthesizers and drum machines available, but to use them for a human, not mechanical effect. When you can strike that balance, it's magic." With *On the Live Side* Sidran hits the mark. **New Age Jazz**

Azra Simonetti

Wind Woman (w/Shapiro) New
   World

Andy Shapiro's majestic compositions inspired Simonetti to create the delectable, shimmering, crystal-clear vocals on *Wind Woman*. This kaleidoscope of translucent sound was created with the latest digital sampling techniques; Shapiro expertly mixes Simonetti's voice with gorgeous cascades of sound. **New Age Vocal**

Avtar Singh, Kulwant Singh, and Others

Healing Sounds of the Ancients, Vols. 2–11 Invincible

This series of chants, some based on ragic scales, uses modern recording, synthesizers, and computers supporting a strong vocal line to reproduce ancient healing effects. In olden times when people wanted to change inner patterns that impeded their growth, they used prayer and music to reach their goals. Here, ethereal music and compelling vocals induce the peaceful mood that leads to inner transformation and transcendence; and with each tape in the series, the listener's power of concentration deepens. *Healing Sounds of the Ancients* is probably the highest-energy meditative music to be found that uses beautiful vocal intonations. **New Age Meditation, New Age Vocal**

Gurumander Singh

Blue Star Invincible

Written with a sense of awe about the universe, *Blue Star* is truly a tribute to Earth. Guitarist Singh's progressive playing style comes through on synthesizer, keyboards, percussion, and occasional vocals. **New Age East/West**

Liv Singh

Music of the Spheres
  Invincible
Music of the Spheres Vol.
  2 Invincible

Music of the Spheres is a collection of soulful, meditative compositions that invites the listener to travel through levels of deepening inner peace. Singh skillfully blends flute, bells, recorder, guitar, tamboura, and harmonium to produce the ancient tonal scales that evoke the ideal fluid, ethereal state for meditation and relaxation. *Vol. 2* contains a haunting rendition of an ancient Indian raga noted for its ability to help the listener achieve spiritual awakenings. The album blends old and modern instruments: sitar, tablas, violin, acoustic and electric guitars with synthesizer. **New Age East/West, New Age Meditation**

Sat Nam Singh
(See Singh Kaur)

Siri Nam Singh

Ten Thousand New
  Waves Invincible

Each selection on the New Age fusion album *Ten Thousand New Waves* unlocks a series of sound pictures. Singh leads us with his acoustic guitar, synthesizer, and percussion, backed by a solid ensemble on keyboards, saxophone, bass, flutes, traps, and congas. **New Age Jazz**

Vikram Singh

Asa Di Var I Invincible
Asa Di Var II Invincible
Evening Raga Invincible

Singh's dynamic voice adds depth to the prayer *Asa Di Var,* an ancient devotion describing man's longing for the supreme being. This rendition contains devoted and spirited singing in Gurumukhi, the language of the Sikhs, accompanied by tamboura, sitar, and tablas. *Asa Di Var II* is a continuation of this lovely musical prayer. *Evening Raga* combines Singh's vocal range with powerful tonal scales designed to simulate the experience of the subtle energy of the hours between day and night. **New Age East/West, New Age Vocal**

Sangit Sirus

Dancing Butterflies
  Nightengale

Sirus creates a dreamy circle of playful melodies led by the seductive song of the violin and accompanied by the charming sounds of sitar and oud. Refreshing tabla rhythms and swaying flute transport the listener to the land of a thousand and one nights. **New Age East/West**

Robert Slap

Atlantis: Crystal Chamber Valley
  of the Sun
East of West Valley of the Sun
In the Caverns of Your
  Mind Valley of the Sun

169

Mystic Memories Valley of the
Sun
New Age Music Sampler 1 Valley
of the Sun
New Age Music Sampler 2 Valley
of the Sun
Reflections of Reflections Valley
of the Sun
Search for Utopia Valley of the
Sun
Sedona Video Soundtrack Valley
of the Sun

Multi-instrumentalist Slap creates the ultimate music for creative visualization. His albums encompass the progressive as well as environmental sides of New Age music, setting specific tones and carrying through with colorful emotional themes that resonate long after the music has ended. Slap points out that "music is made to generate emotional response, and life is a tapestry of ever-changing moods, colors, textures, and emotion. Music reflects life and touches our souls' strings, pulling feelings out with passion into the open." *Reflections of Reflections* explores the interplay between acoustic, synthesized, and natural sounds in a free-form improvisation featuring pentatonic and wind chimes, voices, triangles, and electronic/synthesizer effects. Interwoven are the sounds of water, caves, forest, and wind. This release is especially well suited for headphones or meditation. *East of West* uses acoustic and electric guitars, synthesizer, and percussion to achieve a soothing blend of Eastern and Western themes. Slap combines elements of East Indian and Asian music with modern, classical, and

jazz influences, generating many relaxing moods and textures. This is moving, inspiring music that will support meditation or any mellow activity. **New Age Traditional**

Don Slepian

Christmas Candlelight Fortuna
*Computer Don't Break
Down* Don and Judy
Largos Fortuna
Reflections Audion
Rhythm of Life Fortuna
Sea of Bliss Fortuna
Sonic Perfume Audion

Slepian describes his New Age Electronic music as the "classical music of the future." On *Sea of Bliss* two extended synthesizer pieces offer effervescent electronic sparkles and rhythmic chimes dancing amid flowing bass tones. The length and upbeat melodic nature of the music makes this release perfect for gentle movement or casual listening. *Largos* is comprised of delicate reworkings of fifteen classical baroque favorites on computer-controlled synthesizers that focus on slow movements; these are peaceful, soothing instrumentals good for meditation and relaxation—fans of Daniel Kobialka or Wendy Carlos will enjoy them. *Sonic Perfume* features algorithmic compositions—a collaboration between the performer and a computer that results in a two-way dialogue and co-creative control—which produce surprisingly warm, vital, and quietly inspiring instrumentals. Classically trained in piano, organ, guitar, and recorder, Slepian is a wizard synthesist/composer. **New Age Electronic**

Mark Sloniker

True Nature Sandstone Music

Keyboardist/composer Sloniker creates very lovely easy-on-the-ears New Age Jazz through a balanced blend of acoustic and electric instrumentation. Slow, sweet ballads of solo acoustic piano are the perfect counterpoint to the more up-tempo melodies sporting saxophones, guitars, horns, drums, and other percussion. **New Age Jazz**

Billy Smiley

New Night Meadowlark

Trumpet and flügelhorn are not usually thought of as New Age instruments. However, under the loving care of Billy Smiley, both add considerable warmth and humanity to the spiritually inspiring compositions found on *New Night*. The fluid and emotional horn lines join acoustic and electronic keyboards (Smiley also performs on synthesizers and synth bass) to create a gentle romantic lyricism. **New Age Pop**

Dallas Smith

Inner Rhythms (w/Mazer) Music West
Lifetide (w/Halpern) Sound Rx
Natural Light (w/Halpern) Hear and Now
Newsound (w/Halpern) Hear and Now
Petals (w/Allen, Bell, Canyon) Rising Sun
Sanctuary II Third Eye
Stellar Voyage Rising Sun
Summer Suite (w/Allen, Bell, Canyon) Rising Sun
Summit (w/Mazer) Pro Jazz
Threshold (w/Halpern) Hear and Now

Smith has a tremendous ability to communicate the "aesthetic joy of making music"—especially when accompanied by his frequent performing and recording partner Susan Mazer. Together they have forged new directions in New Age Jazz. Smith's instruments are many, but he is foremost a composer and performer on woodwinds; a lifelong devotee of the Indian bansuri flute, Smith considers it his discipline and a form of meditation. He chooses his acoustic and electronic instruments to create music that, in his own words, "has to be accessible and not overly intellectual." He is also a pioneer in the development of the Lyricon wind synthesizer. He says, "Its power is in the subtle woodwind expressiveness which comes through the technology. It's earthbound and very effective for my compositions which represent a fusing of classical, jazz, and international music styles." *Inner Rhythms* matches Mazer and Smith in an exciting, uplifting, and rhythmic series of improvisation-based pieces that thrill, delight, and inspire the listener. Each player is given room to breathe as well as soar, yet the dynamic interplay between Mazer's electrified harp and Smith's woodwinds is absolutely captivating. **New Age Jazz**

Sandy Smith and Jack Montgomery (Platero)

Arpa de las Americas Platero
Aventuras Vol. I (out of print)
Aventuras Vol. II Platero

Aventuras Vol. II is a journey through the diverse sounds of the many Latin American cultures. Acoustic Paraguayan harp and guitar as played by Smith and Montgomery, respectively, are the featured instruments in an ensemble that includes bass, panpipes, quena flutes, and other exotic instruments. This is delicate, melodic New Age World music—warm, easygoing, and accessible. **New Age World**

Larry Snyder and Dennis McCorkle

Peaceful Fantasy
Vital Body

Multi-instrumentalists Snyder and McCorkle create richly woven sonic tapestries of space music by combining guitars with synthesizers. More ambient than exploratory in tone, the music creates a subtly shaded background for meditation, contemplation, and relaxation. **New Age Space**

Software
(See Peter Mergener and Michael Weisser)

Solitudes

By Canoe to Loon Lake Solitudes
Dawn on the Desert Solitudes
Giant Trees of the Wild Pacific Coast Solitudes
Heavy Surf on a Rocky Point Solitudes
Listen to the Loon Solitudes
National Parks and Sanctuaries Solitudes
Niagara Falls Solitudes
Night in a Southern Swamp Solitudes
Sailing to a Hidden Cove Solitudes
Seascapes Solitudes
Solitudes Sampler Solitudes
Solitudes II—Opus One: Land of the Loon Solitudes
Solitudes II—Opus Two: Under Sail Solitudes
Storm on a Wilderness Lake Solitudes
Tradewind Islands Solitudes

Solitudes presents remote-recording pioneer Dan Gibson's environmental soundtracks with no music added to detract from the beautiful "music" of nature. The listener is enveloped in the calming, mentally cleansing, and relaxing sounds of North American wildlife. As background for meditation, body work, lovemaking, dining, or other activities, these albums stand up to repeated listenings as the subtle yet dense textures of sound reveal something new each time the release is played. *By Canoe to Loon Lake* is a marvelous blend of languid water sounds, the eerie cry of loons, and other wilderness accents. *Seascapes* is a popular release as it features ocean waves with seabird calls. Solitudes

172

has also issued two videocassettes that feature wilderness scenes with only natural sounds—no music or narrative. **New Age Environmental**

Sotavento

Cuicani Redwood

Sotavento is an ensemble of musicians from El Salvador, Puerto Rico, Mexico, and the United States that formed in 1981. The six members collectively play more than twenty-five instruments, some classically familiar and others exotic and indigenous to their historic cultures. Sotavento blends elements of Western classical and jazz with traditional folk melodies from Peru, Brazil, Chile, and Puerto Rico on *Cuicani,* an all-instrumental album that offers a well-arranged but eclectic mix of sweet ballads and danceable up-tempo tunes. Strings, flutes, and percussion instruments are featured predominantly, making this one of the most accessible and pleasing examples of New Age World music to be found. Other releases by the group are strictly ethnic, not New Age. **New Age World**

Soundings of the Planet Records

MHP Peace: Soviet Experience Collection Soundings of the Planet
Music Makes the Snow Melt Down Soundings of the Planet
Peace Through Music Sampler Soundings of the Planet
Soundings Tapestry Soundings of the Planet

Soundings of the Planet is an artist-owned record company featuring musicians who sincerely believe in creating "peace through music." *Soundings Tapestry* blends the sounds of nature with piano, guitar, bells, harp, flute, sitar, and other instruments in serene, melodic improvisations by Dean and Dudley Evenson, Tom Barabas, and D'Rachael. This is true New Age music in both intent and delivery. **New Age Traditional, New Age World**

Richard Souther (aka Douglas Trowbridge)

Heirborne (Souther) Meadowlark
Inner Mission (Souther) Meadowlark
Songs Unspoken (Trowbridge) Meadowlark

Let's get it straight: Richard Souther is Douglas Trowbridge, and both record for Meadowlark Records. Souther creates New Age synthesizer music while his alter ego, Trowbridge, is known for his New Age acoustic piano records, notably the uplifting *Songs Unspoken.* Pianos and keyboards have fascinated Souther since he began playing at the age of two. Discovering computers and synthesizers in the eighties, he turned his prodigious talents toward making humanistic electronic music. On *Heirborne,* Israeli, Irish, and British influences are evident throughout his original compositions. Those who summarily dismiss synthesizers as too mechanical haven't listened to the compelling, emotional selections on this album. As Souther explains, "I prefer the synthesizer over other instruments because of its expressiveness. For *Heirborne* I used twenty of them." **New Age Electronic, New Age Solo**

Paul Speer

Collection 983 Spectral Voyages Catero
Desert Vision (w/Lanz) Narada Equinox
Natural States (w/Lanz) Narada Equinox

A remarkable collaboration between two major New Age talents, pianist David Lanz and guitarist Speer, *Natural States* was inspired by the scenery of the Pacific Northwest. The album also features flute solos by guest artist Chaitanya Hari Deuter. Speer's sensitive fingerwork on guitar delivers rich and resonant timbres for a lyrical, mellifluous sound. *Natural States* and *Desert Vision* are also available on video; the lovely landscapes enhance the cinematic quality of the music. **New Age Traditional**

Chris Spheeris

Desires of the Heart CBS

Keyboardist Spheeris performs romantic, simple, melodic piano and synthesizer pieces. *Desires of the Heart* speaks eloquently of love and passion through spare arrangements that keep the theme from bogging down in sentiment. And there's just enough electronic spice to make the music fresh, warm, and inviting. **New Age Traditional**

Spirit Music Records

Spirit Music Sampler Spirit Music
Windows of Sound Spirit Music

Don Campbell, Laraaji, Lyghte, Spirit Sounds, Sam McClellan, David Collett, and Kano each create spacious ambient music on this sampler designed to "enhance well-being and provide a soothing oasis of sound in an increasingly hectic world." Featured instruments include piano, synthesizer, zither, and bells. Each selection is a quiet instrumental piece that washes away tension effortlessly, leaving the listener feeling renewed, inspired, and uplifted. **New Age Sound Health**

Debbie Spitz

Pipedreams Life

On *Pipedreams* Spitz creates New Age Vocal music backed with violin, flute, and synthesizer—a jazz- and pop-influenced, positive alternative to the Top Forty sound. Spitz's vocal delivery is suitably emotional, matching the lyrical themes without being demanding. **New Age Vocal**

Stairway

Aqua Marine New World

James McCarty, a founding member of the seminal rock-blues band the Yardbirds, and Louis Cennamo, a top session musician for such artists as James Taylor and Al Stewart, com-

174

bine their talents as the duo Stairway. On *Aqua Marine,* along with vibrant guitar and shimmering keyboards, they feature the endearing voice of the dolphin to evoke the power of the sea. **New Age Traditional**

Andy Statman

Flatbush Waltz Rounder
Mandolin Abstractions (w/David Grisman) Rounder
Nashville Mornings, New York Nights Rounder

When Statman plays mandolin, he makes magic. On *Mandolin Abstractions* he crosses the line from ethnic folk to New Age by combining those trilling strings with guitar, bass, percussion, drums, violin, and cello. At times languid and loose, at other times spirited and spiritely, the music has a way of moving that livens the heart and eases the mind. **New Age Folk**

Michael Stearns

Ancient Leaves Continuum Montage
Chronos Sonic Atmospheres
Encounter Hearts of Space
Floating Whispers Sonic Atmospheres
Jewel Sonic Atmospheres
Light Play Continuum Montage
Lyra Sound Constellation Continuum Montage
M'Ocean Sonic Atmospheres
Planetary Unfolding Sonic Atmospheres
Plunge Sonic Atmospheres
Sustaining Cylinders Continuum Montage

Stearns is one of New Age music's outstanding synthesists; he mixes dramatic orchestral textures with upbeat and innovative rhythms to yield visionary electronic music of unusual depth. Stearns is also skilled on guitar and on the Beam (a twelve-foot aluminum C beam that has twenty-four piano strings attached to it). Although his music is sometimes startling and otherworldly, *Jewel* reflects his appreciation of ambient sounds—birds, insects, chanting monks, and natural resonances recorded in large reverberant spaces. Mixing synth drones, angelic choir voices, and environmental sounds, *Jewel* is a hypnotic yet jubilant album. *Chronos* is the soundtrack to the innovative film of the same name that is featured exclusively at IMAX theaters (which feature fifty-foot-high picture screens and a Sensurround sound system). Here Stearns's arrhythmic sounds (long-sustained chords and microtonal scales) create an eerie feeling that accompanies the dreamlike images propelling across the screen. Utilizing many exotic native instruments as well as state-of-the-art technology, *Chronos* is a real workout for the listener's imagination. **New Age Electronic, New Age Space**

Ira Stein and Russell Walder

Elements Windham Hill
Transit Windham Hill

Stein and Walter combine piano and oboe on the fluid, colorful album

NEW AGE WORLD MUSIC

by Rick Bleiweiss*

Bleiweiss's thirty-year music industry career includes roles as a recording artist, songwriter, Grammy-nominated producer, and top executive at several major record companies.

World music is music that transcends national boundaries and is appreciated by varied cultures throughout the world. It can be derived solely from one culture and accepted by others or can be created when music indigenous to one culture is combined with the music of one or more other cultures. In the latter case various cultures with vastly differing music styles and heritages are integrated to create a new, exciting sound that can then be appreciated the world over; for example, a fusion of the melodic structures and rhythms of India with the improvisation of European pop music. World music can also draw from or unite both ancient and contemporary music. Balinese gamelan and Japanese folk choruses might blend with soft piano ramblings, and South American flutes could mix with Spanish guitar and modern synthesizers to set a desired mood. World music is proof that music is the universal language.

OBO ADDY	SPENCER BREWER
ANANDA	OSCAR CASTRO-NEVES
ANCIENT FUTURE	CLANNAD
DAN AR BRAS	STEPHEN COUGHLIN
AZYMUTH	SHAWNA CULOTTA AND
PATRICK BALL	EDITH LEICESTER

*Artist listing compiled by Patti Jean Birosik.

Elements. Their delicate interplay covers many subtle mood changes from quiet and inwardly focused to grand and sweeping musical statements. Adding wordless vocal effects, percussion, and synthesizer on *Transit,* the duo picks up the pace a bit to offer a contrapuntal interpretation of urban life. **New Age Traditional**

Greg Stewart

Transparent Views Beyond

CUSCO

BILL DAVILA

JORDAN DE LA SIERRA

DO'A

ETERNAL WIND

DEAN AND DUDLEY EVENSON

GLOBAL PACIFIC RECORDS

GREEN LINNET RECORDS

STEFAN GROSSMAN

JON HASSELL

DANNY HEINES

INTI-ILLIMANI

ALAP JETZER

BRIAN KEANE

TERESA LAWLOR

MAGICAL STRINGS

STEPHAN MICUS

NIGHT ARK

RUDIGER OPPERMANN

BILLY OSKAY AND MICHAEL
   O'DOMHNNAILL

POPUL VUH

ALI JIHAD RACY

RADIANCE

G. S. SACHDEV

KARL SCHAFFNER

JIM SCOTT

SEARCH FOR SERENITY
   RECORDS

BOLA SETE

SHARDAD

SANDY SMITH AND JACK
   MONTGOMERY

SOTAVENTO

SOUNDINGS OF THE PLANET
   RECORDS

JORGE STRUNZ AND
   ARDESHIR FARAH

SUKAY

TRI ATMA

ANNE WILLIAMS

XOCHIMOKI

*The Voyage Beyond
Sampler* Beyond

As a Synclavier programmer, Stewart has contributed to Michael Jackson's "Captain Eo" 3-D film and video project at Disneyland as well as to the soundtrack for *Little Shop of Horrors.* He brings the same cinematic feel to his original compositions on *Transparent Views.* Stewart's synthesizer-based music ranges from slow-moving, deeply meditative pieces to uplifting innovative compositions. Blending holistic and high-tech interests, Stewart's work is a delightful find for electronic music fans. New Age Space

Michael (aka Maitreya) and Maloah Stillwater

Michael Stillwater Solo:
Celebration Heavensong
One Light Heavensong
Serenade Heavensong
Set Your Heart Free Heavensong
Toddtmos, Germany Heavensong
Wings of Prayer Heavensong

Maloah Stillwater Solo:
Shores of Paradise Heavensong

Michael and Maloah Stillwater:
Heavensong Celebration Live Heavensong
Himmlische Muzik Lichtquell Musik
Voices of the Heart Heavensong

Together and separately the Stillwaters create inspirational and transformational New Age Vocal music. As Michael explains, "I believe that the healing of this world, beginning with the consciousness of each person, is accelerated through the spiritual application of music and song. By communicating directly with the heart, a song has the ability to transcend the barriers built between people and offers a new perception, a gateway to true vision." Michael is a singer/guitarist while Maloah performs on zither and sings. On *Heavensong Celebration Live* their intent is to inspire the remembrance of God through songs with affirmative lyrics, beautiful ballads, and gently in-vigorating light jazz arrangements. Michael's melodious and fluid guitar style is a perfect counterpoint to his warm, rich vocal stylings on *Set Your Heart Free;* Maloah's sweet, clear soprano is showcased on *Shores of Paradise.* New Age Vocal

Alan Stivell

Celtic Symphony Rounder
Harpes du Nouvel Age Rounder
Journée à la Maison Rounder
Reflets Fortuna
Renaissance of the Celtic Harp Rounder

Stivell revived the traditional Celtic harp during the midsixties folk-rock era, influencing such groups as Fairport Convention, Pentangle, and the Incredible String Band. His classic recording, *Renaissance of the Celtic Harp,* was even used as background music for some of Timothy Leary's LSD experiments at Harvard; and he continues to create mind-expanding sounds. *Harpes du Nouvel Age* is entirely performed on solo harp, including the electro-acoustic harp Stivell has experimented with over the past decade, and blends classical, jazz, New Age, and Celtic influences. Delicate arpeggios and glissandi—with every note ringing clear as a bell—along with percussive effects make *Harpes du Novel Age* one of the finest harp albums to come along since Stivell's original, groundbreaking *Renaissance of the Celtic Harp.* New Age Folk

Bob Stohl
(See Emerald Web)

Diana Stork

(See Geist)

David Storrs

Aerobic Exercise Valley of the Sun
Channel for the Light Valley of
the Sun
*Manifestation of the
Pyramids* Valley of the Sun
Sedona Sunrise Valley of the Sun

Multi-instrumentalist Storr's *Channel for the Light* has an ethereal quality that stimulates without being distracting. Subliminal spoken-word suggestions such as "You are a channel for the light," "You walk in the light and are harmonious and self-fulfilled," and "You radiate the Divine Light," are mixed deep within the music so that only the unconscious can pick up the message. On *Sedona Sunrise* wooden flute, harp, chimes, and celestial voices merge for a haunting and mystical sound inspired by Storrs's visit to the vortexes (the rock formations in Sedona, Arizona) that emanate energy. **New Age Traditional**

Liz Story

All Things Considered Novus/RCA
Part of Fortune Novus/RCA
Solid Colors Windham Hill
Unaccountable Effect Windham
Hill

"I think of my music as a translation of spirit. Society has broken down, and the human psyche is in a critical state. The whole culture needs a myth that works, and New Age comes right out of that need," Story said in an *L. A. Weekly* interview. Still, most of keyboardist Story's music fits snugly into the New Age Jazz subgenre rather than the meditate-and-heal category. *Solid Colors,* for example, balances sacred and profane musical themes through contrapuntal use of dissonance and melody. Story's keyboard technique has expanded greatly on the more current release, *Part of Fortune;* this singularly moving release adds cello, percussion, strings, and choir voices to her original piano compositions. **New Age Pop**

Tim Story

Glass Green Windham Hill
In Another Country Uniton
Piano Sampler Windham Hill
*The Soul of the Machine
Anthology* Windham Hill
Three Feet from the Moon Uniton
Untitled Uniton

Story composes mellow atmospheric music for both synthesizer and acoustic piano, influenced by classical, jazz, and minimalist sounds. *Glass Green* is a dreamy and uplifting album well suited to casual listening and quiet pursuits. **New Age Traditional**

Jorge Strunz and Ardeshir Farah

Frontera Milestone
Guitarras Milestone
Mosaico Milestone

Strunz and Farah blend Latin and Persian influences to create an especially exotic brand of acoustic guitar fusion music. As Strunz explains, "The guitar alone can create a feeling of intimacy, and without the other instruments to compete with it, it has more room to breathe. The percussion doesn't get in the way but enhances the natural beauty and richness of the guitars." *Mosaico* integrates multifaceted arrangements for guitar with subtle yet strong support from electric bass and percussion. It also features a guest appearance by Indian violin master L. Subramanian. The selections here are floating improvisations rather than blinding-speed wizardly star turns; if you love guitars, Strunz and Farah create New Age fusion music for you. **New Age Jazz, New Age World**

Sukay

Mama Luna Flying Fish
Pachasiku Flying Fish
Socovon Flying Fish
Sukay: Music of the Andes Flying Fish
Tutayay Flying Fish

Sukay is an Andean word that means "opening the earth to prepare for planting." On *Socovon* this group has broken cultural ground with its exotic Andean flute-based music. Their sometimes haunting, sometimes vibrant music features pan-pipes, bomba (hollowed out log drum), charango (mandolinlike instrument fashioned from an armadillo shell), notched flutes called kenas, as well as other instruments native to South America. **New Age World**

David Sun

Deep Enchantment New World
Harmony New World
An Island Called Paradise New World
Peace New World
The Secret Garden New World
Serenity New World
Sunrise New World
Sunset New World
Tranquility New World

Sun creates music for meditation, healing, or relaxed listening. *Harmony* is an expansive album that celebrates nature with its soothing harp and exalting flute. *Tranquility* maintains a centered, reflective continuity, a wash of soft, delicate sound. The keyboards on *Serenity* seem to create ripples of healing tones. **New Age Meditation, New Age Sound Health**

Tomoko Sunazaki

Moon at Dawn (w/Masayuki Koga) Fortuna
Sound of Silk Strings Fortuna
Spring Night Fortuna

A distinguished master of the Japanese string instrument, the koto, Sunazaki offers a selection of traditional and modern Japanese classics spanning more than four centuries. Joining her on *Moon at Dawn* is shakuhachi flutist Masayuki Koga. The music is at once elegant and vivacious, refined and uplifting. Sunazaki's interchange of Eastern and Western sensibilities bring this traditional music into the realm of New Age. **New Age East/West**

Paul Sutin

Serendipity Real to Reel/
Lifedance

Multi-instrumentalist Sutin creates ambient music that features subtle melodies and exquisite harmonies. Synthesizers, acoustic piano, and Spanish guitar combine for a lush sound on *Serendipity.* Poised between background and foreground music, this album can be used as a gently reflective anti-stress aid. **New Age Sound Health**

Yoshio Suzuki

Morning Picture Innovative
Communication
Touch of Rain Attic

Suzuki plays keyboards with a masterly touch on his original compositions for *Morning Picture,* and accompanies himself on synthesizer, Linn drums, and his first love, the bass. The cuts are melodic, harmonious works reminiscent of some of the compositions of Pat Metheny, Andreas Vollenweider, and George Winston. **New Age Traditional**

Ric Swanson

Urban Surrender American
Gramaphone
Windsock American Gramaphone

Showcasing the talents of percussionist/drummer Swanson and his ensemble Urban Surrender, *Wind-sock* is an exciting New Age Jazz offering that ranges from exuberant Latin street rhythms to the lush beauty of acoustic ballads. Guest artist Richie Cole adds saxophone, and Larry Coryell contributes a stellar electric guitar intro on one track and a beautiful counterpoint on a delicately sweet ballad. **New Age Jazz**

Synchestra

Daydreams Elfin
Electric Snowflake Elfin
Mother Earth's Lullaby Elfin
Noah Elfin
The Phoenix Tape Elfin
Silver Ships Elfin
Timeless Flight Elfin

On *Mother Earth's Lullaby* Synchestra's electronic orchestra music mixes acoustic guitar and layered synthesizers with the natural sound of birds, crickets, and whales. Simple refrains and progressions are repeated, strengthened, and augmented, eventually inundating the listener with sound. Raindrops are the background on *Silver Ships,* which blends synthesizer and percussion into music that rolls like a summer thunderstorm. Side one is playful, colorful, and animated, while side two is mysterious, reflective, and deep. **New Age Electronic, New Age Environmental**

Synergy
(See Larry Fast)

T

Masanori Takahashi
(See Kitaro)

John Michael Talbot

Come to the Quiet Birdwing
Empty Canvas Meadowlark
The Quiet Meadowlark
Songs for Worship Vol. 1 Birdwing
*Troubadour for the Great
    King* Birdwing

In the sixties Talbot teamed up with his brother Terry to form the commercially successful Talbot Brothers, then went on to perform issue-oriented country-rock music in the early seventies under the group name Mason Proffitt. By 1976 he began the spiritual odyssey that led to his becoming a Franciscan monk. As Talbot studied the early music of the church, he developed a classical, contemplative musical style that has been embraced by the New Age music movement. *Empty Canvas* is a release of hope celebrated through the use of guitar, flute, recorder, oboe, cello, harp, and horns. It is lyrical, sensitive, deeply emotive music that attunes the listener's consciousness to the Divine. **New Age Traditional**

Paul Temple

Gentle Healing Sunray

Ethereal harp and sensitive flute playing combine on this relaxing, soothing and, yes, healing release. Temple's improvised audio environment is pure and restful, conducive to meditation, massage, yoga, and coffee breaks. It was "created to help harmonize the energy flows [chakras] in the body"—a veritable sonic acupressure session. *Gentle Healing* will leave you feeling refreshed, renewed, and balanced. **New Age Sound Health**

Ian Tescee

Continua Startsong/Backroads
Io Startsong/Backroads

Electronic composer Tescee creates imaginative New Age Space music using numerous synthesizers and other state-of-the-art electronic gear. His debut album *Io* is a must for all astral travelers. Inspired by the Voyager spacecraft explorations of Jupiter, Tescee uses warm, layered textures that are alternately atmospheric and energetic to describe the terrifying beauty of the most volcanically active world in the solar system. The music is lyrical, expressive, and full of the joy of new discovery. *Continua* is the aural equivalent of a zoom lens, with the music concentrating on the infinitely small and the inconceivably, cosmically grand. As Tescee says, "The big picture consists of both inner and outer space. I would hope that the functionality of my compositions would be as a bridge between the two." New Age Space

John Themis

Atmospheric Conditions
Landscape

On *Atmospheric Conditions* Themis has created a jazzy set of pleasing guitar instrumentals. While the title might lead you to expect space or electronic sound, Themis's music is earthy and emotional, charged with unusual chordal patterns, liquid melodies, and rhythmic lines. New Age Jazz

Lisa Thiel

Prayers for the Planet Earthsong

This pop-based offering from New Age vocalist Thiel is dedicated to "the healing of ourselves, each other, and the Earth who is our mother." Thiel states that the songs "came through a variety of traditions and forms to teach the underlying unity in all religions, all peoples, all pathways to the spirit." A variety of instruments, including guitar, keyboards, and percussion, support Theil's uplifting lyrics and warm, lilting vocals. New Age Vocal

Gloria Thomas

When I Become the Wind Valley of the Sun

A successful commercial songwriter, Thomas has been active in the metaphysical community since the midseventies, along with her husband, singer B. J. Thomas. "Different people add different flavors to music," she says. "New Age music will range all the way from jazz-oriented fusion to transcendental music. What music has done throughout the history of man is to reflect the mass consciousness. The powerful emergence of New Age music shows the spiritual evolution of mankind." On *When I Become the Wind* Thomas combines pop, country, and New Age influences for a very accessible, melodic release. New Age Vocal

Mattias Thurow

Cornucopia Life Style

Thurow is a world-renowned composer / multi - instrumentalist from West Germany whose previous works (records, ballets, plays, and so forth) have spanned jazz, classical, theater, rock, and opera. *Cornucopia* combines these disparate influences to yield subtle textures, varied tempos, and lovely, colorful sounds executed on tenor saxophone, oboe, and keyboards with computer and other sound programming devices. This is music for active listening rather than background. **New Age Traditional**

Charley Thweatt

(See Rosie Lovejoy)

Eric Tingstad

Emerald (w/Rumbel and
  Brewer) Narada Lotus
The Gift (w/Rumbel) Sona Gaia
On the Links Cheshire
Urban Guitar Cheshire
Woodlands (w/Rumbel and
  Lanz) Narada Lotus

The music on *Woodlands* flows from the collaboration of three distinguished musicians: guitarist Tingstad, oboist Nancy Rumbel, and pianist David Lanz. The result is a warmly elegant album ranging in tone from sunny and playful to shadowed and mysterious. Inspired by the music of guitar virtuoso Ralph Towner, Tingstad decided to dedicate his life to the instrument. After receiving encouragement from George Winston, he began to record his original New Age compositions, influenced by both classical and pop styles. He blends a delicate touch with innate sense of arrangement, especially notable when creating pattern after pattern of intricate coun-

terpoint and melody with Rumbel and Lanz. **New Age Traditional**

Richard Tintl

(See Ariel Kalma)

Isao Tomita

Back to the Earth RCA
Bermuda Triangle RCA
Bolero RCA
Firebird Suite RCA
Grand Canyon Suite RCA
Greatest Hits Vol. 1 RCA
Greatest Hits Vol. 2 RCA
Kosmos RCA
Night on Bald Mountain RCA
Pictures at an Exhibition RCA
Planets RCA
*Prelude to the Afternoon of a
  Faun* RCA
Snowflakes Are Dancing RCA
Syncopated Clock RCA

Tomita's commercial breakthrough album, *Snowflakes Are Dancing,* brought computerized music into the average American's consciousness long before the rise of New Age Electronic music or the various experimental offerings of the late seventies. Using state-of-the-art technology, he has created fresh, exciting arrangements of masterworks by Bach, Stravinsky, Holst, Debussy and others. *Back to the Earth* was recorded live in New York during the spectacular bicentennial celebration; as dazzling laser displays and fireworks lit up the night, synthesist Tomita united musicians from the Soviet Union, China, Japan, and the United States to perform ultramodern interpretations of classics such as

Holst's *The Planets* and Stravinsky's *Firebird Suite.* Tomita's two greatest hits collections also offer an insightful overview of one of the best-known electronic composers of our time. **New Age Electronic**

Michael Tomlinson

Run This Way Forever Desert Rain
Still Believe Cypress

Tomlinson creates warm and optimistic New Age Vocal music. *Still Believe* features an interesting blend of soft jazzy pop and folk-influenced guitar-based music. As Tomlinson says, "[*Still Believe*] is a real reflection of my awakening. . . . I still find it very important to put a lot of meaning into the lyrics and into the structures of the songs, but I didn't feel I had to make them all ballads to do that." The vocal styling is akin to Michael Murphey, Jesse Colin Young, or Dan Fogelberg; but what aligns Tomlinson with New Age is the spiritual feeling of his records. As he says, "I am a spiritual person, trying to put more warmth and honesty into the music. . . . There has to be a reason for hope and for being positive." **New Age Vocal**

Michael Trew

Dolphin Celebration Invincible

On *Dolphin Celebration* Trew has captured the joyful freedom of dolphins. Keyboardist Trew combines his experience as a music therapist with his skill at electronic instrumentation for an extraordinarily uplifting

audio outing, backed up by guest musician Graham Mason on keyboards, synthesizer, and percussion. **New Age Traditional**

Tri Atma

Ka Jakee Music Life Style
Yearning and Harmony Fortuna

The group Tri Atma makes melodious, rhythmic, sometimes meditative and always magical instrumental music combining German, Indian, and other exotic influences. The trio's original recordings were produced with mainly acoustic and analogous musical instruments marked by Indo-European elements, but *Ka Jakee Music* finds the band using the latest digital technology to move gently away from the narrow East Meets West musical marriage and into open-future world music. Using acoustic guitars, keyboards, and tablas with computers and other electronic gear, *Ka Jakee Music* develops two totally different moods. Side one is dubbed "The Mobile Side" and features lively danceable New Age Pop instrumentals. Side two, "The Relaxation Side," enables the listener to cool down into a calmer, more inwardly directed mode. **New Age World**

Douglas Trowbridge
(See Richard Souther)

Tsumi

Meetings Fonix

Tsumi is a duo consisting of multi-instrumentalists Ravi and Anudeva. *Meetings* could be about the meeting of two hearts, heart and mind, mind and spirit, or spirit and the Spirit above. The compositions are spacious enough to allow the listener room to make his or her own interpretation(s) of these harmonic themes. Some of the instruments featured are Celtic harp, guitar, keyboards, hammered dulcimer, viola, and saxophone, giving *Meetings* a melodic liquidity with some bright shimmering highs. **New Age Traditional**

Will Tuttle

Awakening Kingdom Pathways
Lost Islands Pathways

Pianist Tuttle is a Dharma Master in the Chogye Order of Korean Zen Buddhism. Recorded live in concert, *Awakening Kingdom* celebrates the splendor of nature and of the creatures of the air, water, and earth by going beyond traditional musical structures and compositional forms. These are joyous improvisations resting somewhere between Eastern and Western culture. **New Age East/West, New Age Solo**

U

Upper Astral

Astral Massage Valley of the Sun
Crystal Cave Valley of the Sun
*Entrance to the Secret
   Lagoon* Valley of the Sun
Higher-Self Rendezvous Valley of
   the Sun
*Journey to the Edge of the
   Universe* Valley of the Sun
Manifestation Valley of the Sun
Skybirds Valley of the Sun
Upper Astral Suite Valley of the
   Sun

Upper Astral creates mellow
inner-harmony music that is perfect
for massage, meditation, healing,
loving, and other gentle pursuits.
Journey to the Edge of the Universe is an
electronic voyage, a soothing, sustained musical astral journey. *Crystal
Cave* is subtitled *Back to Atlantis* and
combines harp, synthesizer, and angelic humming voices with tinkling
chimes that evoke the legendary harmony of the vanished continent. This
high vibrational atmosphere is conducive to an altered state of consciousness or past-life regression.
Manifestation and *Higher-Self Rendez-
vous* encourage the listener to communicate with a Higher Intelligence.
These albums provide a transcendental audio environment for any New
Age activity. **New Age Electronic,
New Age Traditional**

Michael Uyttebroek

All in All Chacra Alternative
Innocence Chacra Alternative
Quiescence Chacra Alternative

His sound is so elegant and crystal
clear, it's no wonder that a growing
number of hospitals and massage
therapists are using Uyttebroek's recordings as "tension-release music."
On *Quiescence* the keyboard instrumentals subtly move the listener into
a state of total relaxation and height-
ened awareness. As the composer
says, "Music is not separate from the
way you live your life. The quality of
interaction and the perception of
self-understanding are manifested in
the way you express your music.

Music is the reflection of the consciousness that produced it. If you are relaxed and in balance, the music shows it." Having studied piano, recorder, and drums, Uyttebroek has found that keyboard improvisations perfectly express his sense of "this movement of learning and growing." **New Age Sound Health**

V

Valley of the Sun Records

New Age Music Sampler Valley of
the Sun
New Age Music Sampler II Valley
of the Sun

Valley of the Sun specializes in two
different styles of New Age music,
types they term "progressive" and
"inner harmony." As the names suggest, one style is energizing while the
other is calming and relaxing. *New
Age Music Sampler* offers an excellent
overview of these two styles as realized by such artists as Upper Astral;
but *New Age Music Sampler II* is even
better, featuring selections from albums by Robert Slap, Steven
Cooper, David Storrs, Upper Astral,
David Naegele, and Natopus. **New
Age Traditional**

Vangelis (Vangelis
Parathanassiou)

Albedo RCA
Antarctica Polydor
Beauborg RCA
Chariots of Fire Polydor
China Polydor
Cosmos RCA
Heaven and Hell RCA
Ignacio Bellaphon
La Fête Sauvage EMI
*L'Apocalypse des
Animaux* Polydor
Mask Polygram
Opera Sauvage Polydor
Soil Festivities Polydor
Spiral RCA
To the Unknown Man RCA

Multi - instrumentalist / composer
Vangelis (full name Vangelis Parathanassiou), is best known for his
sweeping, majestic soundtrack to the
film *Chariots of Fire*, which was most
likely the first New Age Instrumental to receive extensive national airplay. The compelling keyboard work
features chimelike electronic accents
and a simple but repetitive instrumental hook that successfully in-
duced listeners to purchase more
than one million copies of the album.
Another Vangelis soundtrack, *Antarctica*, is a deeply spiritual instru-

mental gem, created with layers of synthesizers, harp, and orchestral arrangements. On *Heaven and Hell* Vangelis plays, as he describes it, "all kinds of keyboards, percussion, and sundry instruments" to create a dizzying tour of the underworld and celestial realms. Opening with a frenetic pace, the album depicts hell as filled with shrieking electronic choral voices and rather grating instrumental bursts of sound. Heaven is suitably light and ethereal with synthesized angelic voices floating above airy electronic arrangements. These three albums represent the best of the New Age sounds in the vast Vangelis catalog; the remaining albums offer majestic but almost overpowering and bombastic instrumentals. That's not to say that such albums as *Mask* and *L'Apocalypse des Animaux* don't make for fine listening; they do, but only if you are willing to accept some dissonance and a more frenetic pace than most New Age music releases. **New Age Electronic, New Age Traditional**

Cyrille Verdeaux

Kundalini Opera Eurock
Messenger of the Son Catero
Offerings Soundings of the Planet
Piano Sampler Windham Hill
Tree O2 Soundings of the Planet

On *Tree 02* pianist Cyrille Verdeaux joins with Dean Evenson on silver flute and Dudley Evenson on cello for a rich, free-flowing symphony of sound. Inspired by the beauty of nature, *Tree 02*'s selections are light and melodic, with a calm-

ing, spacious quality to the arrangements. This is stress-reducing, relaxation music. **New Age Traditional**

Ben Verdery
(See Latitude)

Vilas

Eternal Mother Fonix
Moonglitter Fonix

Pianist Vilas terms his album, *Eternal Mother,* "deep music." These inspired piano solos use the techniques of deep-tone bass and cross-echo to give the music an ethereal sound. Like the cassette cover, the music is sensual, evocative, and earthy, full of lush imagery and rich tones. On *Moonglitter* Vilas offers a glittering cascade of music that leads the listener through many moods. At times the music is quiet and contemplative, while at other times bouncy and alive, rather like moonlight glistening on the tide. **New Age Solo**

Richard Vimal

Aquarhythmies Fortuna
Migrations Polydor France
Transparencies Polydor

Graceful melodies and rich harmonic settings characterize the compositions on *Aquarhythmies*. French synthesist Vimal combines the synthesized sounds of church organ, string voices, and bright, crisp electronic tones to create an album that is alternately majestic and proud, soft and delicate. The record was inspired by images of Vimal's Burgundy, France, homeland—a fairy tale landscape dotted with medieval castles, rich vineyards, and romantic towns. **New Age Electronic**

Andreas Vollenweider

Behind the Garden CBS
Caverna Magica CBS
Down to the Moon CBS
Eine Art Suite CBS
Pace Verde CBS
White Winds CBS

Drawing from his experience in scoring nature documentaries, harpist Vollenweider endeavors to create a calm, supportive sonic atmosphere on each of his releases. In general, Vollenweider's compositions are structurally simple but gain texture through the multitimbred orchestrations of his talented ensemble, who add percussion, brass, and woodwinds. Having modified his electro-acoustic harp so that he can program each string differently, Vollenweider is able to create unusual customized sounds for a unique and identifiable aural personality. He has also doctored the koto (the Japanese stringed instrument most similar to a guitar) by replacing the traditional silk strings with steel and adding electronic pickups. Using a minimum of synthesizers on his albums, Vollenweider prefers an alternative approach to texture, mixing percussion, keyboards, brass, and woodwinds to his center stage harp. The poignant and luscious *Down to the Moon,* which won the 1987 Grammy Award for Best New Age

Recording, has a subtle lunar theme throughout; the music is a flowing series of transitory, Zen-inspired impressions that relax, inspire, and gently energize. Vollenweider told *Jazziz* magazine that there is a parallel between the music and the moon, both being capable of "touching the flow of moods and propelling the times of change." **New Age Traditional**

Thilo Von Westernhagen and Band

Pleasureland Life Style

Pianist Von Westernhagen has, on *Pleasureland,* synthesized jazz and classical influences for a contemporary, progressive sound. Saxophone (contributed by guest artist Herb Geller), electric guitar, piano, organ, bass, drums, and various percussion are united in a series of cinematic pieces that beg the listener to enter the aural landscape that is *Pleasureland.* **New Age Progressive**

Voyager

Contact Voyager
Horizon of Hope Voyager
Sound Dreams Voyager

Voyager is the name used by the multi-instrumentalist/composer Tom Moore for his optimistic and visionary music that speaks to people thematically of hope, love, and peace. Synthesizers, guitars, acoustic and electronic percussion, electronic special effects, and nature sounds are incorporated on each album. *Sound Dreams* is characterized by its relaxed, meditative, and peaceful sounds, while *Contact* explores the dances of energy and time in the mysterious Sonoran Desert through an almost hypnotizing rhythm. **New Age Pop, New Age Traditional**

W

Fred Wackenhut

Orianna Twilight
  Mu-Psych

On *Orianna Twilight* Wackenhut uses synthesizers and acoustic piano to create emotional, sometimes moody, New Age Jazz, punched up with some exotic world music accents. **New Age Jazz**

Richard Wahnfried

Time Actor Innovative
  Communications

Producer and electronic music pioneer Klaus Schulze collaborates with synthesist Wahnfried on *Time Actor*, a musical discussion revolving around time and time-keeping themes. Wahnfried's compositions are spacious, kinetic, and progressive in tone, making use of cyclic, repetitive rhythms to interpret the main theme. This is intellectual, crown-chakra entertainment. **New Age Electronic**

Russell Walder
(See Ira Stein)

Johannes Walter

Heal Yourself Fortuna
Letting Go of Fear Fortuna
Music Mantras Fortuna

The mantra is a combination of words and sounds that cleanse and enlighten the consciousness through constant repetition. Played on flute, synthesizer, and guitar, Walter's *Music Mantras* are attractively hypnotic without becoming boring, powerful psycho-acoustic tools to achieve altered mental states. Walker has also produced several self-help and -discovery cassettes that combine affirmations and soothing music to help achieve a relaxed, harmonious body and mind. **New Age Meditation**

David Ward-Hunt
(See Wavestar)

Mary Watkins

Something Moving Olivia
Spiritsong Redwood
Winds of Change Palo Alto

The seven original solo piano pieces on *Spiritsong* dance and sparkle with a melodic New Age lightness, combining Watkins's classical and jazz training and pop, gospel, and blues influences. Unlike *Winds of Change,* which features a forty-two-piece orchestra and some of Watkins's own string arrangements, *Spiritsong* relies solely on the clean, pure resonance of acoustic piano for its uplifting mood. **New Age Solo**

Wavestar

Mind Journey Wavestar
Moonwind Audion
Zenith Wavestar

Instrumental duo Wavestar is comprised of David Ward-Hunt and John Dyson who play numerous keyboards, synthesizers, sequencers, and a few guitars. *Moonwind* is a cerebral blend of relentlessly rhythmic sequencer tracks and electronic instrumentation that weaves a hypnotic and cinematic tapestry. The tones and textures are richly layered; each side offers a provocatively eclectic palette of moods and atmospheres in which to revel, stimulating both brain and body chakras. **New Age Electronic**

Darryl Way

The Human Condition
  Venture/Virgin

Perhaps best known for his work with the group Curved Air, violinist Way mixes classical and progressive influences on the highly accessible, melodic *Human Condition.* Working with Opus 20, a fourteen-piece string ensemble, he plays solo violin to piano and percussion accompaniment to achieve an emotional, lyrical, fluid sound. **New Age Progressive**

John Weider

Intervals in Sunlight Gold Castle

Having collaborated with such top rock acts as the Rolling Stones, Eric Burdon and the Animals, John Mayall, and Suzi Quatro, guitarist Weider has finally returned to the gentle music he was composing before his hit-making phase. *Intervals in Sunlight* is a collection of acoustic guitar solos that reflect his classical violin training and have more to do with J. S. Bach than Johnny B. Goode. Its influences and moods range from seventeenth-century baroque to twentieth-century avant-garde. Added instrumentation—a synthesizer, percussion—create the colorful backdrop for his stellar guitar performances. Emotional, adventurous, and spirited, this is New Age Pop instrumental music that shines with crystalline purity. **New Age Pop**

Tim Weisberg

High Risk Cypress
Hurtwood Edge A&M
Nadia's Theme A&M

Rotations Liberty
Smile (Best Of) A&M
Tim Weisberg A&M
Tim Weisberg Band A&M
Twin Sons of Different Mothers
(w/Dan Fogelberg) Epic

Flutist Weisberg anticipated the success of New Age music on the early seventies album *Tim Weisberg;* this ethereal and sometimes hauntingly melodic release of solo flute compositions would fit snugly into today's contemporary instrumental radio formats. Weisberg's sound evolved over the years to include digital drums, synthesizers, and other computerized instruments on *High Risk,* yielding energetic instrumental music that borrows from both pop and jazz. **New Age Jazz, New Age Pop**

Phil Wells

Crystal Dancer New World
The Crystal Piano New World

On *Crystal Piano* Wells's solo piano compositions alternate between exultation and tranquility, between intimate ballads and uptempo, pop-influenced pieces. *Crystal Dancer* is a more spirited release; filled with lively pop-jazz keyboard numbers, it's a musical tonic for both the mind and body. **New Age Solo**

Tony Wells

Collage Karma

Collage blends widely disparate instruments into original and inspired compositions under multi-instrumentalist Wells's loving supervision. His performances on flute, Tibetan bells, singing bowls, African slit drums, Brazilian whistles, and Hopi clay flutes mix with the natural sounds of birds, wolves, and water for a lushly textured work. At times quiet and meditative, at other times vibrant and energizing, the music slides into easy rhythms that are gentle on the ears. **New Age Environmental, New Age Traditional**

Tim Wheater

Awakenings New World
The Enchanter New World

On *Awakenings* flutist Wheater adds synthesizer to his pop-influenced instrumental compositions. The sound is bright and cheery, though the liner notes suggest a more spiritual, inwardly directed theme. *The Enchanter* is an evocative kaleidoscope of sound that was inspired by the legends of Merlin— king maker, bard, enchanter. Wheater's flute spins a web of multitextured music that is spellbinding; featuring renaissance-influenced arrangements, *The Enchanter* is perfect for armchair voyaging or casual relaxation. **New Age Traditional**

Andrew White

Conversations Sona Gaia

On *Conversations* guitarist/keyboard player White blends contemporary acoustic and traditional folk influences with the sounds of nature for sensitive, introspective music. As White describes the relationship between music and listener, "It's really a question of being in tune and keeping in tune—and sometimes you need to change your strings." White's music encourages private time dedicated to relaxed meditation, especially with headphones on. **New Age Environmental, New Age Traditional**

Rob Whitesides-Woo

From Heart to Crown Search for Serenity
Miracles Search for Serenity
Sojourn Search for Serenity

On *From Heart to Crown* keyboardist/composer Whitesides-Woo combines ancient woodwind melodies with majestic French horns, delicate Asian harps, and flutes as well as cellos and violins. The music is gentle and loving yet also powerful. Acting as an acoustic acupressure session, *From Heart to Crown* uses certain tones and arrangements of notes to subtly encourage pentup energy release from these two chakra centers. **New Age Traditional**

Arden Wilken

The Brain Tape New World
Deep Touch New World
Dream Time New World
Heart Music New World
Inner Focus New World
Inner Harmony New World
Music for Children New World
Music for Healing New World

Synthesist Wilken has developed an original system of music therapy called Inner Sound that she uses on each of her releases. *The Brain Tape* exercises the brain, taking listeners on an inward journey through the four brain wave states (beta, alpha, theta, and delta), balancing the left and right hemispheres of the brain to allow flow between the listener's inspirational, intuitive self and analytical, structural self. *Music for Healing* is gently transferred from tape to listener by droplets of sound that comfort and renew. *Deep Touch* was created for massage, and the soothing flow of the melodies creates a state of tranquility. *Music for Children,* one of the few New Age music cassettes designed specifically for youngsters, is divided into "Day Play," a gently stimulating flow of music to accompany daily adventures, and "Night Rest," which allows for a smooth transition into sleep. **New Age Sound Health**

Richard Wilkins

Color and Sound Meditations Wilkins Sounds

Color and Sound Meditations helps the listener focus on each chakra by using the color spectrum and compositions created in specific musical keys, as detailed in the liner notes. Saxophonist Wilkins and guest artist pianist Jeffrey Bayles have created well-thought-out instrumentals that are peaceful and melodic. Each cut on the album evokes a specific theme and emotional response, founded on the piano and accented by the warm, rich resonance of the sax. **New Age Meditation**

Anne Williams

Lotus Returning Earthsong
Sky Dance Earthsong
Song of Isis Earthsong
Summer Rose Earthsong
Violets in Spring Earthsong

Williams uses harps and wind instruments to create songs of Earth and spirit. As she says, "I ask Spirit for music to reflect the essence of a particular flower, tree, canyon, stone, circle . . . and I play what I hear. The Earth needs to hear our songs." Her harp music is contemplative and relaxing, and the compositions weave together sounds from many cultures: Egyptian, Mayan, Celtic, and Native American. On *Sky Dance* harps, flutes, synthesizer, guitar, and bells dance together in smooth orchestrated sound inspired by the soaring birds of mountain plateaus. *Violets in Spring* offers up ancient harmonies with harps, flutes, ocarina, tabla, Tibetan bells, wind chimes, and Williams's own voice creating unusually pure resonance. *Song of Isis* was recorded in the pyramids and temples of ancient Egypt over the time of the Harmonic Convergence (August 16–18, 1987). The power of spirit sings out through these inspired songs featuring harp, voice, double pipes, flute, and bells. **New Age Traditional, New Age World**

Windham Hill Records

An Evening with Windham Hill Live Windham Hill
A Piano Sampler Windham Hill
Piano Sampler II Windham Hill

Sampler 81 Windham Hill
Sampler 82 Windham Hill
Sampler 84 Windham Hill
Sampler 86 Windham Hill
Soul of the Machine Windham Hill

Windham Hill is popularly acknowledged as the world's largest and first New Age music record label, although founder/guitarist William Ackerman has publicly rejected the appellation "New Age." Nonetheless, the artists on the label record a wide variety of solo and folk- and jazz-influenced instrumentals that have set the standard for all New Age releases to date. The many samplers Windham Hill releases provide a good introduction to its artists. For those who love piano music in all its diverse and beautiful styles, *Piano Sampler* features both the familiar arrhythmic and the polyrhythmic staccato styles that Windham Hill artists are known for. Featured artists are Michael Harrison, Peggy Stern, Philip Aaberg, Richard Dworsky, Tim Story, Paul Dondero, Allaudin Mathieu, Cyrille Verdeaux, and Rick Peller. *Sampler 84* is perhaps the most cohesive and satisfying compilation from the label, featuring Michael Hedges, Mark Isham, William Ackerman, George Winston, Shadowfax, Alex de Grassi, Scott Cossu, Billy Oskay, and Michael O'Domhnaill. **New Age Folk, New Age Jazz, New Age Traditional**

Stephen Winfield

Forest Flower Sona Gaia

Forest Flower mixes acoustic instruments with the sounds of nature to yield relaxing, stress-relieving compositions. Winfield performs on chimes, saxophone, piano, and flute, combined with bird songs added. This melodic, mellow music is suitable for meditation or such quiet activities as yoga or tai chi. New Age Meditation

George Winston

Autumn Windham Hill
Ballads and Blues Windham Hill
Country Windham Hill
December Windham Hill
Evening with Windham Hill Live Windham Hill
Sampler 81 Windham Hill
Sampler 82 Windham Hill
Sampler 84 Windham Hill
Sampler 86 Windham Hill
Variations on the Kanon by Pachelbel Windham Hill
Velveteen Rabbit Dancing Cat
Winter into Spring Windham Hill

Pianist Winston is one of the great popularizers of minimalist, acoustic solo piano music. Each of his best-selling albums, such as *Autumn* and *December,* features intimate, emotional compositions that encourage the listener to relax into the pretty, uncomplicated melodies. Winston's spacious keyboard work on *Autumn* uses lush, rich, middle tones; and each selection interprets a different aspect of this colorful season. For classical music buffs, *Variations on the Kanon by Pachelbel* should be a welcome crossover release. Winston updates what may be the most well-known classical theme with his original arrangements. You can actually appreciate each note's sustain

and decay as the slow, meditative piece progresses. In Winston's original compositions, the notes he plays are as important as the notes he eliminates; his music is never cluttered, never frenetic, never aggressive—a perfect example of what New Age music is all about. New Age Solo, New Age Traditional

Paul Winter (Paul Winter Consort)

Callings Living Music
Canyon Living Music
Common Ground A&M
Concert for the Earth Living Music
Earthdance A&M
Icarus Epic
Living Music Collection 86 Living Music
Missa Gaia Living Music
Road A&M
Something in the Wind A&M
Sun Singer Living Music
Whales Alive (w/Leonard Nimoy) Living Music
The Winter Consort A&M
Wintersong Living Music

Winter's music cannot be distinguished from his philosophy: "Through music the diverse cultures of the world can find common ground." To that end he combines elements of classical, jazz, and international folk traditions with themes drawn from the natural environment. Winter's career began during college when he formed the jazz group, the Paul Winter Sextet. The group recorded numerous albums for Columbia Records and became one of the first jazz bands to play the

200

White House. However, in the midst of the tumultous sixties, Winter decided to create a new performing entity that reflected his evolving concern for cultural unity and environmental harmony. In 1967 the Paul Winter Consort was launched. The Beatles' producer, George Martin, worked with the Consort on *Icarus*. Now considered a New Age classic, this ground-breaking release mixed jazz, rock, pop, and symphonic elements into a majestic, sweeping fusion of sound suitable for the popular "mind voyaging" activities of the time. Based on the ancient Greek myth, *Icarus* is a musical interpretation of the rise and fall of youthful ambition. Piano, guitar, organ, drums, and accent instruments create densely layered arrangements that should be appreciated through focused listening, preferably with headphones. Ten years later, *Common Ground* became the first Paul Winter Consort album to mix the actual voices of animals and the sounds of nature into the rhythmic, world music–influenced compositions. Expanding this concept, *Callings* features the voices of thirteen different sea mammals woven into the suitably liquid and flowing instrumental tracks; keyboards, guitar, and flute blend in perfect harmony with the sounds of whales, dolphins, and other creatures. One of Winter's less appreciated achievements is recognizing great talent; during the Consort's existence, many fine musicians have been members and then gone on to release successful solo records or form chart-topping groups. These musicians, profiled elsewhere in this book, include Eugene Friesen, David Darling, and Oscar Castro-Neves. Winter's discovery of these artists, as well as his own work, have made him a founding father of New Age music. **New Age Traditional**

Henry Wolff and Nancy Hennings

Tibetan Bells Vol. 1 Island
Tibetan Bells Vol. 2 Kuckuck
Yamantaka Kuckuck

The trance-inducing power of Tibetan bells has been known for hundreds, perhaps thousands, of years. As an aid to meditation, they are invaluable. Wolff and Hennings make fine recordings featuring these sonorous bells in solo compositions as well as in pairs and groupings. *Tibetan Bells Vol. 1* is a classic recording of distinctly tuned bells, eminently suitable for deep inward voyaging or concentration. *Tibetan Bells Vol. 2* is an intense experience as the crystal pure tones of the bells resonate vigorously; the overtones and harmonics work calming, peaceful miracles on the mind. **New Age Meditation**

Sylvia Woods

The Harp of Brandiswhiere Tonmeister
Three Harps for Christmas Tonmeister

Woods is one of the leaders in the worldwide renaissance of folk and Celtic harp playing. She has written nine books of harp music, including the popular *Teach Yourself to Play the*

Folk Harp. After three years of recording and touring with Robin Williamson and His Merry Band, Woods embarked on a solo career and recorded the seminal *Harp of Brandiswhiere,* an original suite for Celtic harp. On *Three Harps for Christmas* Woods performs on the nylon-strung neo-Celtic harp, the metal-strung ancient Celtic harp, and the rare and lovely triple-strung harp. **New Age Solo**

X

Xochimoki

*Flower of the Ancient
 Ones* Earthsong
*New Music, Ancient
 Sources* Earthsong
*Quetzal: Music from the Heart
 of Maya* Earthsong

Jim Berenholtz and Mazatl Galindo formed Xochimoki to create exotic music using instruments comparable to those of pre-Colombian civilizations in Mexico and Central and South America. On *New Music, Ancient Sources,* clay and wooden flutes, rattles, and skin drums evoke a mental return to the heights of Mayan culture; the percussion-based music is highlighted by the soulful and sometimes eerie sound of clay whistles. Berenholtz and Galindo have also put together comprehensive liner notes for this album that offer useful insights into the duo's artistic vision. **New Age World**

Stomu Yamashta

Kukai JVC
Red Buddha Van
Sea and Sky Kuckuck

Yamashta is a visionary composer/synthesist who creates vivid, uplifting space music releases, notably *Sea and Sky*. Using numerous synthesizers and other electronic gear, Yamashta's instrumental voyages on this release balance swirling washes of undertones representing the sea, with shimmering, airy synth accents. *Sea and Sky* is well suited for headphone enjoyment. **New Age Space**

Yanni

Keys to Imagination Private Music
Optimystique Varese Sarabande
Out of Silence Private Music

Out of Silence is the cultural and musical union between Yanni's Greek upbringing and his current American residency. Utilizing state-of-the-art synthesizers, computers, and other electronic media, Yanni custom-programs an unusual plucked-string sound into his keyboards, reminiscent of bouzoukis and mandolins. Yanni's sound can be summed up in one word: emotion. Dramatic and sensitive, his epic tone poems evoke a myriad of pastoral and urban images as they address themes inspired by his visit home to Greece after a ten-year absence. Romantic string sounds combine with subtle synthesized undertones for soothing, gentle, and intimate music on one track; another cut offers pumping percussion, percolating electronic leads, and majestic string accents for an invigorating New Age anthem. **New Age Electronic, New Age Progressive**

Yas-Kaz

Egg of Purana
 Gramavision/Gravity
Jomon Sho Gramavision/Gravity

The group Yas-Kaz is known for its self-designed and crafted musical instruments that are Asian in sound, encompassing influences from Japan, Polynesia, and China. On *Egg of Purana* they perform on these instruments as well as on guitar synthesizer, flute, and violin. The resulting music is delicate and interesting, like a well-remembered favorite dish with an added exotic but unknown spice. Overall the compositions are based on unusual harmonies yet have a relaxing effect on the listener. **New Age East/West**

Beth York

Transformations Ladyslipper

Music therapist York utilizes such instruments as oboe, flute, alto sax, harp, acoustic guitar, percussion, and synthesizers in addition to her own featured piano performances to create New Age fusion music. The sounds ebb and flow with soothing rhythms and cycles, perfect for relaxation or meditation. York began formal training at an early age because, in her own words, she was "searching for the intimacy I have always felt for my music and the healing communication it always held." On *Transformation* York also uses wordless vocalization to stimulate the chakras with appropriate vibrations through each composition. **New Age Sound Health**

Hiroshi Yoshimura

Green Sona Gaia

Opening with the soothing sound of a burbling brook, Yoshimura adds birdcalls and other natural sounds to his synthesizer soloings on *Green*. The music uses repetition and cycles of sound to induce a tranquil, relaxed state in the listener while providing verdant images of pastoral settings. This is healing music for the senses; perfect for relaxation, meditation, quiet activities, and inwardly directed explorations. **New Age Environmental**

Masakazu Yoshizawa

Kyori: Innervisions
  Fortuna

Kyori: Innervisions blends Western and Japanese musical idioms. Entrancing shakuhachi (wooden flute) solos are balanced by ensemble pieces featuring guest artist Osamu Kitajima on koto, biwa, and guitar, plus Geoffrey Hales on percussion. Yoshizawa is classically trained and has performed everything from chamber music to avant-garde music to film scores. He is also a specialist in Hiyashi, the percussion and flute music used in Kabuki presentations. *Kyori: Innervisions* features musical evocations of Yoshizawa's childhood in Japan, of its rivers and streams and the peaceful harmony found within his village. One of the pieces on the album was totally improvised by the musicians—only the scale was agreed upon beforehand. Without being able to see one another or even agreeing who would begin the piece, the musicians waited, listened, and then created exceptional music. **New Age East/West**

Z

Gheorgie Zamfir

Fantasy Polygram
Harmony Polygram
The Light of Experience Epic
The Lonely Shepherd Polygram
Meditations and
  Celebrations Polygram
Music by Candlelight Polygram
Reflections Polygram
Romance of the
  Panflute Polygram
Solitude Polygram

Zamfir is a virtuoso on the nai, the haunting pan flute of his native Romania. Commonly recognized as one of the oldest instruments in the world, the pan flute's origin is described in the pages of Greek mythology. Yet the instrument is still rather rare outside of Europe and even more rarely featured as a lead instrument. Zamfir's flutes are capable of playing twenty octaves; combining this capacity with his own phenomenal breath control (it's not surprising to learn that Zamfir is an advocate of transcendental medita-tion and yoga) yields sweet tunes that entrance and delight the listener. Zamfir released *The Lonely Shepherd* in 1976, heralding the arrival of a sound that was quite unlike anything heard in Euro-pop music and offering a soothing break from its frenetic stylings. Many of Zamfir's releases offer instrumental panpipe versions of contemporary hits or classics from the great baroque and classical composers. **New Age Pop**

Zavijava Orchestra

Rivers of Light
  Mu-Psych Music

Rivers of Light, the Zavijava Orchestra's impressive debut album, showcases the harmonic creations of Charles Townsend and Christopher Faris. Their synergistic improvisational interplay is underscored by microcosmic attention to sound color and precisely defined rhythmic structures. Guest contributor Suzanne Bonnen's cascading harp arpeggios on several selections complement the duo's performances on electronic keyboards, piano, violin, contrabass, vibraphone, and recorder. This is music to meld into; it will leave you with an afterglow of pleasure. Zavijava Orchestra creates New Age music suitable for relaxation, meditation, or inward travels. **New Age Traditional**

Denny Zeitlin

Homecoming Living Music

Zeitlin has recorded more than twenty albums of traditional jazz that feature his piano-based compositions. *Homecoming* celebrates his earliest and deepest roots: the solo acoustic piano. Co-producer Paul Winter worked closely with his friend of twenty years to bring out the most lyrical, heartfelt qualities of Zeitlin's music. The result is spirited, flowing compositions that are sweeping and vigorously lyrical, blending classical, pop, and jazz influences. **New Age Solo**

NEW AGE RECORD LABELS

Alcazar Inc.
P.O. Box 429
Waterbury, VT 05676
802 244-8657

Allegiance Records
1419 N. La Brea Blvd.
Los Angeles, CA 90028
213 851-8852

Allegro/Pacific Arts Records
P.O. Box 5455
Mill Valley, CA 94942
415 435-2772

Ambient Music
18633 Topham St.
Reseda, CA 91335

American Gramaphone
9130 Mormon Bridge Rd.
Omaha, NE 68152
402 457-4341

Antiquity
1845 N. Farwell Ave.
Milwaukee, WI 53202
414 272-6700

Arhoolie
10341 San Pablo Ave.
El Cerrito, CA 94530
415 525-7471

Ark Records
P.O. Box 230073
Tigard, OR 97223
503 620-5680

Atlantic
75 Rockefeller Plaza
New York, NY 10019
212 484-6000

Attic
624 King St., W.
Toronto, Ontario,
Canada M5V1M7
416 862-0352

Audion
c/o JEM Records
3619 Kennedy Rd.
S. Plainfield, NJ 07080
201 753-6100

Audiophile Imports
P.O. Box 32247
Pikesville, MD 21208
301 484-7752

Awakening
930 N. Wetherly Dr., #303
Los Angeles, CA 90069
213 659-6238

Back Road Records
417 Tamal Plaza
Corte Madera, CA 94925
415 924-4848
800 825-4848

Beyond
648 N. Fuller Ave.
Los Angeles, CA 90036
213 934-2221

Birdwing
(See Sparrow Records)

Black Sun
P.O. Box 30122
Tucson, AZ 85751
602 326-4400

Blue Note
1370 Ave. of the Americas
New York, NY 10019
212 603-8700

Callisto Records
5909 N. 6th St.
Philadelphia, PA 19120

Canadian Music Centre
20 St. Joseph St.
Toronto, M4Y1J9, Canada
416 961-6601

Canyon Records and Indian Arts
4143 N. 16th St.
Phoenix, AZ 85016
602 266-4823
602 266-4659

Capitol
1750 N. Vine
Hollywood CA 90028
213 462-6252

Catero
1301 Chestnut St.
San Carlos, CA 94070
415 593-6720

CBS Masterworks
51 W. 52nd St., 13th Fl.
New York, NY 10019
212 975-4321

Celestial Harmonies
4549 E. Ft. Lowell
Tucson, AZ 85712
602 326-4400

Chacra Alternative Music
35 Parklane Pl., Dept. 3
Dollard-des-Ormeaux
Quebec, Canada H9G1B8
514 624-0278

Chameleon Music Group
3355 W. El Segundo Blvd.
Hawthorne, CA 90250
213 973-8282
800 423-6935 (outside California)

Chidvilas
P.O. Box 17550
Boulder, CO 80308
303 665-6611

Cinema Records
6500 River Chase Circle E.
Atlanta, GA 30328
404 955-1550

Composers' Recordings Inc.
170 W. 74th St.
New York, NY 10023
212 873-1250

Coda Landscape Records
(See JEM)

Columbia
(See CBS Masterworks)

Concept Synergy
279 S. Beverly Dr., #604
Beverly Hills, CA 90273
213 285-1507

Cooper Sound Waves
P.O. Box 5910
Santa Monica, CA 90405-0190
213 392-7784

Crescendo/GNP-Crescendo
8400 Sunset Blvd.
Los Angeles, CA 90069
213 656-2614

Cypress Records
1523 Crossroads of the World
Hollywood, CA 90028
213 465-2711

Dali
(See Innovative Communications)

Dancing Cat
P.O. Box 639
Santa Cruz, CA 95061
408 429-5085

Dark Stream Records
P.O. Box 5494
Lynnwood, WA 98046

Digital Music Product
P.O. Box 2317
Rockefeller Center Station
New York, NY 10185
212 627-0840

Earthsong
P.O. Box 780
Sedona, AZ 86336

Eastern Gate Publishing Co.
P.O. Box 1485
Front Royal, VA 22630
703 636-3788

ECM Records
810 Seventh Ave., 12th Fl.
New York, NY 10019
212 333-8478

Editions EG
c/o JEM
3619 Kennedy Rd.
S. Plainfield, NJ 07080
201 753-6100

Elektra
9229 Sunset Blvd., #718
Los Angeles, CA 90069
213 205-7400/4700

E-N Records
(See Startsong)

Epic
51 W. 52nd St.
New York, NY 10019
212 975-4321

Eurock
P.O. Box 13718
Portland, OR 97213
503 281-0247

Expansion
P.O. Box 996
Cardiff by the Sea, CA 92007
619 944-3456

Express Music Catalog
175 Fifth Ave.
New York, NY 10010
212 254-6161

Fantasy Records
10th and Parker
Berkeley, CA 94710
415 549-2500

Flying Fish
1304 W. Schubert St.
Chicago, IL 60614
312 528-5455

Flying Heart
4026 N.E. 12th Ave.
Portland, OR 97212
503 287-8045

FM
(See CBS Masterworks)

Folkways
c/o Birch Tree Group
180 Alexander St.
Princeton, NJ 08540
609 683-0090

Fortuna
4549 E. Ft. Lowell
Tucson, AZ 85712
602 326-4400

Foundation for Shamanic Studies
Box 670, Belden Station
Norwalk, CT 06852
203 454-2825

Fylkingen
P.O. Box 4514
S-102 65 Stockholm
Sweden
46-8-845-443

Gaia
121 W. 27th St.
New York, NY 10001
212 645-5252

Geffen
9130 Sunset Blvd.
Los Angeles, CA 90069
213 278-9010

Global Pacific
589 First St., W.
Sonoma, CA 95476
707 996-2748

Gold Castle
3575 Cahuenga Blvd., #470
Los Angeles, CA 90068
213 850-3321

Golden Voyage
(See Awakening)

Gramavision
260 W. Broadway
New York, NY 10013
212 645-5252

Green Linnet
70 Turner Hill Rd.
New Canaan, CT 06864
203 966-0864

Halpern Sounds
(See Sound Rx)

Hannibal
P.O. Box 667
Rocky Hill, NJ 08553
609 466-9320

Harmonia Mundi
P.O. Box 64503
Los Angeles, CA 90064
213 474-2139

Heartbeat
(See Rounder)

Hearts of Space
P.O. Box 31321
San Francisco, CA 94131
415 759-1130

Heavensong
P.O. Box 450
Kula, HI 96790
808 878-6415

Heru Records
845 Via de la Paz, #454
Pacific Palisades, CA 90272

Higher Octave Music
8964 Wonderland Park Ave.
Los Angeles, CA 90046
213 856-0039

Hi-Rise Records
P.O. Box 975
Union, NJ 07083

Important
149-03 Guy R. Brewer Blvd.
Jamaica, NY 11434
718 995-9200

Innovative Communications
c/o Chameleon Music Group
3355 W. El Segundo
Hawthorne, CA 90250
213 973-8282
800 423-6935 (outside California)

Invincible Records
P.O. Box 13054
Phoenix, AZ 85002
602 252-0077
602 899-8496

JEM
3619 Kennedy Rd.
S. Plainfield, NJ 07080
201 753-610

Kicking Mule
P.O. Box 158
Alderpoint, CA 95411
707 926-5312

Kuckuck
P.O. Box 30122
Tucson, AZ 85751
602 326-4400

Ladyslipper
P.O. Box 3130
Durham, NC 27705
919 683-1570

Landmark
(See Fantasy Records)

Liberty
(See Capitol)

Lifedance Distribution
3479 N.W. Yeon Ave.
Portland, OR 97210
503 228-9430

Li-Sem Enterprises
490 El Camino Real, #215
Belmont, CA 94002
415 592-4901

Living Music
1047 Amsterdam Ave.
New York, NY 10025

Lost Lakes Arts
(See Windham Hill)

Lovely Music Ltd.
463 West St.
New York, NY 10014
212 243-6153

Magenta
P.O. Box 9388
Stanford, CA 94305

Magic Wing Records
P.O. Box 1373
Ashland, OR 97520
503 535-2894

MCA
70 Universal City Plaza
Universal City, CA 91608
818 777-1000

Meadowlark
9255 Deering Ave.
Chatsworth, CA 91311
818 709-6900

Mercury
(See Polygram)

Milestone
(See Fantasy Records)

Mistral Music
337 Greenwood Ave.
Waukegan, IL 60087
312 336-0445

Moss Music Group
200 Varick St.
New York, NY 10014
800 422-4869
212 293-4800

Multiphase
P.O. Box 15176
St. Louis, MO 63110

Mu-Psych
973a Bristol Pike
Bensalem, PA 19020
215 639-2441
800 338-8873

Musical Heritage Society
1710 Hwy. 35
Ocean, NJ 07712
201 531-7000

Music of the Spheres
c/o Potentials Unlimited
Dept. NR
4606 44th St., S.E.
P.O. Box 891
Grand Rapids, MI 49518
616 949-7894

Music of the World
P.O. Box 258
Brooklyn, NY 11209

Music West
2200 Larkspur Landing Circle, #100
Larkspur, CA 94939
415 925-9800
415 459-6000

Narada
1845 N. Farwell
Milwaukee, WI 53202
414 272-6700

Nebula Records
P.O. Box 23764
Baton Rouge, LA 70893
504 769-0632

New Albion
584 Castro St., #463
San Francisco, CA 94114
415 621-5757

New Era Records
P.O. Box 11179
Edmonton, Alberta,
Canada T5J3K4

New Music Distribution Service
500 Broadway
New York, NY 10012
212 925-2121

New World
179 Water St.
Torrington, CT 06790
800 233-1337

Novaphonic
1731½ N. Bronson Ave.
Los Angeles, CA 90028
213 469-5603

Novus
c/o RCA Records
1133 Ave. of the Americas
New York, NY 10036
212 582-0028

Open Air
(See Windham Hill)

Optimism Records
3575 Cahuenga Blvd. W., #247
Los Angeles, CA 90068
213 850-3350

Oriental
P.O. Box 1802
Grand Central Station
New York, NY 10017
212 557-7851

Palo Alto
755 Page Mill Rd.
Palo Alto, CA 94304
415 856-4355

Pangaea Records
1776 Broadway
New York, NY 10019
212 262-7194

Paradise Boutique
4465 Katherine Ave.
Sherman Oaks, CA 91403
818 990-4935

Passport
c/o JEM Records
3639 Kennedy Rd.
S. Plainfield, NJ 07080
201 753-6100

Pathways
1173 Hearst Ave.
Berkeley, CA 94702
800 888-PATH

Philo
(See Rounder)

Platero
P.O. Box 415
Forest Knolls, CA 94933

Plumrose Music
28400 Greenwood Rd.
Elk, CA 95432
707 877-3223

Polygram
810 Seventh Ave.
New York, NY 10019
212 399-7100

Prestige
(See Fantasy Records)

Private Music
220 E. 23rd St.
New York, NY 10010
212 684-2533

Progressive Records
P.O. Box 846
Livermore, CA 94550
415 447-3248

PVC
(See JEM)

Pyramid Dist.
1577 Barry Ave.
Los Angeles, CA 90025
213 207-4127/2944

Pythagoras Press
P.O. Box 1153
Carmel Valley, CA 93924
408 659-2086

Quaver
P.O. Box 272
Evanston, IL 60204

RB International
200 Varick St.
New York, NY 10014
212 243-4800

RCA/Victor
1133 Ave. of the Americas
New York, NY 10036
212 930-4000

Reckless
P.O. Box 4675
Portsmouth, NH 03801
603 659-5673

Redwood Records
6400 Hollis St., #8
Emeryville, CA 94608
415 428-9191

Revere Records
(See Lifedance Distribution)

Rhythmythology Music Productions
P.O. Box 5704
Santa Rosa, CA 95402
707 538-7122

Rising Sun
P.O. Box 8878
Aspen, CO 81612-8878
303 945-1227

RMM Records
P.O. Box 185
Sebastopol, CA 95473-0185
707 523-2805

Rounder
1 Camp St.
Cambridge, MA 02140
617 354-0700

Roundup Records
P.O. Box 154
N. Cambridge, MA 02140
617 354-0700

Rykodisc
200 N. Third Ave.
Minneapolis, MN 55401
612 375-9162

Sandstone Music
8300 Tampa Ave., #G
Northridge, CA 91324
818 993-8822

Search for Serenity
180 W. 25th St.
Upland, CA 91786-1113
714 981-2318

Sense of Purpose
(See Voyager Music)

Sequoia
13906 Ventura Blvd.
Sherman Oaks, CA 91423
818 703-5190

Seven Arrows Trading Company
P.O. Box 4904
Taos, NM 87571
505 758-0513

Shanachie Records
Dalebrook Park
Ho-Ho-Kus, NJ 07423
201 445-5561

Shining Star
200 Tamal Vista Blvd., #417
Corde Madera, CA 94925
800 825-4848

Silver Wave Records
P.O. Box 7943
Boulder, CO 80306
303 443-5617

Solitudes
c/o Moss Music Group
200 Varick St.
New York, NY 10014
212 243-4800

Sona Gaia
1845 N. Farwell Ave., 2nd Fl.
Milwaukee, WI 53202
414 272-6700

Songs for a Small Planet
c/o The Songsmith Society
P.O. Box 2601
Northbrook, IL 60065
312 272-9199

Sonic Atmospheres
14755 Ventura Blvd., #1776
Sherman Oaks, CA 91403
818 505-6022

Sound Currents
P.O. Box 5044
Mill Valley, CA 94942
415 459-2041

Soundings of the Planet
P.O. Box 43512
Tucson, AZ 85733
602 883-1784

Soundless Sound Recordings
P.O. Box 8005, Ste. 283
Boulder, CO 80306-8005
303 440-4431

Sound Rx
P.O. Box 2644
San Anselmo, CA 94960
415 491-1930

Sparrow Records
9225 Deering Ave.
Chatsworth, CA 91311
818-709-6900

Spirit Music
42 Baker Ave.
Lexington, MA 02173
617 861-1625

Spring Hill Music
5216 Sunshine Canyon
Boulder, CO 80302
303 938-1188

Startsong (*also* E-N Records)
3218 E. La Salle
Colorado Springs, CO 80909
303 634-2045

Storyville
(See Moss Music Group)

Suite Beat
(See Chameleon Music Group)

Takoma
(See Allegiance Records)

Tape Masters
176 Forest Ave.
Pacific Grove, CA 93950

TMB Music
24256 Hatteras St.
Woodland Hills, CA 91367
818 884-5741

Tonmeister
P.O. Box 29521
Los Angeles, CA 90029
818 956-1363

Triangle Publishing
P.O. Box 452
New York, NY 10021
212 661-1180

Turnabout
(See Moss Music Group)

Turquoise
P.O. Box 947
Whitesburg, KY 41858
606 633-0485

United Artists
(See Capitol)

Valley of the Sun
P.O. Box 3004
Agoura, CA 91301
213 457-1547

Vanguard/Terra
c/o Welk Record Group
1299 Ocean Ave.
Santa Monica, CA 90401
213 451-5727

Varrick
(See Rounder)

Venture
(See Virgin/Venture)

Verve and Verve/Forecast
c/o Polygram
810 Seventh Ave.
New York, NY 10014
212 333-8000

Victor
(See RCA)

Virgin/Venture
9247 Alden Dr.
Beverly Hills, CA 90210
213 278-1181

Vital Body
P.O. Box 1067
Manhasset, NY 11030
516 759-5200

Voyager Music
P.O. Box 24733
Tempe, AZ 85282
602 897-7761

Warner Bros.
3300 Warner Blvd.
Burbank, CA 91510
818 846-9090

Wayside Music
P.O. Box 6517
Wheaton, MD 20906-0517

Windham Hill
1416 N. La Brea Blvd.
Hollywood, CA 90046
213 469-2411

Yansa Music
6925 Fifth Ave., #E436
Scottsdale, AZ 85251
602 481-0696

ABOUT THE AUTHOR

Patti Jean Birosik owns Ready to Rock/Vox Talent, an entertainment conglomerate that includes management, consulting, production, recording, and public relations companies as well as a full service talent agency. She is listed in *Who's Who in Entertainment;* is a voting member of the National Academy of Recording Arts And Sciences; former vice president and current advisory board member of Los Angeles Women in Music; a contributing editor/writer for *Yoga Journal, Body/Mind/ Spirit, Science of Mind, Cymbiosis, New Frontier,* and the *Sedona Red Rock News,* among others; and a member of the New Age Music Network.

Birosik previously worked as an air personality and music director for several California radio stations; spent several years "on the road" as a tour publicist and account executive with various public relations firms; contributed freelance articles to *Billboard, Cashbox, Record World, Bam,* and *Music Connection;* and was part of Warner Bros. Records' Artist Development department specializing in music videos and television exposure.

Birosik divides her time between Sedona, Arizona, and Los Angeles, California.